Popular Culture

and

Corrections

ROBERT M. FREEMAN, Ph.D.

American Correctional Association

This book is dedicated to my wife, Diane; my sons, Eric and Brian; my daughter-in-law, Sonya; and the newest edition to the clan: our grandson Andrew.

American Correctional Association Staff

Richard L. Stalder, President
James A. Gondles, Jr., CAE, Executive Director
Gabriella M. Daley, Director, Communications and Publications
Harry Wilhelm, Marketing Manager
Alice Fins, Publications Managing Editor
Michael Kelly, Associate Editor
Book production and cover design by Capitol Communication Systems, Inc.

Printed in the United States of America by Victor Graphics, Baltimore, Maryland

For information on publications and videos available from ACA, contact our worldwide web home page at: http://www.corrections.com/aca

ISBN 1-56991-126-6

This publication may be ordered from:
American Correctional Association
4380 Forbes Boulevard
Lanham, Maryland 20706-4322
1-800-222-5646

Library of Congress Cataloging-in-Publication Data
Freeman, Robert M.
    Popular culture and corrections/Robert M. Freeman.
        p. cm.
    Includes bibliographical references.
    ISBN 1-56991-126-6 (pbk.)
        1. Corrections—United States. 2. Prisons—United States. 3. Prisons in mass media. 4. Prisoners in popular culture—United States. I. Title
    HV9304 .F74 2000
    365'.973—dc21   00-32759

Table of Contents

Foreword

What does the public know about corrections? What do our politicians expect? What do the movies portray? What type of stories are carried on the television networks and in newspapers about corrections? Unfortunately, seldom do our media outlets reveal the hard work and the honest labor of the people in corrections. Too often, we and our neighbors see sensationalized, distorted, or inaccurate depictions of corrections. In *Popular Culture and Corrections*, Robert Freeman addresses these problems and suggests some ways to counteract these images. Dr. Freeman examines the many aspects of popular culture and describes how horror stories on the news and stereotypes in movies and on television help create a negative public perception for corrections. His book introduces a "process of community education" in which professionals take an active role in informing news media, Hollywood, elected officials, and the general public about the reality of corrections.

This is one of the most important books that ACA has published because it gets to the heart of how the public views corrections and how that view impacts the field. Throughout its history, ACA has stood for improving the image of those who work in corrections. We have done this by improving the conditions of corrections professionals and those who are incarcerated through the development of standards. ACA is proud of the facilities that have met or exceeded these standards and become accredited. We are ensuring that individuals can benchmark their professionalism through our new program of individual certification. These issues get to the essence of professionalism. Our members know this. This book will help readers understand how they can make a difference in forming the public's image of corrections.

It is vital for corrections to have an image that reflects the challenges, opportunities, demands, and rewards that working in this field entails. This not only helps maintain a positive environment for those in corrections, it also helps attract talented people into the profession.

James A. Gondles, Jr., CAE
Executive Director
American Correctional Association

Preface

The day before work on this book began, I watched a prison movie classic, *The Shawshank Redemption*. I have always enjoyed this movie. The characters are sharply defined, the dialog crisp, and the imagery outstanding. I never fail to be moved by the plight of the inmate protagonist as he matches wits with a corrupt warden and brutal guards before effecting the dramatic escape to freedom and a life of leisure on a Mexican beach. In pre-*Shawshank* years, my family and I had derived similar enjoyment from such prison movies as *Cool Hand Luke*, *Escape From Alcatraz*, and *The Longest Yard*. We had cheered the inmates and detested the sadistic guards, just as millions of other viewers were doing. It was all good clean fun, an enjoyable way to kill a couple of hours. My family and I, like so many others, are avid consumers of the popular culture of corrections.

Yet, there was always in the back of my mind the disquieting thought that I really should not be cheering the inmates and detesting the correctional staff in these classic prison movies. After all, I was one of those staff. I was employed in public corrections with the Pennsylvania Department of Corrections for nearly twenty years and in private corrections for eighteen months before moving on to earn my Ph.D. in Criminal Justice and Criminology at the University of Maryland at College Park. I started my career with the Pennsylvania Department of Corrections as a government career trainee and ended it as a senior corrections superintendent. During the nearly twenty-one years I was in corrections, I saw both the good and the bad in corrections, including the last major prison riot of the 1980s. As I rose through the ranks, I grew increasingly aware of the fact that the public perception of corrections is generally negative. The more contact I had with elected officials, the news media, academicians, and members of the general public, the more I realized they had, with very rare exception, no conception of the reality of modern corrections. Their reality was the distorted reality shown time and time again in the classic prison movies. It was a reality made timeless by skilled professionals working tirelessly in the offices and editing rooms of the popular culture of corrections. It was a reality that created an intertwined set of negative stereotypes that fueled a negative public perception of corrections.

And, once I became a superintendent, I realized that this negative public perception of corrections had a more serious dimension than just making corrections professionals feel unappreciated. It had a negative impact on the profession itself. Good people with the potential to make a significant contribution to corrections were not considering it as an acceptable choice for employment because they could not see themselves working in such a negative environment. Other individuals with too high a potential for participating in brutality or corruption were drawn to the field because they thought the negative stereotypes reflected reality. Worse, elected officials defined corrections only in terms of prisons, which were to be used as dumping grounds for the tens of thousands of marginalized people caught up in a system of draconian mandatory-minimum sentencing structures.

When I entered academia in 1994, I finally had both the opportunity and the resources to methodically explore the question of why the public has such a negative perception of corrections. My first conclusion—the immediate response you get most often from practitioners—was that corrections is the victim of news media sensationalism and stereotypical prison movies. In short, corrections is a victim of the popular culture of corrections. From that conclusion, it was a short step to the most frequently expressed solution: the answer to bad press and bad Hollywood is "a good public relations campaign." In fact, my original discussions with the editor of this book were organized around the concept of it being organized as a public relations manual for correctional managers.

However, further research into the subject of how popular culture in general, and the popular culture of corrections specifically, is created and able to maintain its incredible power to influence public perception convinced me that my initial conclusion was analogous to saying that an individual is obese because that individual eats too much. From that hasty conclusion, it is only a short step to the solution: go on a diet. The relationship between the corrections known to practitioners, the corrections presented to the general public in the popular culture of corrections, and the negative public perception of corrections is much more complicated than the proposed solution of a good PR campaign would suggest, just as the issue of fighting obesity is far more complicated than simply eating less food. Proposals for the development of PR campaigns all too often emphasize the dissemination of professional press releases and use of techniques to help maintain a good relationship with the news media. This is, at best, a partial solution because this approach does not take into account the complex processes that have shaped the popular culture of corrections—conveying negative stereotyping of corrections over the past 200 years.

This book is informally divided into two sections. The first five chapters explore the complex interrelated processes involved in defining the popular culture of corrections that contains the powerful, negative correctional stereotypes that provide such a solid foundation for the overwhelmingly negative public perception of corrections and the individuals employed in that field. The last five chapters detail the proposed antidote to the popular culture of corrections: a process of community education whose many elements are designed to assist in the decertification of negative correctional stereotypes.

I have written this book with the goal of providing current and future practitioners, faculty, students, and citizens with some thoughts on a very complex subject. I hope my efforts are of assistance. I am open to any comments or suggestions that readers believe will improve the quality of this book. Comments or suggestions can be sent directly to me at:

Robert M. Freeman, Ph.D.
Chair, Department of Criminal Justice
Shippensburg University
Shippensburg, Pennsylvania 17257—2299
rmfree@ARK.SHIP.EDU

The Popular Culture of Corrections:

An Overview

In an October, 1995 episode of the popular *The X-Files* television series, FBI agents Dana Scully and Fox Mulder investigate a series of bizarre murders in a maximum-security prison. The location of their investigation is the prison's death row, a bleak, dreary cellblock housing desperate men grimly awaiting their date with the executioner. The maximum-security prison is run by a corrupt warden who is so brutal that he *personally* (on two separate occasions) beats to death a death-row inmate in a shower room while a bored guard leisurely smokes a cigarette and keeps watch in a corridor, indifferent to the frantic pleas from other death-row inmates that he intervene and stop the beatings.

Ask any group of corrections professionals how closely *The X-Files* episode corresponds to the correctional reality that they experience on a daily basis, and they will laugh and shake their heads in disbelief that the question is even being asked. However, ask those same individuals if they think the general public would consider *The X-Files* episode to be an accurate reflection of correctional reality and the smiles will fade.

The Correctional View of the Public Perception of Corrections

Many corrections professionals are concerned that the general public views them with the same disdain and contempt that they view criminals. They fear that they are not perceived as being valuable and contributing members of society. They are concerned that the general public is too likely, and too willing, to uncritically accept as truth the negative images of corrections that routinely appear in prison movies and on television shows like *The X-Files*. They worry that the news media focuses only on negative stories about corrections.

This concern about a negative public perception of corrections is so pervasive that the editors of *Corrections Today*, the official publication of the American Correctional Association, decided in 1989 and 1998 to devote entire issues to examining the public perception of corrections. Both issues of *Corrections Today* presented the opinions of corrections professionals and those opinions were not encouraging:

> Many corrections workers believe the public image of the corrections field is quite bad. Actually, it is nowhere that good. . . . The public view of corrections

in this country is, frankly, terrible. The major stories that reach the public about corrections are almost universally negative (Schwartz, 1989: 38).

Jack Cowley, who retired from the Oklahoma Department of Corrections in 1996 after thirty years of service, observes that:

> No one complains of being misunderstood by the public more than corrections professionals. I can recall countless conversations with wardens who lamented the fact that they could not manage their prisons as they believed necessary due to public opinion regarding proper prison management (Cowley, 1998: 39).

Dennis Avery, manager of Parole and Victim Services in the Hennepin County Bureau of Community Corrections, Minneapolis, Minnesota believe that in corrections, "We have a good product, but it's been hard to sell" (Avery, 1989: 6). The belief that there exists a negative public perception of corrections extends beyond the ranks of the corrections professional. Marie Rosen of *Law Enforcement News*, a publication of the John Jay College of Criminal Justice, states that "The public has a terrible image of prisons" (quoted in Meddis, 1989: 26).

Are these individuals accurate in their belief that the general public has a negative perception of corrections? Attend any correctional conference and attendees easily can provide anecdotal accounts of public mistrust and inaccurate perceptions that they personally have encountered. But we must be cautious about relying too heavily on personal anecdotes and opinions. Both are useful in defining the parameters of an issue, but they are not science. Opinions and beliefs frequently are colored by personal biases, conflicts, and misunderstandings resulting from a mutual failure to communicate. And one negative experience, or even a cluster of negative experiences, does not necessarily define an entire reality. Therefore, to address the issue of the public perception of corrections objectively, we need to review the relevant research that has been conducted.

Research on the Public Perception of Corrections

Researchers have produced very little empirical information about the public perception of corrections. In fact, a search of the literature reveals only two studies that focus specifically on this subject: the 1979 Graber Criminal Justice System study and the 1997 Florida Department of Corrections—commissioned study.

The Graber Study. In her 1979 study of the influence of the print media on public opinion about the criminal justice system, Doris Graber surveyed four panels of registered voters in Illinois, Indiana, and New Hampshire. Each panel of voters was asked to rate the job performance of the police, courts, and corrections on a ranking scale of good, fair, and poor. The overall ratings (by percent) were as follows:

Ranking of Job Performance in Corrections (by percentage)

	Good	Fair	Poor
Police	57	43	0
Courts	11	47	42
Corrections	15	20	65

Clearly, in 1979, the public perception of corrections was that it had the poorest performance of the three components of the criminal justice system. Only 15 percent of the survey respondents believed corrections was doing a good job. But what about the public perception of corrections today? Has the passage of time made any difference in how the public views corrections?

The Florida Department of Corrections—Commissioned Study. A 1997 Florida Department of Corrections—commissioned survey of 936 Florida citizens and news media representatives found that Floridians provided somewhat higher approval ratings of corrections than did the midwesterners in the Graber study. In response to a forty-four question survey that examined selected elements of Department of Corrections' performance, .9 percent of the respondents rated the agency's overall performance as excellent; 22.5 percent as good; 52.7 percent as fair; and 23.9 percent as poor. Although these findings are more positive than those in the Graber study, it is clear that fewer than one in four Floridians believe the Florida Department of Corrections is doing a good job. A good performance rating by 22.5 percent of the Florida respondents is only $7\frac{1}{2}$ percentage points higher than the 15 percent of the respondents in the Graber study who viewed corrections as doing a good job. This increase represents a less than spectacular improvement in eighteen years. The fact that 76.6 percent of the survey respondents provided performance ratings in only the poor-to-fair range of the approval continuum suggests that corrections professionals still have a long way to go in "selling" the general public on their accomplishments.

Although the Florida results may not generalize to the other forty-nine states, they do provide a basis for the conclusion that there is room for cautious optimism in the finding that the percentage of Floridians (23.9) giving the Department of Corrections a poor rating is much lower than the 65 percent of respondents Graber reported. This suggests that the public perception of corrections can change. However, any attempts by corrections professionals to promote that change must be based on a thorough knowledge of the basic dynamics of a complicated process known as the social construction of reality.

The Social Construction of Reality

All individuals, in their attempt to understand the complex world around them, engage in the social construction of reality. This psychological phenomenon can be defined as the cognitive process of "organizing and circulating the knowledge which people have of their own everyday life and of the more remote contexts of their lives" (McQuail, 1972: 13). Any occupation, organization, group, or other social entity about which an individual has no personal knowledge is a remote context. The remote contexts in an individual's life constitute the uncharted regions in that individual's cognitive map of society. The people who inhabit an uncharted region can be classified as insiders and the individuals existing outside of that uncharted region can be classified as outsiders. Every remote context represents the unknown because its reality is a mystery. Consequently, outsiders will lack the personal knowledge base necessary for evaluating and understanding the reality of the insiders for whom the remote context is part of "their own everyday life." They will have no personal experience on which to rely when a remote context is the subject of popular culture or the focus of public policy formulation.

Corrections as a Remote Context

Corrections, particularly institutional corrections, is not a part of the daily life of most Americans. Because the activities of corrections traditionally have been hidden from public view, the public perception of corrections cannot be based on personal knowledge. Most members of the general public have no personal knowledge of the field.

They are outsiders who do not even think about corrections unless they happen to be watching a prison movie or a newscast. For most Americans, corrections is an outstanding example of a "remote context." As Gene Wilder's character in *Stir Crazy* (1980) notes:

> You know . . . people see movies about prison life, but until you've actually spent a little time here you can't get the real flavor. I think more Americans should spend some time behind bars.

The "flavor" of corrections can be created by three organizers of social perception. These organizers are identified in the literature as social construction of reality engines.

The Three Social Construction of Reality Engines

According to Ray Surette, there are three "dominant social construction of reality engines" (Surette, 1998: xvii): (1) personal experiences and information received from family and friends; (2) knowledge supplied by various organizations and agencies that collect and disseminate data and information about specific fields and organizations; and (3) popular culture.

The First Social Construction of Reality Engine: Personal Experience. Individuals' personal knowledge of their occupation provides the "real flavor" of that occupation because it is based on personal experiences. Employees in corrections are in an excellent position to make accurate assessments about the issues involved in that field because they are insiders. If the employees see other correctional employees portrayed in a movie or TV show, or if corrections in general, or the specific organization to which the employees belong, is the focus of a news report, they have the insider's knowledge necessary to evaluate the accuracy of that portrayal or news report. Based on their personal experiences, employees can look at the information that is being presented to the public and ask: How does this information square with what I know to be true because of my own experiences? Is it congruent or incongruent? Or, put another way, is it the "real flavor?" If the information is congruent, they can accept it, and the image of corrections it creates, as valid. If the information is incongruent, they can reject it with the confidence born of personal experience.

Employees have at their command the factual information that can be used successfully to challenge and invalidate negative information that is being presented as the "real flavor." (This process will be defined in Chapter 5 as *decertification*).

The "Conversational Knowledge Base." If the correctional employee has family or friends in an occupation other than corrections, these outsiders can be exposed to the "real flavor" of corrections simply by talking to the employee about job-related activities. The outsider's perception of the remote context of corrections may be strongly influenced by information received during these social interactions. The information that is received from those people who are the closest to us creates what Surette refers to as an individual's "conversational knowledge base" (Surette, 1998: xvii).

Personal experiences combine with the "conversational knowledge base" to create the foundation of individuals' social reality, to organize their personal life. However, it is not possible to have a personal relationship with a member of every remote context that exists. When issues related to a specific remote context are encountered, and no conversational knowledge base exists, the information needed to inform perceptions can come from two nonpersonal sources: the second and third social construction of reality engines.

The Second Social Construction of Reality Engine: Information Agencies. The second engine is the knowledge "supplied by various organizations, institutions, and agencies that collect and disseminate data, information, and claims about the world" (Surette, 1998: xvii). During the daily routine of their job, correctional employees are provided data and information by public agencies and other organizations that have a vested interest in their field. They can read trade publications; attend training sessions, seminars, and conventions; and spend time interacting with people in corrections-related industries. The information they receive usually will tend to reinforce those perceptions of corrections that are based on personal experience.

Individuals for whom corrections is a remote context may read correctional trade journals such as *Corrections Today*, *The Corrections Professional*, *The Prison Journal*, or *Corrections Management Quarterly* if they are curious enough about corrections to do so, or attend American Correctional Association seminars and conferences. They can browse the Internet and click onto department of corrections' websites that provide a wealth of factual information. All of these sources will provide them with information that will color their perception of corrections with the "real flavor." But most outsiders do not engage in these types of activity because they have neither the time nor the interest required to do so. Instead, outsiders tend to rely on the third social construction of reality engine as their primary source of information about corrections.

The Third Social Construction of Reality Engine: Popular Culture. Popular culture consists of vibrant sets of reinforcing images that provide the general public a factual and emotional perspective from which they can understand a remote context.

> Popular culture comprises the amusements that occupy the nation's leisure time; it reflects the interests, manners, and tastes of its diverse audience. It includes the popular arts—the movies, stage, television and radio, journalism, fictional writings, and the poetry and other forms of expression that appeal to the majority; and it includes fads and fashions in dress and speech, sports, and styles of interaction that draw the interest of audiences (Inciardi and Dee, 1987: 85).

If the "popular arts" fully and accurately presented the intricate complexities of corrections, then corrections professionals might have fewer complaints about public perception of the field. However, this is not the case because popular culture presents the general public a constructed image of reality.

Popular Culture as a Constructed Image of Reality

What does the term constructed image of reality mean? Surette says:

> popular culture is an extract of reality. Even when it is presented as a snapshot of reality as in the popular news, aspects of reality are extracted, recast, and marketed. Popular culture takes a specific, narrow slice of the world and reconstructs it as a constructed image of reality (1998: XV).

Because popular culture presents only a reconstructed image of a very "narrow slice of the world," there is a powerful tendency for that constructed image of reality to be distorted and not represent the "real flavor" of the remote context that is being presented. *The X-Files* episode cited at the beginning of this chapter is an excellent example of the constructed image of the reality of corrections. When exposed to this image of corrections, the typical viewer suspends disbelief and accepts the story line. This willingness to suspend disbelief and accept a constructed image of reality involves more than a lack of experience-based personal knowledge or the inability to create a conversational knowledge base. The attraction of the "popular arts" lies in their singular ability to meet a strong psychological need: the universal need to temporarily escape one's personal reality with all of its attendant stresses, issues, and challenges.

Popular Culture as Escapism. Popular culture's presentation of a remote context such as corrections to its vast audiences represents the opportunity for the members of those audiences to engage in a pleasurable escape from their personal reality: "Popular entertainment allows me to escape my reality; popular news gives me filtered, molded, snippets of the abnormal events of the world" (Surette, 1998: XV). Herein lies the attraction of corrections for the consumers of popular culture. People, in general, are fascinated with abnormal people, behaviors, and events. And it cannot be denied that prisons are abnormal environments:

> Basic survival tactics are necessary to endure even a short stay. Inmates learn to strike first and seek strength in gangs often comprised of dangerous offenders. Sexual assaults are frequent and often go unpunished. The prison experience is one in which the code of survival is survival of the fittest, in which weakness is a crime, and in which the expression of vulnerable feelings can jeopardize the survival of the prisoner (National Criminal Justice Commission, 1997: 33).

Correctional work involves an intense focus on abnormal people and their abnormal behavior. The people under the jurisdiction of corrections are murderers, rapists, pedophiles, serial killers, drug addicts, violent personalities, and alcoholics: the traditional outsiders of civilized society. The behavior of prison inmates is often abnormal: self-mutilation, suicide, violent assaults, escapes, gang fights, homosexual rapes, riots, and bizarre episodes of mental illness. Many inmates demonstrate morally repugnant personal philosophies of cruelty, hypermasculinity, physical and psychological violence, contempt for authority, and among the male prisoners, degradation of women.

Thus, prisons are unpleasant environments, which members of the public do not want to personally enter, but they do want to be able to have a window into those environments because of their fascination with the abnormal. The window that is provided by the "popular arts" provides outsiders with an opportunity to be removed from their personal reality and taken into the exotic realm of the remote context. But, popular culture does something else when it takes outsiders into a remote context. It introduces those outsiders to a broad range of stereotypes that describe the nature of the individuals who inhabit the remote context being presented.

Stereotyping is a form of social distortion that can be either positive or negative. Popular culture has a profound ability to define specific remote contexts through the manipulation of stereotypes that are readily identified with those remote contexts. Corrections is a remote context full of emotion-arousing negative stereotypes that can easily grab and hold the attention of the audience. But popular culture presents to the general public two diametrically opposed sets of negative stereotypes to define corrections and its employees. The first, and most pervasive, set of stereotypes defines a constructed image of corrections that we can term smug hack corrections. The second set of stereotypes, much less pervasive but still influential, defines a constructed image of corrections that we can term country club corrections.

The World of Smug Hack Corrections

Smug hack corrections is a world of dangerous, dark prisons populated by inmates awash in despair because their keepers are smug hacks. Toch and Klofas (1982: 238-54) identify the smug hack as a custody-oriented "guard" known for brutality, incompetence, low intelligence, indifference to human suffering, and an obsession with routine. The smug hack is not a figment of a writer's imagination. The smug hack actually has existed in correctional history. The essential characteristics of this category of individual can be identified in the following inmate description of a speech given by a Texas "guard" with unblinking icy-blue eyes set in a heavily tanned, weathered face:

> I'm gonna tell ya'll one time, and one time alone how I'm gonna deal. First off, if airy one uv you tries to run off, I'm gonna kill ya. If airy one uv you 'sputes my word, I'm gonna kill ya. If airy one uv you don' do lak I tell ya, I'm gonna kill ya. If you lay th' hammer down under me [refuse to work], I'm gonna kill ya. And if I jes take a notion to, I'm gonna kill ya (Crouch and Marquart, 1989: 59).

If this Texas guard becomes the popular culture standard for defining all correctional officers in all types of correctional environments, then negative stereotyping has occurred. The term for this process of stereotyping is gratuitous vilification.

Negative Stereotyping through Gratuitous Vilification. The smug hack identified by Klofas and Toch can be considered the focal point, or symbolic core, of smug hack corrections. For this reason, some suggest that corrections is the victim of "gratuitous vilification" (Kerle, 1996: 5), a specific form of stereotyping that creates for the general public a powerful negative image of corrections that is congruent with the Texas officer identified by Crouch and Marquart (1989). Gratuitous vilification constructs an image of the correctional officer as:

> a harsh (if not sadistic), power-hungry illiterate—an ignorant, rigid, authoritarian individual who is vigorous only when demanding inmate compliance, when opposing inmate's rights, when criticizing management policies or when scuttling rehabilitation programs . . . thugs . . . clones or zombies . . . uniformed automatons performing routine, mundane and mindless tasks which anyone could do, which permit no individual excellence, and require no notable skills (Ross, 1981: 3).

Because of gratuitous vilification "the image of the subhuman and senselessly brutal custodian lives on . . . " (Johnson, 1996: 199). The prisons run by the smug hacks are horrible, bestial places typified by the following statement:

> Prisons hurt, maim, and kill. Prisons demoralize and feed the self-hatred generated by failed human potential. To be a person caged, shackled, and bound is a humiliation which makes one feel subhuman. The slow and methodical rape of the spirit continues day after day: men and women inside our prisons are convinced that they have no worth, no purpose, no hope, no rights, no chance (Philip Brasfield, as quoted in Irwin and Snedeker, 1991: 96).

Over time and through constant repetition, the stereotypes created by gratuitous vilification are distilled, concentrated, and hardened into the oversimplified caricature of corrections known as smug hack corrections. The sadistic guards and despairing inmates of smug hack corrections define an ugly reality that is both repugnant and fascinating. However, popular culture provides the public with a correctional symmetry. Counterbalancing the ugly stereotypes of smug hack corrections are the public anger-arousing stereotypes of a far more pleasant correctional environment: country club corrections.

The World of Country Club Corrections

According to popular culture, country club corrections is a world in which inmates laze away the days in relative luxury at taxpayers' expense, unconcerned about being incarcerated because life in prison is so much better than life on the street. In this constructed image, inmates are served by correctional staff ever eager to respond to their every need and desire as quickly and effectively as possible. Inmates inhabit a world in which they routinely receive luxuries, such as cable TV and college educations, that are denied to the hard working taxpayers of America. It is a world in which there is no concern about deterrence or retribution. There is only a pervasive systemic concern that inmates have as comfortable an incarceration as possible. The stereotypes of country club corrections reflect the imagery of relaxed inmates and servile correctional employees more concerned about inmates being comfortable than they are about the suffering of the criminals' victims.

Both of these constructed images of corrections contain powerful negative stereotypes, but does it really matter if popular culture presents corrections in terms of stereotypes? As it turns out, it matters a great deal.

The Power of Popular Culture

Popular culture is a powerful social construction of reality engine for millions of members of the general public. Therefore, its role as a primary source of the general public's information about corrections is of concern for three reasons.

Correctional Dependence on Elected Officials. Corrections does not exist in a vacuum. It is a field which is dependent upon elected officials for the definition of its mission and the resources to carry out that mission. The general public:

> forms the constituency of the elected legislatures of the states, and the legislature is the direct source of the funding necessary for any change or improvement in the correctional system. Each legislator is necessarily concerned with the attitudes of his or her constituents toward the funding, design, and implementation of correctional programs within the state. The assumed perceptions of this vague, often unspecified and unorganized voting mass constitute the foundations on which our correctional structures are built (Cheatwood, 1998: 209).

In other words, an electorate ignorant of corrections as it truly exists will not be in a position to influence elected officials to take those actions which are in the best interests of both corrections and society. The result will be legislative actions, such as mandatory minimum sentences for drug offenders and actions designed to increase the harshness of prison life, which create serious (and unnecessary) problems for corrections.

Meeting the Personnel Needs of the Future. Today's correctional managers must look to the future needs of their agencies. If good people do not want to enter corrections as a profession because of their negative perception of the nature of the work, how is corrections going to manage the multitude of challenges it faces in the twenty-first century? As Gido (1996: 276) has noted, the corrections of the twenty-first century is likely to be confronted by smaller, less qualified labor pools; the loss of the most experienced managers and line staff at a time when they are desperately needed; increased numbers of women and minorities as staff in an environment which has historically been antagonistic to both groups; and the need to continue to evolve an organizational structure which will truly empower employees. The corrections of the future will function within a complex environment in which "transformational leaders must move boldly to change inflexible cultures and practices" (Gido, 1994: 280). These types of leaders are not going to exist when they are most needed if popular culture is able to convince the best and the brightest of our youth that correctional employment is undesirable and to be avoided at all costs.

The Self-image of the Corrections Professional. The problem popular culture creates for the individual corrections professional is, quite simply: "no matter how hard we strive to maintain our professionalism, our own self-image is damaged by these misperceptions" (Kniest, 1998: 46). As Richard J. Koehler, commissioner of the New York City Department of Corrections in 1989, said:

> Nothing can be more frustrating than working diligently on a day-to-day basis to manage correctional institutions; cope with the stress of crowding; deliver services in an acceptable fashion; and maintain a humane and effective system, only to read in the morning newspaper that your efforts and hard work have been crystallized into one newspaper story about a female inmate injured on her way to court, or the inmate who was erroneously discharged from one of your institutions. It is difficult under these circumstances to escape by saying, "These things happen" (Koehler, 1989: 16).

It is not just the self-image of the individual corrections professional that can be damaged. How they conduct themselves on the job can be called into question by their loved ones:

> The misrepresentations of a correctional officer's role can even follow him or her home. Dinwiddie [sergeant in the Missouri Department of Corrections] says that after his wife saw a videotape on the news of an inmate being maced by a correctional officer, she asked her husband if that was how he treated inmates (Kniest, 1998: 47).

Damaged self-image and familial questions about the nature of one's work and job performance can lead to stresses, which can damage both the individual and the people about whom he or she cares. In addition, the negative impact of popular culture can extend beyond the personal life of the correctional employee. It can negatively effect employee job performance:

> Because corrections staff rely on one another for support and assistance in their day-to-day work, morale and camaraderie are important ingredients to success. [Misrepresentations of corrections in the media] can fractionalize staff, reduce teamwork and affect how a unit and agency functions (Bill Bates, unit supervisor for the Missouri Department of Corrections, quoted in Kniest, 1998: 47).

If correctional staff experience low morale, their ability to accomplish the multifaceted mission of corrections can suffer. The "misrepresentations of corrections" noted by Kniest are the negative stereotypes that constitute the vast reservoir of correctional imagery known as the popular culture of corrections.

The Popular Culture of Corrections

The fundamental premise of this book is that there is a profound gap between the world of corrections experienced by corrections professionals and the world defined by the negative stereotypes that compose the constructed images of corrections. These stereotypes are presented to the general public through a specialized, and quite entertaining, category of popular culture known as the popular culture of corrections. The terms "popular culture" and "the popular culture of corrections," are not synonymous. Popular culture defines a much broader societal context while the popular culture of corrections refers very specifically to corrections and corrections-related issues. The terms should not be considered interchangeable.

Defining the Popular Culture of Corrections. The popular culture of corrections can be defined as multiple, intertwined sets of negative imagery based on correctional stereotypes and abnormal and unusual events assigned a greater prominence in fiction than they actually possess in the real world. The people and the events that create this negative imagery combine to produce a steady stream of stereotypes that are guaranteed to shock and titillate those individuals for whom corrections is a remote context. Whether presented on the printed page, the big screen of the local theater, in video form, or on the Internet, all of the stereotypes are disturbing and powerful. They easily move the consumers of the popular culture of corrections to tears, anger, disgust, and a variety of other powerful negative emotions. When they move the consumers to laughter, it is frequently laughter at the expense of the correctional employees being presented. These emotions will create a negative public perception of corrections.

The Mass Media as a Dissemination Vector. The power of the popular culture of corrections to influence the public perception of corrections derives from its array of powerful stereotypes and the dissemination of these stereotypes to the general public through the technology of the mass media (a term that includes both the entertainment media and the news media). According to Ray Surette, popular culture has become such an important element in the social construction of reality process because "the media establish powerful frames for perceiving the world while they control the distribution of shared social knowledge" (Surette, 1998: xvii). Put another way, because any given individual personally can experience only a limited number of world events, we are all dependent on the mass media for the social construction of reality (Hans and Dee, 1991; Nimmo and Combs, 1983; and Tuchman, 1978):

> In modern societies, the media often play a more crucial role than personal social networks in constructing social reality because knowledge of many social phenomenon is obtained solely from the media. Because few people have direct experience with crime and because the media are a primary source of crime-related information, the process of social construction of reality and the role of the media have been proposed as particularly important for crime and justice (Surette, 1995: 337).

The social construction of the reality of corrections is no exception to this principle of dependency on the mass media.

The Creation of the Popular Culture of Corrections

The popular culture of corrections is the product of a complicated, ongoing evolutionary process organized around the creation and consistent reinforcement of a core set of negative stereotypes and their associated imagery. This core of negative stereotypical imagery defines the constructed image template of corrections (referred to hereafter as the corrections template).

The Source of the Corrections Template. There are two intertwined streams of imagery-laden information that constitute the source of the corrections template. The first stream of imagery-laden information is the rich sociological literature documenting the history of corrections that has been compiled by sociologists and other academics. The sociological literature is a robust blend of people, activities, philosophies, and events, some of which were positive; some of which were negative. The negative people and events contained in the sociological literature are the primary source of raw material for the corrections template. The negative imagery associated with this raw material is given additional vitality by the second source of information that has developed in tandem with, and complements, the sociological literature. This second stream of imagery-laden information is the inmate-authored prison literature. These imagery streams merge to create a deep pool of raw material for the architects responsible for creating the popular culture of corrections: the collective of entertainment media professionals known as Hollywood.

Hollywood's Selective Editing of the Sociological Literature and Creation of the Corrections Template. The raw material contained in the sociological and prison literature, in and of itself, lacks the power to influence the public perception of corrections. It must be extracted and transformed into a polished finished product that will stimulate and hold the interest and attention of the general public. This process of extraction and transformation (selective editing) is accomplished through the myriad skills and technologies of Hollywood professionals.

When Hollywood writers, producers, and directors decide to produce a work of fiction involving corrections, they strive to emphasize the elements most likely to produce an exciting story line in accordance with the Hollywood requirement that there be a readily identifiable villain who will be confronted by an equally identifiable hero (Freeman, 1996: 11). It is the search for these elements that draws Hollywood professionals to the sociological and prison literature. These works provide the foundation for the powerful stereotypes deemed to be so essential by the creators of "popular arts." Because it is the correctional employees who are the keepers, and inmates who are at their mercy for all that they need for their survival, Hollywood's portrayal of the inmate as hero and the staff as the villain becomes inevitable. To sharply contrast hero and villain, and gain audience sympathy for the hero, Hollywood extracts from the raw material of the sociological and prison literature those elements that are most likely to be perceived as dehumanizing, brutal, and shocking.

These elements continuously are shaped, molded, and reshaped using a variety of techniques to produce highly entertaining work products, the most significant of which are the prison movies. As a result, Hollywood, over a period of decades, has skillfully crafted a corrections template composed of the most negative and virulent stereotypes of correctional history. It then has used its powerful technology to provide the sharp visibility that will present most effectively those stereotypes to the general public and influence their perception of corrections.

However, Hollywood deals in fiction and the public knows that fact. This raises the question of why the public will accept historical imagery presented in fictionalized form as a valid reflection of current reality. If Hollywood were the only source of correctional imagery, the impact of the popular culture of corrections on the public perception might not be as powerful. But Hollywood is not alone in presenting corrections to the public. Time after time history-based stereotypes of corrections seen in the prison movie are directly reinforced by news media coverage of examples of current correctional employee misconduct.

News Media Documentation of Current Employee Misconduct as a Direct Reinforcer of Stereotyping. A minority of correctional employees will engage in behavior that is prohibited by agency codes of ethics and codes of conduct. This negative behavior can be viewed as providing "proof" that the stereotypes contained in the corrections template, in fact, are based on reality. But current employee misconduct cannot reinforce Hollywood stereotyping unless it first comes to the attention of the news media.

The news media directly reinforces the Hollywood stereotypes of corrections by ensuring that current employee misconduct is widely reported to vast numbers of people who otherwise would not have heard about that behavior. Thus, members of the general public who hear, or read, news media reports of correctional officers beating inmates, or engaging in corruption, can mentally compare that information with the prison movies they have seen, even if this only occurs at an unconscious or subliminal level. The most obvious conclusion to be derived from this comparison is that corrections is indeed an ugly world run by smug hacks.

However, the news media can introduce a twist in the corrections template at this point. Reporters can present modern rehabilitation programming and activities in a manner which suggests the existence of country club corrections. Although this type of imagery deviates from the corrections template, it also can be defined as negative imagery because of the public's aversion to inmates receiving what are perceived to be luxuries.

Thus, the entertainment media and the news media converge to create a mutually reinforcing interface of negative imagery. But the power of the corrections template to influence the public perception of corrections is a function of more than the mass media. There also exist two sources of indirect reinforcement of corrections template stereotypes: the silence of corrections' executive managers (referred to as correctional silence—as we will see in Chapter 5, this term is not entirely accurate, but the discussion of the limitations of the term requires a degree of elaboration that would be inappropriate here) and the rhetoric and legislative actions of elected officials.

Correctional Silence: The First Indirect Reinforcer. Correctional silence does not play a role in the creation of the constructed image of corrections. It does not create or present historically derived stereotypes. Instead, it is an element that supports popular culture's influence by giving credibility to its stereotypical imagery. This credibility is the product of the fact that correctional managers (and, by extension, line staff) are limited in their ability to publicly challenge crime-control policy that is based on the political assumption that country club corrections actually exists. This limited ability to speak out is the product of organizational constraints that are political, ethical, legal, and operational in nature. These constraints create an information vacuum that allows correctional stereotypes to be the only view of corrections to be seen by the general public when crime-control policy is being debated.

The "Get Tough On Crime" Activities of Elected Officials: The Second Indirect Reinforcer. The public acceptance of country club corrections' stereotypes encourages elected officials to engage in two types of legislative actions. The first type involves the passage of "get tough on crime" mandatory sentencing and abolition of parole legislation. The second type involves legislation that mandates a harsher prison regimen, for example, the removal of inmate exercise equipment, the return to striped inmate uniforms, denial of television privileges, reduction in rehabilitation programs, and, in a minority of states, the revival of chain gangs. These legislative actions converge to create the prison conditions that are most destructive to the overall quality of prison life and most conducive to negative inmate behavior and employee misconduct. The news media reporting of any subsequent employee misconduct will directly reinforce the imagery of smug hack corrections.

In summary, selective editing of the sociological literature, augmented by the prison literature, creates a corrections template that is presented to the general public by Hollywood, directly reinforced by the news media, and indirectly reinforced by correctional silence and political activity. The result is a continuous cycle of negative stereotyping that produces a negative public perception of corrections.

Points to Consider

1. For the typical person, what other occupations constitute a remote context? Does popular culture treat these occupations as stereotypically as it does corrections? Explain.

2. Are corrections professionals justified in their belief that the public has a negative perception of them? Or are they just being overly sensitive to legitimate criticisms of their job performance? Defend your answer.

3. Why is the research literature on the subject of the public perception of corrections so limited?

4. What stereotypes of corrections are most frequently featured in the popular culture of corrections? Why?

5. Does the concept of gratuitous vilification apply only to corrections? If not, what other groups or occupations have experienced this type of negative stereotyping? How have these groups or occupations confronted gratuitous vilification? What can corrections professionals learn from these confrontations?

6. Which constructed image of corrections most upsets the public: smug hack corrections or country club corrections? Why?

7. Does the popular culture of corrections really have a negative impact on the public perception of corrections? Defend your answer.

References

Avery, D. S. 1989. Corrections—The Hard Sell. *Corrections Today*. (51)1:6.

Cheatwood, D. 1998. Prison Movies: Films About Adult, Male, Civilian Prisons: 1929-1995. In F. Bailey and D. Hale, eds. *Popular Culture, Crime and Justice*. Belmont, California: West/Wadsworth Publishing. pp. 209-231.

Cowley, J. 1998. Changing Public Opinion: Correctional Administrators Have an Obligation to Attempt to Influence Public Policy. *Corrections Today*. (59)1:38-40.

Crouch, B. M. and J. W. Marquart. 1989. *An Appeal to Justice*. Austin: University of Texas Press.

Florida Department of Corrections. 1998. *Corrections in Florida: What the Public, News Media, and DC Staff Think*. Tallahassee, Florida: Florida Department of Corrections.

Freeman, R. 1996. Correctional Staff as the Villain and the Inmate as Hero: The Problem is Bigger than Hollywood. *American Jails*. (10)3:9-16.

Gido, R. L. 1994. Organizational Change and Workforce Planning: Dilemmas for Criminal Justice in the Year 2000. In R. Muraskin and A.R. Roberts, eds. *Visions for Change: Crime and Justice in the Twenty-First Century*. Upper Saddle River, New Jersey: Prentice-Hall. pp. 272-282.

Graber, D. 1979. Evaluating Crime-Fighting Policies: Media Images and Public Perspective. In R. Baker and F. A. Meyer, Jr., eds. *Evaluating Alternative Law Enforcement Policies*. Lexington, Massachusetts: D.C. Heath and Company. pp. 179-199.

Hans, V. and J. Dee.1991. Media Coverage of Law: Its Impact on Juries and the Public. *American Behavioral Scientist*. 235: 136-149.

Inciardi, J. A. and J. L. Dee. 1987. From the Keystone Cops to Miami Vice: Images of Policing in American Popular Culture. *Journal of Popular Culture*. 212: 84-102.

Irwin, J. and M. Snedeker. 1991. Prisons are Violent and Dehumanizing. In D. L. Bender and L. Bruno, eds. *America's Prisons: Opposing Viewpoints*. San Diego, California:.Greenhaven Press. pp. 92-98.

Johnson, R. 1996. *Hard Time: Understanding and Reforming the Prison*. Belmont, California: Wadsworth Publishing.

Kerle, K. 1996. The Jail Image and the Caring Factor. *American Jails*. (10)3: 5.

Klofas, J. and H. Toch.1982. The Guard Subculture Myth. *Journal of Research in Crime and Delinquency*. 192: 238-254.

Kniest, T. 1998. Old Habits Die Hard: Corrections Professionals Constantly Struggle Against Negative Stereotypes. *Corrections Today*. (59)1: 46-49.

Koehler, R. J. 1989. Like It or Not: We Are News. *Corrections Today*. (51)1: 16-17.

McQuail, D. 1972. Introduction. In D. McQuail, ed. *Sociology of Mass Communications*. Harmondworth:Penquin.

Meddis, S. 1989. A Reporter's Notebook—Forming Partnerships with the Press. *Corrections Today*. (51)1: 22-26.

National Criminal Justice Commission. 1997. Imprisonment Is not Beneficial. In B. Leone, S. Barbour, B. Stalcup, and C. Cozic, eds. *America's Prisons: Opposing Viewpoints*. San Diego, California: Greenhaven Press. pp. 32-38.

Nimmo, D. and J. Combs. 1983. *Mediated Political Realities*. New York: Longman.

Ross, R. R. 1981. Introduction. In R. R. Ross, ed. *Prison Guard/Corrections Officer*. Ontario, Canada: Butterworths.

Schwartz, J. A. 1989. Promoting a Good Public Image: Effective Leadership, Sound Practice Makes the Difference. *Corrections Today*. (51)1: 38-42.

Surette, R. 1995. A Serendipitous Finding of a News Media History Effect: A Research Note. *Justice Quarterly*. 122: 355-364.

———. 1998. Prologue: Some Unpopular Thoughts about Popular Culture. In F. Bailey and D. Hale, eds. *Popular Culture, Crime and Justice*. Belmont, California: West/Wadsworth. pp. xiv-xxiv.

Tuchman, G. 1978. *Making News: A Study in the Construction of Reality*. New York: Free Press.

Zimmer, L. E. 1986. *Women Guarding Men*. Chicago, Illinois: University of Chicago Press.

Sociological Literature and Prison Literature:

CHAPTER 2

Raw Material for the Corrections Template

Corrections, like every other American institution, has a history that creates a rich tapestry of people, events, activities, and philosophies. This historical tapestry is a mixture of positive and negative imagery that has been documented in sociological literature developed over the past 200 years. Any creator of a fictionalized work involving corrections who is seeking information on reality-based events, activities, personalities, and imagery that can be woven into a stimulating story line can turn to the sociological literature as a primary source of raw material. Incorporating elements of reality into the structure of the final artistic product is done to enhance the marketability of that product by making it more "authentic," even if that incorporation involves stereotyping achieved through the selective editing of the literature

Sociologists and Corrections

The sociological literature consists of a rich body of scholarly books and articles in professional journals that discuss and evaluate specific correctional issues. Box 2-1 provides a listing of a representative sample of the scholarly books found in the sociological literature. Although some of the authors, especially those after 1980, were not sociologists, the term *sociological literature* will be used because the bulk of the books have been authored by sociologists.

There are four points to be made about the nature of this sociological literature. First, the vast majority of the authors of books on prisons focused their investigation on the male prison, especially the maximum-security prison. Any observations about corrections that were based solely on the examination of that environment might not be equally valid for lower-security institutions and community-based corrections. Thus, the raw material on corrections to be found in the sociological literature consists primarily of information about only one slice of correctional reality, and this is the most abnormal slice of all because the maximum-security prison environment is one of the most abnormal environments possible. The nature of the maximum-security prison is tailor-made for stereotyping.

Second, the vast majority of authors were white males who were interested in the study of male inmates. The result was a focus on male behavior and male issues.

15

Box 2-1 Books in the Sociological Literature

J. R. Brice, *Secrets of the Mount-Pleasant State Prison, Revealed and Exposed: An Account of the Unjust Proceedings Against James R. Brice, Esq., By Which He was Convicted of the Crime of Perjury, accompanied by affidavits to prove his innocence: Also an account of the Inhuman treatment of Prisoners by some of the keepers; and an authentic statement of the officer and salaries, with other curious matters before unknown to the public* (1839)*

F. H. Wines, *Punishment and Reformation: A Historical Sketch of the Use of the Penitentiary System* (1895).

G. Ives, *A History of Penal Methods: Criminals, Witches, Lunatics* (1914/1970).

F. Tannenbaum, *Darker Phases of the South* (1924/1969).*

H. E. Barnes, *The Story of Punishment: A Record of Man's Inhumanity to Man* (1930/1972).

J. F. Fishman, *Sex in Prison: Revealing Sex Conditions in American Prisons* (1934).

D. Clemmer, *The Prison Community* (1940/1958).

R. G. Caldwell, *Red Hannah* (1947).

A. E. Smith, *Colonists in Bondage: White Servitude and Convict Labor in America, 1607-1776* (1947/1963).

V. Fox, *Violence Behind Bars* (1956).

J. V Barry, *Alexander Maconochie of Norfolk Island: A Study of Prison Reform* (1958).

G. M. Sykes, *The Society of Captives* (1958).

E. Goffman, *Asylums: Essays on the Social Situation of Mental Patients and Other Inmates* (1961).

W. H. Blumenthal, *Brides from Bridewell: Female Felons Sent to Colonial America* (1962).

J. A. Leibert, *Behind Bars: What a Chaplain Saw in Alcatraz, Folsom and San Quentin* (1965).

D. Ward and G. Kassebaum, *Women's Prison: Sex and Social Structure* (1965).

R. Giallombardo, *Society of Women: A Study of a Women's Prison* (1966).

C. B. Hopper, *Sex in Prison: The Mississippi Experiment in Conjugal Visiting* (1969).

T. Murton and J. Hyams, *Accomplices to the Crime: The Arkansas Prison Scandal* (1969).*

J. Irwin, *The Felon* (1970).

O. J. Keller and B. S. Alper, *Halfway Houses: Community-centered Correction and Treatment* (1970).

D. J. Rothman, *The Discovery of the Asylum: Social Order and Disorder in the New Republic* (1971).

M. T. Carleton, *Politics and Punishment: The History of the Louisiana State Penal System* (1971).

G. W. Kassebaum, D. A. Ward, and D. M. Wilner, *Prison Treatment and Parole Survival: An Empirical Assessment* (1971).

E. Heffernan, *Making it in Prison: The Square, The Cool, and the Life* (1972).

R. Goldfarb, *Jails: The Ultimate Ghetto* (1973).

W. G. Nagel, *The New Red Barn: A Critical Look at the Modern American Prison* (1973).

Box 2-1 Books in the Sociological Literature (continued)

L. Carrol, *Hacks, Blacks and Cons: Race Relations in a Maximum Security Prison*
    (1974).

T. R. Davidson, *Chicano Prisoners: The Key to San Quentin* (1974/1983).

G. Hawkins, *The Prison* (1976).

R. Johnson, *Culture and Crisis in Confinement* (1976).

J. T. Sellin, *Slavery and the Penal System* (1976).

J. B. Jacobs, *Stateville: The Penitentiary in Mass Society* (1977).*

C. W. Thomas and D. W. Petersen, *Prison Organization and Inmate Subcultures*
    (1977).

B. McKelvey, *American Prisons: A History of Good Intentions* (1977).

H. Toch, *Living in Prison: The Ecology of Survival* (1977).

H. Toch, *Police, Prisons, and the Problem of Violence* (1977).

J. Q. Burstein, *Conjugal Visits in Prison* (1977).

J. W. Moore, *Homeboys: Gangs, Drugs, and Prison in the Barrios of Los Angeles*
    (1978).

S. Sheehan, *A Prison and a Prisoner* (1978).

R. Berkman, *Opening the Prison Gates: The Rise of the Prisoners' Movement* (1979).

D. Fogel, *We are the Living Proof: The Justice Model for Corrections* (1979).

J. Smykla, *Coed Prisons* (1980).

A. Stanton, *When Mothers Go To Jail* (1980).

D. J. Rothman, *Conscience and Convenience: The Asylum and its Alternatives in*
    Progressive America (1980).

J. Irwin, *Prisons in Turmoil* (1980).*

L. H. Bowker, *Prison Victimization* (1980).

B. M. Crouch, *The Keepers: Prison Guards and Contemporary Corrections* (1980).

D. Lockwood, *Prison Sexual Violence* (1980).

R. J. Wicks, *Guard! Society's Professional Prisoner* (1980).

E. Freedman, *Their Sisters' Keepers: Women's Prison Reform in America, 1830-1930*
    (1981).

L. X. Lombardo, *Guards Imprisoned: Correctional Officers at Work* (1981/89).

I. Hirliman, *The Hate Factory* (1982).

J. G. Fox, *Organizational and Racial Conflict in Maximum Security Prisons* (1982).

R. Johnson and H. Toch, *The Pains of Imprisonment* (1982).

W. S. Wooden and J. Parker, *Men Behind Bars: Sexual Exploitation in Prison*
    (1982).

J. B. Hirst, *Convict Society and Its Enemies* (1983).

M. Bell, *The Turkey Shoot: Tracking the Attica Cover-up* (1985).

J. Irwin, *The Jail: Managing the Underclass in American Society* (1985).

N. H. Rafter, *Partial Justice: State Prisons and their Inmates, 1800-1935* (1985).

S. Chaneles, *Prisons and Prisoners: Historical Documents* (1985).*

J. Pollock, *Sex and Supervision: Guarding Male and Female Inmates* (1986).

R. R. Ross and E. Fabiano, *Female Offenders: Correctional Afterthoughts* (1986).

L. Zimmer, *Women Guarding Men* (1986).

R. P. Dobash, R. E. Dobash, and S. Gutteridge, *The Imprisonment of Women*
    (1986).

Box 2-1 Books in the Sociological Literature (continued)

R. Johnson, *Hard Time: Understanding and Reforming the Prison* (1987/1996).*

J. J. DiIulio, Jr., *Governing Prisons* (1987).*

S. J. Martin and S. Eckland-Olson, *Texas Prisons: The Walls Came Tumbling Down* (1987).

P. S. Embert and D. B. Kalinich, *Behind the Walls* (1988).

B. M. Crouch and J. W. Marquart, *An Appeal to Justice: Litigated Reform of Texas Prisons* (1989).*

J. Pollock-Byrne, *Women, Prison and Crime* (1990).

N. H. Rafter, *Partial Justice: Women, Prisons and Social Control* (1990).

L. E. Sullivan, *The Prison Reform Movement: Forlorn Hope* (1990).

A. Butler and C. M. Henderson, *Angola: Louisiana State Penitentiary A Half-Century of Rage and Reform* (1990).*

L. T. Fishman, *Women at the Wall* (1990).

P. W. Keve, *Prisons and the American Conscience: A History of U.S. Federal Corrections* (1991).

J. J. DiIulio, Jr., *No Escape* (1991).

W. B. Taylor, *Brokered Justice: Race, Politics, and the Mississippi Prisons, 1798-1992* (1993).

A. W. Pisciotta, *Benevolent Repression* (1994).*

K. C. Haas and G. P. Alpert, *The Dilemmas of Corrections: Contemporary Readings* (1995).**

O. L. Lewis, *The Development of American Prisons and Prison Customs, 1776-1845* (1996).

---

* *Examples from these books are provided in the discussion that follows.*

** *The example cited is from Bowker's "The Victimization of Prisoners by Staff Members," pages 123-146.*

Even after 1980, there were very few female authors of books on corrections. Those who did venture into this male-dominated field helped to broaden the perspective of the literature by examining issues specific to female offenders and female inmates. However, this female-based sociological literature is just as vulnerable as the male-based literature to serving the function of providing raw material for negative stereotyping. Women in conditions of confinement offer a wide range of scenarios for stereotyping.

Third, the issues being examined most frequently in both male and female-based literature were those of violence; sexual behavior (both consensual and forced); the repressive nature of corrections; the exploitation of inmate labor; the failure of corrections as a social institution; and racial conflict, both interpersonal and systemic. As a result, much of the sociological investigation of corrections is framed by a focus on the types of negative issues that Hollywood finds most useful for the process of creating dynamic story lines and the correctional stereotypes that drive those story lines. Titles such as Fishman's *Sex in Prison: Revealing Sex Conditions in American Prisons*; Goldfarb's *Jails: The Ultimate Ghetto*; Sellin's *Slavery and the Penal System*; and Hirliman's *The Hate Factory* nicely define the historical focus that Hollywood finds most useful for presenting corrections and inmates to the general public.

Fourth, the study of corrections by management theorists and researchers interested in examining corrections from the perspective of its managers and employees is relatively new. As already noted, the primary contribution to the formal study of corrections has been provided by sociologists. Their most frequently used approach to understanding corrections was to view the inmates as their main source of information (Houston, 1995). This approach is known as *constitutive criminology*, in other words, studying the prison through "the voices of the prisoners, not the voices of the administration" (Vaughn and Smith, 1999: 910). Because these sociologists were primarily interested in the experiences of the prison inmates and their perceptions of corrections, the conclusions they reached about corrections were not always positive, as many of the book titles in Box 2-1 suggest.

In addition, the social turmoil created in the 1960s by the Vietnam War, Watergate, urban riots, the 1968 Chicago Democratic Convention police riot, the rise of feminism, the civil rights movement, and the misuse of state authority at Kent State University and Jackson State University influenced the sociological view of corrections.

> Beginning in the 1960s much of the sociological writing on prisons became informed by countercultural assumptions, chief among them that prisons are the oppressive instruments of an oppressive, racially discriminatory, and vengeful society (DiIulio, 1987: 19).

Some of the most disturbing examples of correctional life are cited in the writings of sociologists trying to expose the evils of a system to which they objected:

> Prison scholars, many of them penologists trained in the social sciences have been almost as prone as the more hard-boiled convicts to assume "automatically" the incompetence and malevolence of officers and to focus upon unrepresentative events (Johnson, 1996: 200).

The result is a body of literature in which the content of the books often matched the negative images to be found in their titles. For example, John Irwin, in his frequently cited book, *Prisons in Turmoil*, writes that:

> guards are more racially prejudiced than the average citizen. . . . Guards' racism takes three forms. First, they do not like, and in fact often hate, nonwhites. . . . Moreover, most white guards believe that nonwhites are inferior. . . . Finally, the guard force, with a rural background and poor education, misunderstand the perspectives of subcultures of most prisoners (Irwin, 1980: 125).

This statement conveys a powerful message to any individual exposed to Irwin's work. For those to whom corrections is a remote context, Irwin's words are confirmation of the powerful theme of blatant racial prejudice that is one of the seven structural themes of smug hack corrections that will be discussed later in this chapter. His words resonate with the vivid imagery of the racial segregation of inmates in the gym and at the movies presented in Carrol's *Hacks, Blacks, and Cons: Race Relations in a Maximum Security Prison*.

Research Articles in the Sociological Literature. Space limitations prevent listing the numerous scholarly journal articles in the sociological literature, but the fact that many of these articles reinforce the themes found in the scholarly books on corrections can be verified by scanning the titles in the sample of research articles listed in Box 2-2.

The focus of the journal articles in Box 2-2 are generally consistent with the focus found in the scholarly books examining corrections. Sociological books and journals have provided a solid historical foundation for the architects of the popular culture of

Box 2-2 A Sample of Sociological Articles on Corrections

R. Martinson, "What Works?—Questions and Answers About Prison Reform" (1974).

L. Carrol "Humanitarian Reform and Biracial Sexual Assault in a Maximum Security Prison" (1977).

E. Poole and R. M. Regoli, "Work Relations and Cynicism Among Prison Guards" (1980).

M. Colvin, "The 1980 New Mexico Prison Riot" (1982).

A. Propper, "Make Believe Families and Homosexuality Among Imprisoned Girls" (1982).

P. L. Nacci and T. R. Kane, "The Incidence of Sex and Sexual Aggression in Federal Prisons" (1983).

J. W. Marquart and B. M. Crouch, "Coopting the Kept: Using Inmates for Social Control in a Southern Prison" (1984).

A. J. Bronstein, "Prisoners and Their Endangered Rights" (1985).

B. Owen, "Race and Gender Relations among Prison Workers" (1985).

J W. Marquart, "Prison Guards and the Use of Physical Coercion as a Mechanism of Prisoner Control" (1986).

R. Tewksbury, "Fear of Sexual Assault in Prison Inmates" (1989).

N. R. Chonco, "Sexual Assaults Among Male Inmates: A Descriptive Study" (1989).

F. T. Cullen, F. E. Lutze, B. G. Link, and N. T. Wolfe, "The Correctional Orientation of Prison Guards: Do Officers Support Rehabilitation?" (1989).

R. L. Dugger, "Life and Death in Prison" (1990).

H. Eigenberg, "Male Rape: An Empirical Examination of Correctional Officers' Attitudes Toward Rape in Prison" (1990).

R. Martin and S. Zimmerman, "A Typology of the Causes of Prison Riots and an Analytical Extension to the 1986 West Virginia Riot" (1990).

M. E. Deutsch, D. Cunningham, and E. M. Fink, "Twenty Years Later—Attica Civil Rights Case Finally Cleared for Trial" (1991).

B. Modlin, "Naked Men and Uniformed Women: The Erotic Element in Cross Gender Supervision" (1991).

G. Bonnyman, "Reform Advances in Tennessee After Decades of Brutality" (1993).

corrections by documenting those negative elements of correctional history so essential to creating and sustaining the intense conflict and human emotion that provides the core of successful correctional drama. The subsequent selective editing of this literature has created and sustained seven negative themes conducive to negative stereotyping. In combination, these themes define the thematic structure of smug hack corrections.

The Thematic Structure of Smug Hack Corrections

The structural themes of smug hack corrections consist of seven interwoven sets of negative imagery: systemic physical brutality in the service of inmate discipline; the exploitation of inmates as a cheap source of labor; the degradation of female inmates; the condoning of homosexual rape; systemic racial prejudice; staff incompetence, corruption, and cruelty; and the timelessness of smug hack corrections. We will briefly review these themes and randomly selected examples of the scholarly literature that support them.

Systemic Physical Brutality in the Service of Inmate Discipline

The sociological literature frequently contains references to correctional systems, particularly during the early phases of their development, relying on a policy of physical brutality to control hostile inmate populations. These policies used the services of both employees and inmates.

The Correctional Staff as Brutalizer. There is documentation of many instances where disciplinary procedures were designed to be both brutal and degrading. The most commonly used form of systemic brutality in state prisons was the formal policy of flogging inmates:

> The victim is stripped naked and beaten with a cruel instrument of torture called a cat, from his neck to his heels, until as raw as a piece of beef. I have seen men flogged until their shirt adhered to the flesh; yes, I have seen the backs of some in such a situation that they smelled of putrefaction. The cat consists of a piece of hickory wood about three feet long for a handle, at one end of which is fastened generally about seven small lashes, which are twisted so hard that they cut and sink into the flesh nearly equal to wire. I have heard those who were suffering under that instrument scream murder so loud that they might be heard a great distance (Brice, 1839: 69).

In most states, the practice of flogging was legislated out of existence by the 1950s, but many of the sociologists studying corrections emphasize that the elimination of flogging did not mean that inmates were to be free from brutalization. For example, it has been reported that in Oklahoma, from the 1900s through the 1960s:

> Officers used deliberate tortures such as forcing the men to eat in the hot sun during the summer when shade was nearby and handcuffing prisoners to the bars in their cells (with knotted rags in their mouths) so that when their legs collapsed, their body was suspended only by the handcuffs (Bowker, 1995: 125).

As late as the 1960s, Arkansas correctional officers used the infamous Tucker Telephone to punish inmates. The Tucker Telephone involved physical torture: a naked inmate strapped to the treatment table at Tucker Hospital had electrodes attached to his big toe and penis. An electric generator from a crank-type telephone was used to send an electrical charge into the inmate's body. Inmates subjected to this torture frequently lost consciousness, suffered irreparable damage to their testicles, and not infrequently became psychotic because of the intensity of the pain (Murton and Hyams, 1969: 7).

The Inmate as System Surrogate Brutalizer. The sociological literature also reports that systemic brutality did not always rely on members of the correctional staff to be the instruments of that brutality. In some systems, inmates were authorized to exercise direct physical control over other inmates. The most notorious example of this delegation of systemic brutality was found in Texas.

In the early 1970s, the Texas Department of Criminal Justice's control of inmates was based on the use of the infamous Building Tenders (BT) system. BTs were inmates who were officially used to control the cell-blocks through the use of tactics organized around fear, intimidation, and physical brutality (Crouch and Marquart, 1989). Building

Tenders have been described as "the meanest characters the administration could co-opt into doing the state's bidding" (Press, 1986: 46). The strategy of maintaining control was simple: "BTs armed with homemade clubs would severely beat stubborn or aggressive inmates, a process called counseling or whipping him off the tank" (Welch, 1996: 360).

However, Texas was not the only system to use inmates as control agents. At Louisiana's State Penitentiary at Angola:

> Under the supervision of camp captains, who dispensed floggings and other harsh punishments at their discretion with little interference from wardens, were no more than a few dozen underpaid guards to oversee several thousand convicts; they were supplemented by hundreds of convict-guards, armed with rifles and shotguns and under orders to shoot to kill anyone foolish or desperate enough to attempt escape (Butler and Henderson, 1990: 9).

Historical events of this nature provide excellent raw material for the recurring images of employee and inmate brutality that are a common thread in prison movies and television shows incorporating a corrections segment into the story line.

The Exploitation of Inmates as a Cheap Source of Labor

The sociological literature emphasizes that prison wardens periodically have been expected to use inmate labor to reduce the cost of prison operation and provide a nontaxpayer revenue flow into the prison. To achieve these challenging fiscal goals, some wardens created chain gangs and work camps that leased inmate labor to community individuals and organizations. In many cases, inmate working conditions were inhumane. The most inhumane conditions existed in the post-Civil War South. During this time, the convict-lease system was used to control blacks after emancipation. Forced to labor under appalling physical conditions, mistreated and abused, fed only enough to keep them alive, black male and female inmates alike were returned to a condition of slavery. The inhuman consequences associated with this system of forced labor included:

> . . . the innocent were made bad, the bad worse; women were outraged and children tainted; whipping and torture were in vogue, and the death-rate from cruelty, exposure, and overwork rose to larger percentages (DuBois, 1901: 112).

The leasing of convicts was not limited to the South. States such as Michigan, Missouri, Indiana, Illinois, California, Nebraska, Montana, Wyoming, Oregon, and Texas all leased out inmates during the 1880s (McShane, 1996: 71). But, regardless of the region or the race of the inmate, for those inmates placed on chain gangs, and in work camps, "Conditions were brutal, and hundreds of prisoners died from beatings, disease, malnutrition, or in attempting escapes" (McShane, 1996: 19).

Some of the popular prison movies that will be noted in Chapter 3 use the chain gang as the primary vehicle for their fictionalized account of conflict between the keepers and the kept. Even today, contemporary prison movies and TV story lines will reference chain gangs or their modern equivalent: the prison sweat shop or work camp.

The Degradation of Female Inmates

The sociological description of corrections' treatment of female inmates is equally grim. Although flogging was not a common practice in women's prisons, discipline was still harsh and physical:

One of the most reliable women officials told me that in her state at the State Farm for Women the dining room contains a sweat box for the women who are punished by being locked up in a narrow place with insufficient room to sit down, and near enough to the table so as to be able to smell the food. Over the table there is an iron bar to which women are handcuffed when they are strapped (Tannenbaum, 1969: 104-5).

Typically, the literature reports that female inmates also labored under the same brutal conditions as men and received the same inadequate food, clothing, shelter, and medical care, especially in the South; their housing was frequently even more substandard than the housing assigned to the men; and they were routinely subjected to sexual assault by both male inmates and guards, with pregnancy being the inevitable result.

The sociological literature on the female offender and the women's prison provides fertile ground for the sexual exploitation themes that dominate the B-Class women's prison movies that will be discussed in Chapter 3.

The Condoning of Homosexual Rape

Some sociologists have documented allegations of a particularly repulsive form of correctional employee misconduct that visits the ultimate degradation onto a male inmate. For example, in one prison where staff members had a practice of presenting homosexuals to inmate leaders as "gifts" for controlling the inmate population, one inmate was given to:

> . . . an entire wing of the prison, as a bonus to the convicts for their good behavior. In this wing, any prisoner who wanted his services, at any time and for any purpose, was given it; the guards opened doors, passed him from one cell to another, provided lubricants, permitted an orgy of simultaneous oral and anal entry, and even arranged privacy (Sagarin and MacNamara, 1975: 21-22).

The discussion of homosexual rape is one of the taboos in corrections; yet, it is a subject that is at least mentioned in virtually every book written by inmate authors or any prison movie created by Hollywood. This theme promotes some of the most vivid stereotypical imagery to be found in prison movies.

Systemic Racial Prejudice

The sociological literature emphasizes that for most of their history, American prisons were racially segregated with the level of brutality directed at black inmates as great, or greater, than it was for white inmates. Reports claim that white guards were especially quick to use violence when black inmates challenged their authority:

> A group of black prisoners refused to return to their cells, and one black prisoner raised his hand in the black power salute. A guard was heard to say, "That one is mine!" and the young man was fatally riddled with five bullets. Testimony before the United States Senate later revealed that approximately 50% of the correctional officers involved in the incident belonged to the Ku Klux Klan (Bowker, 1995: 127).

Prison movies and television shows using a prison segment tend to have at least an undercurrent of racial tension present even if there is no overt racial conflict. It has become a staple of the popular culture of corrections that racial prejudice in corrections is systemic.

Staff Incompetence, Corruption, and Cruelty

The sociological literature often has viewed correctional employees, especially the security staff, as having a competence status only slightly above that of the inmates:

> The guards are politically appointed, untrained for their work by even an institutional school of instruction, with no assurance of tenure or pension, underpaid, many physically unfit for the crises (escapes, mutiny, pursuit, and supervision), [and] inexperienced in prison conditions (Jacobs, 1977: 21).

More damaging than allegations of incompetence, however, was the documentation of brutality and indifference to suffering by top institutional managers. A classic example of this is seen in the case of Zebulon Brockway of the Elmira Reformatory, where legislative investigators discovered "a widespread conspiracy to supply tobacco, opium and other contraband articles to prisoners" (quoted in Pisciotta, 1994: 106) as well as a homosexual "sex ring" openly operated by correctional staff. Worse were the brutal disciplinary methods personally applied by Brockway:

> Brockway admitted that he whipped inmates, punched them in the face, struck them with the clublike handle of his whip, chained them for months in rest cure cells on a diet of bread and water, used corporal punishment to extract confessions, and sent threatening notes to terrorize offenders into compliance. . . . He conceded that his trusted inmate-monitors were the backbone of Elmira's "sex ring" and that escapes and violence were, indeed, serious concerns (Pisciotta, 1994: 53).

This theme of staff incompetence, corruption, and cruelty can be considered the glue that holds the other themes together in a cohesive structure because they could not exist without it. Bell's *The Turkey Shoot: Tracking the Attica Cover-up*, provides an excellent illustration of this point. Staff incompetence, corruption, and cruelty is an ugly theme that has become a virtual cliche in the popular culture of corrections because it is continually repeated with numerous variations, none of which reflect kindly on correctional managers and line staff.

The final structural theme of smug hack corrections is more difficult to define, but it is just as important as the first six themes because it stipulates that it is futile to attempt to introduce positive changes into the world of smug hack corrections.

The Timelessness of Smug Hack Corrections

There is support in the sociological literature for the theme that Smug Hack Corrections has always been, and always will be, the dominant expression of correctional reality in the United States:

> A sober fact about the prison: alone among all the major social institutions serving as the keystone of the American social structure for the past two centuries, the prison has changed the least—hardly at all. . . . Only one institution has not been battered by either the tidal waves of progress or the shock waves of social trauma: recessions, mass unemployment, depression, riots, civil war, armed insurrections, law enforcement run amok, civil disobedience, arson, domestic psychological warfare—the prison (Chaneles, 1985: xi-xii).

This statement suggests that any evils that occurred in the past are destined to reappear in the present and the future. This is a theme emphasized in such books as Sullivan's

The Prison Reform Movement: Forlorn Hope (1990). The practical implication of this theme is the conclusion that the popular culture of corrections will be unchallengeable because it will be continuously fed a steady stream of current examples that maintain its power.

These examples represent a very small sample of the sociological literature that provides the architects of the popular culture of corrections with a ready supply of raw material that can be crafted into riveting fictionalized accounts of an exploitative, brutal, sexist, and racist corrections with little or no redeeming features. But the sociological literature is only the first source of raw material for negative stereotyping.

The second source of raw material is those inmates who are sufficiently intelligent and literate to create an articulate prison literature based on the novelization of their personal experiences with incarceration and, to a much lesser extent, parole. This prison literature consistently has emphasized the theme of the oppressed inmate as the victim of a corruptly lethal system. Inmate-authored novels reinforce all seven of the negative structural themes documented in the sociological literature by giving them credibility through the validation of inmates' personal experiences.

Inmate-authored Prison Literature

There is a rich prison literature that has been created by inmates. Box 2-3 provides a list of some of the best known of the inmate-authors and their novels.

In his review of the inmate-authored prison literature, Dennis Massey defines the emotional mood that drives every inmate-authored prison novel and continuously reinforces the theme of the timelessness of smug hack corrections:

> What is depressing about the prison novels is the lack of change not in individual inmates, but in the criminal justice system itself. The main characters in Brown's *Iron City* are all eventually released, with a resounding sense that the movement has prevailed over the system, but this victory is an isolated one in the development of the prison novel, especially novels by minority writers. More often the system prevails, even when there is significant change among individuals (Massey, 1989: 189-190).

A selection of inmate-authored novels have been chosen for a brief review because they have been particularly successful in presenting the seven structural themes of smug hack corrections to the general public.

The Inmate-authored Novels as Validation of Smug Hack's Structural Themes. In 1871, J. H. Banka wrote an intelligent account of his incarceration at the Southern Indiana State Prison at Jeffersonville. This book established the path that future inmate-authors would follow:

> ... the most vivid scenes [of the book] are of the shop labor and its drudgery, the drunken warden and his corrupt staff and incredibly poor management, and the debauchery and torture of the female inmates. ... and the assorted punishments meted out to violators of prison rules. (Massey, 1989: 25).

Four structural themes are easily identified in this single paragraph. In 1927, the intertwined structural themes of employee corruption and the ugly brutality of the contract labor system were highlighted exceptionally well by Charles L. Clark in his autobiography *Lockstep and Corridor*.

In 1967, Malcolm Braly wrote *On the Yard*, a work of fiction which was clearly based on his experiences during confinement in San Quentin and other prisons. *On the Yard*

Box 2-3 Inmate-authored Novels about the Prison Experience

J. H. Banka, *State Prison Life by One Who Has Been There, Written By a Convict, in a Convict's Cell* (1871).

C. L. Clark, *Lockstep and Corridor* (1927).

R. J. Tasker, *Grimhaven* (1930).

R. E. Burns, *I Am A Fugitive From A Chain Gang* (1932).

V. F. Nelson, *Prison Days and Nights* (1933).

J. Odlum, *Each Dawn I Die* (1938).

L. L. Brown, *Iron City* (1952).

C. Himes, *Cast The First Stone* (1952).

F. Elli, *The Riot* (1964).

B. Sands, *My Shadow Ran Fast* (1964).

D. Pearce, *Cool Hand Luke* (1965).

M. Braly, *On The Yard* (1967).

S. Elkin, *A Bad Man* (1967).

G. Jackson, *Soledad Brother* (1970).

E. R. Johnson, *Cage Five is Going to Break* (1970).

H. J. Griswold, M. Misenheimer, A. Powers, and E. Tromanhauser, *An Eye For An Eye* (1970).

E. Bunker, *No Beast So Fierce* (1973).

D. Goines, *White Man's Justice: Black Man's Grief* (1973).

P. Thomas, *Seven Long Times* (1974).

M. Braly, *False Starts: A Memoir of San Quentin and Other Prisons* (1976).

E. Bunker, *The Animal Factory* (1977).

E. Bunker, *Little Boy Blue* (1981).

J. H. Abbott, *In The Belly of the Beast* (1981).

N. C. Heard, *House of Slammers* (1983).

J. Harris, *Stranger in Two Worlds* (1986).*

D. E. Martin and P. Y. Sussman, *Committing Journalism: The Prison Writings of Red Hog* (1993).

J. Washington, *Iron House: Stories From The Yard* (1995).

V. Hassine, *Life Without Parole: Living in Prison Today* (1996).

L. Peltier, *Prison Writings* (1999).

---

* Female inmate author.

An exceptionally good discussion of many of the books authored prior to 1989 can be found in Dennis Massey's 1989 *Doing Time in American Prisons: A Study of Modern Novels*.

Note: Although he is not a prison author, Stephen King's *The Green Mile* (1996) should also be noted at this point because it has been a very popular, and undoubtedly influential, book. The 1999 Tom Hanks movie based on Stephen King's book will be discussed in Chapter 3.

attempted to present the underlying futility of corrections as a corrective social institution. In the introductory note to the book, an individual identified as Philip T. Brylke, Jr, A-71991, California Prisoners' Union, notes that "The book details in trembling simplicity the essential nature of the diseased beast we call Prison" (Brylke, 1967). *On the*

Yard presents a generally negative picture of correctional employees. At one point in the book, for example, an inmate reflects that he is happy that the correctional employee who is his boss is not "some dreary time server, or one of the pompous blanks or vicious little opportunists who infested the administrative staff" (Braly, 1967: 89).

In 1970, *An Eye for an Eye* was published. Written by four inmates (H. Jack Griswold, Mike Misenheimer, Art Powers, and Ed Tromanhauser), this book was more clearly biographical in nature than *On the Yard*. The credentials these men possessed to write the book consist of their serving a combined total of more than fifty years for crimes ranging from burglary to kidnaping. The stated premise of the book is the "crime of punishment." In the preface of the book, H. Jack Griswold, an inmate-journalist, writes that the motivation for the book is the belief that he and his three coauthors have a responsibility to:

> verbally kick the affluent cushions from beneath the sleeping public, tell them what's really going on in this nation's prisons, and inform them that they're victims of a gigantic fraud with regard to the so-called "rehabilitation" programs in vogue today. . . . present state of affairs in corrections in this country is appalling, and nothing can or will be done until you demand something more workable and humane (H. Jack Griswold in Griswold et al., 1971: ix).

Griswold then goes on to state that the prisons of America "are in reality catacombs of misery and perversion, caldrons of bitterness and hatred that must be torn down and replaced with scientifically oriented centers of social adjustment" (H. Jack Griswold in Griswold et al., 1971: ix). *An Eye for an Eye* provides so many examples of correctional brutality and indifference to human suffering that Ed Tromanhauser (one of the inmates) makes the argument that it is the prison which makes men into criminals. In other words, the prison environment is so corrosive that a descent into criminality is inevitable. He states that if 1,000 typical men were suddenly incarcerated:

> 40 percent of the men would become so inured to the prison way of life, so indoctrinated by the criminogenic outlook on life, that they would be future serious lawbreakers upon release (Ed Tromhauser in Griswold et al., 1970: 209).

In 1974, Piri Thomas presented *Seven Long Times* to the public. Piri Thomas is a minority from two worlds: African-American and Puerto Rican. He effectively presents the imagery of racial discrimination, homosexual violence, and brutal guards in a prison system run by white males. Thomas places a particular emphasis on the threat posed by inmates who desire to turn other inmates into their "punks" through sexual assault and verbal intimidation. This is a theme that will be graphically repeated in Nathan Heard's 1983 *House of Slammers*.

In 1981, another articulate inmate, Jack Abbott, presented inmates as victims of a consciously racist corrections system. In his book, *In the Belly of the Beast*, he writes:

> At Leavenworth and Atlanta, I was always thrown into all-black cells. . . . The idea was to get me to be attacked by blacks. The idea was to get me to hate blacks. I personally have never had any problems with them. . . . This is because I am known among them. But my case is exceptional, and as a rule whites are turned into active racists by this method (Abbott, 1981: 182).

This statement by Abbott echoes and reinforces the imagery of overt racial prejudice and hostility to minorities presented so powerfully by Donald Goines in *White*

Man's Justice: Black Man's Grief (1973) and Piri Thomas in *Seven Long Times* (1974).

Inmate author Victor Hassine, in his 1996 book about the travails of his incarceration in several of the correctional facilities in the Pennsylvania Department of Corrections, has noted the prevailing theme of prison violence:

> Violence and hatred in prison means more money, more guards, more overtime, and more prisons. What incentive is there to keep prisons safe and humane? All staff has to do is sit back and let the men tear each other apart (Hassine, 1996: 65).

Hassine's book is unique in one respect. In the Appendix, he praises a Deputy Superintendent for Operations at the State Correctional Institution at Camp Hill for testimony he provided to a Senate Judiciary Committee:

> In his testimony he graphically outlined incident after incident of corruption, violence, drug dealing, and incompetence. This disturbing account will give outsiders a clearer sense of the grim realities of prison life (Hassine, 1996: 144).

Victor Hassine is careful to note that the Deputy Superintendent in question was fired by the Department of Corrections.

The Female Inmate Contribution to the Prison Literature. As with the sociological literature, the primary contributors to the prison literature have been men, possibly because there are so many more of them. One exception is Jean Harris, the murderer of Dr. Herman Tarnower, the Scarsdale Diet Doctor. In her 1986 book, *Stranger in Two Worlds*, she documents, among other themes, the overall incompetence of many of the correctional employees. In general, however, her book is relatively benign compared to the scathing prose of many of the male inmate authors.

Adding to the Sociological Literature. The sociological literature is not static. It is constantly being updated and, in some cases, this updating of the literature involves inmate activities that demonstrate the lengths to which inmates will go to protest their conditions of confinement. For example, in February 1951, thirty-seven inmates at Angola used a single-edged razor blade to slash their Achilles tendons in a protest against inhumane working conditions (Butler and Henderson, 1990: 18-19). In 1967, a labor camp of young male inmates was assigned to a quarry in Georgia where they spent the hot days breaking rocks with sledge hammers. During an inmate uprising, fifty-two inmates protested their inhumane working conditions by using their state-issued hammers to break their own legs (American Correctional Association, 1995: 3).

These types of incidents confer validity onto the books of the inmate authors and increase the imagery in the sociological literature that will support the seven structural themes of smug hack corrections.

The Sociological Literature and Country Club Corrections

In contrast to the voluminous sociological literature cited in our discussion of smug hack corrections, there is very little in that literature to support the stereotypes of country club corrections. There is certainly nothing in the inmate-authored prison literature to support the idea that inmates live a country club existence. Rather, this set of stereotypes appears to be a much more recent phenomenon that is the creation of contemporary writers of magazine and newspaper articles. An excellent example of this view of corrections is found in a 1994 *Reader's Digest* article, "Must Our Prisons Be Resorts?" As the biased title suggests, the author paints a very rosy picture of incarceration. According to this article:

Hard labor is out, physical fitness is in. From aerobics to strength training to boxing, today's thugs and armed robbers can return to the streets bigger, stronger and faster than ever. When they're tired of working out, they can join theater groups, take music lessons or college courses—all for free. Or they can tune into the latest R-rated movies (Bidinotto, 1994: 66).

The article provides a variety of examples of the resort life of the inmate, including the annual "Outta Joint" picnic at the New Mexico State Penitentiary at Santa Fe where inmates "were entertained by a clown, a puppet show, a political satire performance, and eight bands" (Bidinotto, 1994: 67). The article describes the annual Lifer's Banquet at the Massachusetts Correctional Institution in Norfolk where "Some 33 convicts, mostly murderers, and 49 invited guests enjoyed catered prime rib dinners" (Bidinotto, 1994: 67). To further drive home the point:

At the high-security Sullivan Prison in Fallsburg, N.Y., twin yards filled with barbells and recreational equipment also have outdoor TVs, so inmates working out don't miss their favorite shows. Inside, prisoners "Jam" in a music room crammed with electric guitars, amplifiers, drums and keyboards (Bidinotto, 1994: 67).

This description of country club corrections concludes with a memo from a Massachusetts policy coordinator which informs inmates of an increase in recreation in the form of the creation of a third baseball field. Because of the addition of this new baseball field:

The horseshoe pits will be temporarily relocated near the golf course. The bocci area will be relocated at the site of the new gym. The soccer field will be relocated to the east Field behind the softball field (Bidinotto, 1994: 71).

The article concludes with the plaintive question: "Hasn't the time come for us to require public officials to explain why prisons need to be resorts?"

Using this example of the type of editorial attacks on corrections that periodically surface, it is safe to say that this type of article suggests three structural themes for country club corrections: no discipline; no work; and no remorse. But there are other themes more disturbing to the general public. These appear in newspaper articles with sensational newspaper headlines such as "Iowa Inmates Granted Right to Read Porn" (Johnson, 1989: A1, A4). Dozens of similar articles have appeared on this subject over the past decade, all giving the impression that prison is a porn lover's paradise. These types of newspaper articles add a fourth theme: sexual immorality.

There is a fifth theme, and this one gravely frightens the general public. It appears in newspaper articles with headlines such as "Slaying Suspects on Early Release" (*Brandenton Herald*, 1993: B6). This fifth theme is the jeopardizing of public safety.

The negative imagery to be found in the sociological and prison literature is powerful. But it will have little effect on the public perception of corrections if it remains in books and articles and is not disseminated in an easily viewed form to the general public.

Points to Consider

1. Why were sociologists so interested in the inmate view of corrections? Why did they pay so little attention to the views of correctional employees? Is this still the case today? Why or why not?

2. What has been the impact of inmate-authors on popular culture and the public perception of corrections?

3. Do you agree that the sociological and prison literature are the primary source of raw material for the corrections template? Why or why not?

4. Why have contemporary writers created the concept of country club corrections? Or are they actually reporting on a correctional reality? Defend your answer.

5. Why are female authors so rare in both the sociological literature and the prison literature? What impact has that had on the content of those literatures?

6. This chapter has cited examples of negative imagery found in the sociological literature on corrections. What are ten examples of positive imagery to be found in that literature?

References

Abbott, J. H. 1981. *In The Belly of the Beast: Letters From Prison*. New York: Vintage Books.

American Correctional Association. 1995. *Historical Overview: Chain Gangs in the United States, 1800s-1995*. Lanham, Maryland: American Correctional Association.

Banka, J. H. 1871. *State Prison Life by One Who Has Been There, Written By a Convict, in a Convict's Cell*. Cincinnati, Ohio: C. F. Vent.

Barnes, H. E. 1930/1972. *The Story of Punishment: A Record of Man's Inhumanity to Man*. Montclair, New Jersey: Patterson Smith.

Barry, J. V. 1958. *Alexander Maconochie of Norfolk Island: A Study of Prison Reform*. London, England: Oxford University Press.

Bell, M. 1985. *The Turkey Shoot: Tracking the Attica Cover-up*. New York: Grove Press.

Berkman, R. 1979. *Opening the Prison Gates: The Rise of the Prisoners' Movement*. Lexington, Massachusetts: Lexington Books.

Bidinotto, R. J. 1994. Must Our Prisons Be Resorts? *Reader's Digest*. November: 65-71.

Blumenthal, W. H. 1962. *Brides from Bridewell: Female Felons Sent to Colonial America*. Rutland, Vermont: Charles E. Tuttle Co.

Bonnyman, G. 1993. Reform Advances in Tennessee After Decades of Brutality. *The National Prison Project Journal*. 84: 1-5.

Bowker, L. H. 1980. *Prison Victimization*. New York: Elsevier.

―――. 1995. The Victimization of Prisoners by Staff Members. In K. C. Haas and G. P. Alpert, eds. *The Dilemmas of Corrections: Contemporary Readings*, 3rd edition. Prospect Heights, Illinois: Waveland Press. pp. 123-146.

Bradenton Herald. 1993. Slaying Suspects on Early Release. September, 23: B6.

Braly, M. 1967. *On The Yard*. Greenwich, Connecticut.: Fawcett Publications.

―――. 1976. *False Starts: A Memoir of San Quentin and Other Prisons*. New York: Penguin.

Brice, J. R. 1839. *Secrets of the Mount-Pleasant State Prison, Revealed and Exposed: An Account of the Unjust Proceedings Against James R. Brice, Esq., By Which He Was Convicted of the Crime of Perjury, accompanied by affidavits to prove his innocence: Also an account of the Inhuman treatment of Prisoners by some of the keepers; and an authentic statement of the officers and salaries, with other curious matters before unknown to the public.* Albany, New York: Printed for the author.

Bronstein, A. J. 1985. Prisoners and Their Endangered Rights. *Prison Journal.* 451: 3-17.

Brown, L. L. 1952. *Iron City.* New York: Masses & Mainstream.

Brylke, P. T. 1967. Introductory Note. In M. Braly. *On The Yard.* Greenwich, Connecticut: Fawcett Publications.

Bunker, E. 1973. *No Beast So Fierce.* New York: W. W. Norton.

———. 1977. *The Animal Factory.* New York: Viking Press.

———. 1981. *Little Boy Blue.* New York: Viking Press.

Burns, R. E. 1932. *I Am A Fugitive From A Chain Gang.* New York: Gosset & Dunlap.

Burstein, J. Q. 1977. *Conjugal Visits in Prison.* Lexington, Massachusetts: Heath.

Butler, A. and C. M. Henderson. 1990. *Angola: Louisiana State Penitentiary, A Half-Century of Rage and Reform.* Lafayette, Louisiana: The Center for Louisiana Studies, University of Southwestern Louisiana.

Caldwell, R. G. 1947. *Red Hannah.* Philadelphia: University of Pennsylvania Press.

Carleton, M. T. 1971. *Politics and Punishment: The History of the Louisiana State Penal System.* Baton Rouge, Louisiana: Louisiana State University Press.

Carrol, L. 1974. *Hacks, Blacks and Cons: Race Relations in a Maximum Security Prison.* Lexington, Massachusetts: Lexington Books.

———. 1977. Humanitarian Reform and Biracial Sexual Assault in a Maximum Security Prison. *Urban Life.* 54: 417-437.

Chaneles, S. 1985. *Prisons and Prisoners: Historical Documents.* New York: The Haworth Press.

Chonco, N. R. 1989. Sexual Assaults Among Male Inmates: A Descriptive Study. *The Prison Journal.* 72-82.

Clark, C. L. 1927. *Lockstep and Corridor.* Cincinnati, Ohio: University of Cincinnati Press.

Clemmer, D. 1940/1958. *The Prison Community.* New York: Holt, Rinehart, and Winston.

Colvin, M. 1982. The 1980 New Mexico Prison Riot. *Social Problems.* 295: 449-461.

Crouch, B. M. 1980. *The Keepers: Prison Guards and Contemporary Corrections.* Springfield, Illinois: Thomas.

Crouch, B. M. and J. W. Marquart. 1989. *An Appeal to Justice: Litigated Reform of Texas Prisons.* Austin: University of Texas Press.

Cullen, F. T., F. E. Lutze, B. G. Link, and N. T. Wolfe. 1989. The Correctional Orientation of Prison Guards: Do Officers Support Rehabilitation? *Federal Probation.* 53: 33-41.

Davidson, T. R. 1974/1983. *Chicano Prisoners: The Key to San Quentin.* Prospect Heights, Illinois: Waveland Press.

Deutsch, M. E., D. Cunningham, and E. M. Fink. 1991. Twenty Years Later—Attica Civil Rights Case Finally Cleared for Trial. *Social Justice.* 183: 13-25.

DiIulio, J. J., Jr. 1987. *Governing Prisons*. New York: The Free Press.

———. 1991. *No Escape*. New York: Basic Books.

Dobash, R. P., R. E. Dobash, and S. Gutteridge. 1986. *The Imprisonment of Women*. Oxford, England: Basil Blackwell, Ltd.

DuBois, W. E. B. 1901. The Spawn of Slavery: The Convict-Lease System in the South. *The Missionary Review of the World*.14: 737-745.

Dugger, R. L. 1990. Life and Death in Prison. *The Prison Journal*. 701: 112-114.

Early, P. 1993. *The Hot House: Life Inside Leavenworth Prison*. New York: Bantam Books.

Eigenberg, H. 1990. Male Rape: An Empirical Examination of Correctional Officers' Attitudes Toward Rape in Prison. *The Prison Journal*. July: 39-56.

Elkin, S. 1967. *A Bad Man*. New York: Random House.

Elli, E. 1964. *The Riot*. New York: Coward-McCann.

Embert, P. S. and D. B. Kalinich. 1988. *Behind the Walls*. Salem, Wisconsin: Sheffield Publishing Co.

Fishman, J. F. 1934. *Sex in Prison: Revealing Sex Conditions in American Prisons*. New York: National Library Association.

Fishman, L. T. 1990. *Women at the Wall*. Albany, New York: State University of New York Press.

Fogel, D. 1979. *We Are the Living Proof: The Justice Model for Corrections*. Cincinnati, Ohio: Anderson Publishing Co.

Fox, J. G. 1982. *Organizational and Racial Conflict in Maximum Security Prisons*. Lexington, Massachusetts: Lexington Books.

Fox, V. 1956. *Violence Behind Bars*. Lexington, Massachusetts: Lexington Books.

Freedman, E. 1981. *Their Sisters' Keepers: Women's Prison Reform in America, 1830-1930*. Ann Arbor, Michigan: University of Michigan.

Giallombardo, R. 1966. *Society of Women: A Study of a Women's Prison*. New York: Wiley.

Goffman, E. 1961. *Asylums: Essays on the Social Situation of Mental Patients and Other Inmates*. New York: Anchor Books.

Goines, G. 1973. *White Man's Justice: Black Man's Grief*. Los Angeles: Holloway House.

Goldfarb, R. 1973. *Jails: The Ultimate Ghetto*. Garden City, New York: Anchor Press/ Doubleday.

Griswold, H. J., M. Misenheimer, A. Powers, and E. Tromanhauser. 1971. *An Eye For An Eye*. New York: Pocket Books.

Haas, K. C. and G. P. Alpert. 1995. *The Dilemmas of Corrections: Contemporary Readings*. Prospect Heights, Illinois: Waveland Press.

Harris, J. 1986. *Stranger in Two Worlds*. New York: Kensington.

Hassine, V. 1996. *Life Without Parole: Living in Prison Today*. Los Angeles, California: Roxbury Publishing.

Hawkins, G. 1976. *The Prison*. Chicago: University of Chicago Press.

Heard, N. C. 1983. *House of Slammers*. New York: Macmillan.

Heffernan, E. 1972. *Making it in Prison: The Square, The Cool, and the Life*. New York: Wiley.

Himes, C. 1952. *Cast The First Stone*. New York: Coward-McCann.

Hirliman, I. 1982. *The Hate Factory*. Agoura, California: Paisano Publications, Inc.

Hirst, J. B. 1983. *Convict Society and Its Enemies*. Sydney, Australia: George Allen & Unwin.

Hopper, C. B. 1969. *Sex in Prison: The Mississippi Experiment in Conjugal Visiting*. Baton Rouge, Louisiana: Louisiana State University Press.

Houston, J. 1995. *Correctional Management: Functions, Skills, and Systems*. Chicago: Nelson-Hall.

Irwin, J. 1970. *The Felon*. Englewood Cliffs, New Jersey: Prentice Hall.

———. 1980. *Prisons in Turmoil*. Boston: Little, Brown.

———. 1985. *The Jail: Managing the Underclass in American Society*. Berkeley, California: University of California Press.

Ives, G. 1914/1970. *A History of Penal Methods: Criminals, Witches, Lunatics*. Montclair, New Jersey: Patterson Smith.

Jackson, G. 1970. *Soledad Brother*. New York: Coward-McCann.

Jacobs, J. B. 1877. *Stateville: The Penitentiary in Mass Society*. Chicago: University of Chicago Press.

Johnson, D. 1989. Iowa Inmates Granted Right to Read Porn. *The Tampa Tribune*. February, 6: A1, A4.

Johnson, E. R. 1970. *Cage Five is Going to Break*. New York: Harper & Row.

Johnson, R. 1976. *Culture and Crisis in Confinement*. Lexington, Massachusetts: Lexington Books.

———. 1996. *Hard Time: Understanding and Reforming the Prison*, 2nd edition. Belmont, California: Wadsworth Publishing Co.

Johnson, R. and H. Toch. 1982. *The Pains of Imprisonment*. Beverly Hills, California: Sage Publications.

Keller, O. J. and B. S. Alper. 1970. *Halfway Houses: Community-centered Correction and Treatment*. Lexington, Massachusetts: Heath Lexington Books.

Leibert, J. A. 1965. *Behind Bars: What a Chaplain Saw in Alcatraz, Folsom and San Quentin*. Garden City, New York: Doubleday and Co.

Lewis, O. L. 1996. *The Development of American Prisons and Prison Customs, 1776-1845*. Montclair, New Jersey: Patterson Smith.

Lockwood, D. 1980. *Prison Sexual Violence*. New York: Elsevier.

Kassebaum, G. W., D. A. Ward, and D. M. Wilner. 1971. *Prison Treatment and Parole Survival: An Empirical Assessment*. New York: John Wiley and Sons.

Keve, P. W. 1991. *Prisons and the American Conscience: A History of U.S. Federal Corrections*. Carbondale, Illinois: Southern Illinois University Press.

King, Stephen 1996. *The Green Mile*. New York: Pocket Books.

Lombardo, L. X. 1981/1989. *Guards Imprisoned: Correctional Officers at Work*. Cincinnati, Ohio: Anderson Publishing Co.

Marquart, J. W. 1986. Prison Guards and the Use of Physical Coercion as a Mechanism of Prisoner Control. *Criminology*. 244: 347-366.

Marquart, J. W. and B. M. Crouch. 1984. Coopting the Kept: Using Inmates for Social Control in a Southern Prison. *Justice Quarterly*. 14: 491-509.

Martin, S. J. and S. Eckland-Olson. 1987. *Texas Prisons: The Walls Came Tumbling Down*. Austin, Texas: Texas Monthly Press.

Martin, R. and S. Zimmerman. 1990. A Typology of the Causes of Prison Riots and an Analytical Extension to the 1986 West Virginia Riot. *Justice Quarterly*. 74: 711-738.

Martin, D. E. and P. Y. Sussman. 1993. *Committing Journalism: The Prison Writings of Red Hog*. New York: W. W. Norton & Company.

Martinson, R. 1974 What Works? Questions and Answers about Prison Reform. *Public Interest*. 35: 22-54.

Massey, D. 1989. *Doing Time in American Prisons*. New York: Greenwood Press.

McKelvey, B. 1977. *American Prisons: A History of Good Intentions*. Montclair, New Jersey: Patterson Smith.

McShane, M. D. 1996. Chain Gangs. In M. D. McShane and F. P. Williams, III, eds. *Encyclopedia of American Prisons*. New York: Garland Publishing. pp. 71-73.

Modlin, B. 1991. Naked Men and Uniformed Women: The Erotic Element in Cross Gender Supervision. *Odyssey*. 67-68.

Moore, J. W. 1978. *Homeboys: Gangs, Drugs, and Prison in the Barrios of Los Angeles*. Philadelphia: Temple University Press.

Murton, T. and J. Hyams. 1969. *Accomplices to the Crime: The Arkansas Prison Scandal*. New York: Grove Press.

Nacci, P. L. and T. R. Kane. 1983. The Incidence of Sex and Sexual Aggression in Federal Prisons. *Federal Probation*. (47)4: 31-36.

Nagel, W. G. 1973. *The New Red Barn: A Critical Look at the Modern American Prison*. New York: Walker and Co.

Nelson, V. F. 1933. *Prison Days and Nights*. Garden City, New York: Garden City Publishing Co.

Odlum, J. 1938. *Each Dawn I Die*. Indianapolis, Indiana: Bobbs-Merrill.

Owen, B. 1985. Race and Gender Relations Among Prison Workers. *Crime and Delinquency*. 31: 147-159.

Pearce, D. 1965. *Cool Hand Luke*. New York: Charles Scribner's Sons.

Peltier, L. 1999. *Prison Writings*. New York: St. Martin's Press.

Pisciotta, A. W. 1994. *Benevolent Repression*. New York: New York University Press.

Pollock, J. 1986. *Sex and Supervision: Guarding Male and Female Inmates*. New York: Greenwood Press.

Pollock-Byrne, J. 1990. *Women, Prison and Crime*. Pacific Grove, California: Brooks/Cole.

Poole, E. and R. M. Regoli. 1980. Work Relations and Cynicism Among Prison Guards. *Criminal Justice and Behavior*. 7: 303-314.

Press, A. 1986. Inside America's Toughest Prison. *Newsweek*. October, 6: 46-61.

Propper, A. 1982. Make Believe Families and Homosexuality among Imprisoned Girls. *Criminology*. 201: 127-139.

Rafter, N. H. 1985. *Partial Justice: State Prisons and their Inmates, 1800-1935*. Boston, Massachusetts: Northeastern University Press.

———. 1990. *Partial Justice: Women, Prisons and Social Control*. New Brunswick, New Jersey: Transaction Publishers.

Ross, R. R. and E. Fabiano.1986. *Female Offenders: Correctional Afterthoughts*. Jefferson, North Carolina: McFarland and Co.

Rothman, D. J. 1971. *The Discovery of the Asylum: Social Order and Disorder in the New Republic*. Boston: Little Brown.

———. 1980. *Conscience and Convenience: The Asylum and Its Alternatives in Progressive America*. Boston: Little Brown.

Sagarin, E. and D. E. J. MacNamara. 1975. The Homosexual as a Crime Victim. *International Journal of Criminology and Penology*. 3: 21.

Sands, B. 1964. *My Shadow Ran Fast*. New York: Signet Books.

Sellin, J. T. 1976. *Slavery and the Penal System*. New York: Elsevier.

Sheehan, S. 1978. *A Prison and a Prisoner*. Boston: Houghton Mifflin.

Smith, A. E. 1947/1963. *Colonists in Bondage: White Servitude and Convict Labor in America, 1607-1776*. Chapel Hill, North Carolina: The University of North Carolina Press.

Smykla, J. 1980. *Coed Prisons*. New York: Human Sciences Press.

Stanton, A. 1980. *When Mothers Go to Jail*. Lexington, Massachusetts: Lexington Books.

Sullivan, L. E. 1990. *The Prison Reform Movement: Forlorn Hope*. Boston: Twayne Publishers.

Sykes, G. M. 1958. *The Society of Captives*. Princeton: Princeton University Press.

Tannenbaum, F. 1924/1969. *Darker Phases of the South*. New York: Negro Universities Press.

Tasker, R. J. 1930. *Grimhaven*. New York: Alfred Knopf.

Taylor, W. B. 1993. *Brokered Justice: Race, Politics, and the Mississippi Prisons, 1798-1992*. Columbus, Ohio: Ohio State University Press.

Tewksbury, R. 1989. Fear of Sexual Assault in Prison Inmates. *The Prison Journal*. 62-71.

Thomas, C. W. and D. W. Petersen. 1977. *Prison Organization and Inmate Subcultures*. Indianapolis, Indiana: Bobbs-Merrill Co.

Thomas, P. 1974. *Seven Long Times*. New York: Praeger.

Toch, H. 1977. *Living in Prison: The Ecology of Survival*. New York: The Free Press.

———. 1977b. *Police, Prisons, and the Problem of Violence*. Washington, D.C.: Government Printing Office.

Vaughn, M. S. and L. G. Smith. 1999. Questioning Authorized Truth: Resisting the Pull of the Policy Audience and Fostering Critical Scholarship in Correctional Medical Research—A Reply to Kerle Et Al. *Justice Quarterly*. 164: 907-918.

Ward, D. and G. Kassebaum.1965. *Women's Prison: Sex and Social Structure*. Chicago: Aldine-Atherton.

Washington, J. 1995. *Iron House: Stories From The Yard*. New York: Vintage Books.

Welch, M. 1996. *Corrections: A Critical Approach*. New York: McGraw-Hill Companies.

Wicks, R. J. 1980. *Guard! Society's Professional Prisoner*. Houston, Texas: Gulf Publications.

Wines, F. H. 1895. *Punishment and Reformation: A Historical Sketch of the Rise of the Penitentiary System*. New York: Thomas Crowell.

Wooden, W. S. and J. Parker. 1982. *Men Behind Bars: Sexual Exploitation in Prison*. New York: Plenum.

Zimmer, L. 1986. *Women Guarding Men*. Chicago: The University of Chicago Press.

Creating and Disseminating the Corrections Template:

CHAPTER 3

Hollywood and the Prison Movie

The references noted throughout Chapter 2 can create the impression that the sociological literature on corrections is uniformly negative. This is not the case. Unlike the inmate-authored prison literature, the sociological literature documents positive elements of correctional history:

- Alexander Maconochie's mark system, a method of positive reinforcement of behavior with upgraded privileges for good behavior
- The reformatory system
- The 1870 National Congress on Penitentiary and Reformatory Discipline's *Declaration of Principles*
- Creation of the Federal Bureau of Prisons
- The introduction of racially integrated prison systems as early as 1916
- The construction of medium- and minimum-security prisons
- Creation of wage-based prison industries
- Hiring of female and minority employees
- The development of objective classification processes
- The introduction of human service professionals into the prison
- The development of inmate treatment programs as early as the 1940s
- The development of employee training programs
- The removal of female inmates from male prisons through the creation of women's prisons
- The creation of the juvenile justice system
- The creation and expansion of probation, parole, and other forms of community corrections

All of these initiatives represented the sincere attempts of prison reformers to create correctional systems that could manage convicted offenders humanely. These initiatives constituted a systemic rejection of the types of behavior reported in Chapter 2.

Creating the Corrections Template: The Selective Editing of the Sociological Literature

The consumers of the popular culture of corrections are rarely exposed to the positive elements of the sociological literature because of the marketing needs that dictate Hollywood's project design decisions. These marketing needs require Hollywood professionals to selectively edit the sociological and prison literature by extracting the imagery that is most vivid, most representative of intense human conflict, and attention-getting: the three qualities that Hollywood needs for the effective creation of the characters with whom the audience can identify and the states of dynamic tension that will enthrall viewers. Once selective editing has provided the most marketable image framework for a project, all that is left to add is the dialog that will define and advance the conflict that is the heart of a good drama (or melodrama, depending on the quality of the production).

The Financial Imperative of Hollywood Image Creation

The primary goal of Hollywood executives is to maximize corporate profitability through the development of financially lucrative work products. To accomplish this goal, every project must be organized around one compelling objective: the creation of imagery that will attract the revenue-generating public, hold their attention, and move them to tears or laughter through arousal of their most basic emotions. In other words, Hollywood must produce movies that contain the proper emotional hooks. Websdale and Alvarex, in their discussion of forensic journalism, define emotional hooks as consisting of:

> . . . those experiences that readers can relate to at some deep level and perhaps even project themselves into. Such projection, if it occurs, might result in readers being considerably relieved that their own lives were not taken or jeopardized (1998: 125-126).

Substitute "viewer" for "reader" and "own freedom was" for "own lives were" and you have a term that appropriately applies to prison movies. Prison movies attract the interest of the movie-going audience because of the artful use of emotional hooks that are organized around the language and imagery of the smug hack corrections structural themes extracted from the sociological and prison literature. Entertainment industry professionals are not concerned with the complex reality of modern corrections because their goal is profitability, not education:

> As products in a competitive high-risk market, the goal of motion pictures is to make money—not to educate, to deliver messages, or to present realistic portraits of prison life. If these things are done, they are by-products of the primary demand for financial return (Cheatwood, 1998: 210).

The end product of decades of selective editing is the corrections template.

In Defense of Hollywood. Hollywood cannot be legitimately faulted for this approach. It only acknowledges the fiscal reality that an audience in search of escapist entertainment will find a movie about a prison riot, escape, rape, or hostage situation to be much more exciting than a movie about inmates in a successful drug rehabilitation program. The Hollywood reality is that when corrections is being done right, things are very boring from the standpoint of the general public who are craving excitement and a temporary escape from their personal reality. For Hollywood, negative correctional behaviors are profitable, but positive correctional behaviors are not. Thus, it is in the best interests of Hollywood to present to their audiences the powerful negative stereotyping of the corrections template while ignoring the more positive elements in the sociological literature that would weaken the power of that imagery. As a result, the complex reality of corrections is filtered through the selective editing needed to create fiction that will attract viewers and revenue.

The Hollywood creation and dissemination of the corrections template is the most powerful source of nonpersonal information about the remote context of corrections. For many members of the general public, their first exposure to the corrections template will be the prison movie, and this exposure usually will take place at a very early age because of the pervasive presence of television, VCRs, and videotapes in the American household.

The Prison Movie

The prison movie has been the primary entertainment-based source of information about corrections for the public since the early 1900s. Between 1929 (when talking movies were introduced) and 1995, more than 100 American-made prison movies have been presented to the public (Cheatwood, 1998). These movies consistently have presented a starkly bleak view of prisons in which "there are few real heroes" (Cheatwood, 1998: 223). The typical prison movie is structured to present the most sensational and dramatic correctional stereotypes while ignoring the complex political and economic issues effecting corrections.

A Typology of Prison Movies

Derral Cheatwood (1998: 216-227) categorizes prison movies in terms of four eras: The Depression Era (1929-1942), The Rehabilitation Era (1943-1962), The Confinement Era (1963-1980), and The Administrative Era (1981-the present).

Depression Era Movies. These films portray the inmate as a victim of injustice: either a good man framed by criminals or pushed into crime by powerful societal forces or an accident. In some movies, the inmate is, however, a gangster who will redeem himself through some heroic or virtuous act. A recurrent theme is the corrupt values of the correctional system and the men who administer that system. These movies provide the foundation for the role reversal dynamic of the criminal as societal underdog and the correctional employee as oppressor, which will be discussed later in this chapter.

Rehabilitation Era Movies. Cheatwood notes two major themes in these movies. The first theme is the violence that occurs in the institutional setting. The second theme is the criminal's personal responsibility for his or her personal actions. These movies are essentially morality plays that emphasize the theme that crime does not pay. They focus more on the flaws of the criminal than on the flaws of the system. The recurring presence of violence, however, provides credibility to the harsh imagery of smug hack corrections.

Confinement Era Movies. These movies take a much more pessimistic view of both criminals and corrections: "Now there is no hope drawn from either the prison system or the individual" (Cheatwood, 1998: 223). The seven smug hack corrections structural themes blossom into the center pieces of the prison movies of this era: riots, escapes, sex, rape, racism, "and all the other facets of prison life that have become subject to big screen observation and exaggeration" (Cheatwood, 1998: 223).

Administrative Era Movies. Many of these films are futuristic or outright science fiction. Cheatwood believes that in this era of prison movies, we are seeing the confusion that currently reigns when the issue is the role of prisons in a modern society. In many of these movies, the violence is extreme, almost to the point of being a caricature of what can happen in a prison environment. The sense of futility and human despair is also a powerful theme used to highlight the extent of the victory that is achieved by the inmate-hero when he overcomes the system.

Categorizing the Prison Movie. An Internet search during the writing of this book produced a list of 603 movies (including movies produced in foreign countries) in which prison was either the setting for the movie, or was at least an important element in the story line. Prison movies can be divided into two broad categories: real life drama in which the subject matter is intended to be taken seriously or B-class movies in which overt sensationalism is the guiding rule and there is little attempt to meet serious dramatic standards. The worst of the B-class movies are the bad girl movies. Box 3-1 provides a limited chronology of the most popular American prison movies in the serious prison movie category.

The movies listed in Box 3-1 are serious dramas in the sense that they claim to portray the reality of prison life. While the setting for most of the movies is an America prison, there are movies which are set in foreign countries. The most obvious of these are the Devil's Island movies such as *Papillon* (1973) which was set in the French penal colony in Guyana in South America; *Midnight Express* (1978) was set in Turkey; and *Brokedown Palace* (1999) was set in Thailand. These films have been included in the list because they were popular with American viewers and their bleak story lines heavily reinforce the smug hack corrections structural themes presented in American-sited prison movies.

There are, of course, other categories of prison movies on the list that do not make the claim of being a serious drama: comedies (*Pardon Me*, 1931; *Stir Crazy*, 1980; *Ernest Goes to Jail*, 1989); musicals (*Hold 'Em Jail*, 1932); and science fiction movies (*Escape From New York*, 1981; *The Fortress*, 1992; *Deadlock*, 1992; *Alien 3*, 1992 and *No Escape*, 1994). Each of these movies has some influence on the public perception of corrections because it presents correctional stereotyping even though its purpose is to create laughs or paint a vision of a bleak future society.

The vast majority of all of these movies featured male actors in the lead role. One of the few exceptions was *Alien 3* (1992), which featured Sigourney Weaver.

The Movie in which Corrections is a Peripheral Element. The impact on the public's perception of movies in which corrections is only a peripheral element of the story line cannot be dismissed. For example, in *Tango and Cash* (1989), the scenes of graphic violence and the subtext of correctional officer corruption, although only a small element of that movie, contained vivid imagery that is not easily forgotten. And the prison sequence presented in *Good Fellas* (1990) was less than five minutes long, but the presentation of correctional officers as casually corrupt was both powerful and shocking.

Bringing the Corrections Template to Life

It is not enough to present the corrections template to the members of the general public. It also must be brought to life for them if it is to influence their perception of corrections. It must arouse their emotions if lasting memories are to be created. Hollywood has the power to create works of fiction designed to leave an indelible impression in the minds of the public through the skillful manipulation of their emotions. The power of

Box 3-1 A Brief Chronology of Popular American Prison Movies

Convict (1919)
The Big House (1930)
Numbered Men (1930)
The Criminal Code (1931)
Ladies of the Big House (1931)
The Last Mile (1932)
I Am a Fugitive From A Chain Gang (1932)*
Tonight's the Night: Pass It On (1932)
Escape From Devil's Island (1935)
San Quentin (1937)
20,000 Years in Sing Sing (1937)
Alcatraz Island (1937)
Prison Break (1938)
Over The Wall (1938)
Each Dawn I Die (1939)*
Mutiny in the Big House (1939)
Fugitive From a Prison Camp (1940)
Murder in the Big House (1942)
Behind Prison Walls (1943)
Within These Walls (1945)
San Quentin (1946)
Brute Force (1947)
My Brother's Keeper (1948)
Train to Alcatraz (1948)
Prison Warden (1949)
Convicted (1950)
Experiment Alcatraz (1950)
Inside the Walls of Folsom Prison (1951)
Carbine Williams (1952)
My Six Convicts (1952)
Riot in Cell Block 11 (1954)
Crashout (1955)
Big House USA (1955)
Cell 2455, Death Row (1955)
Behind The High Wall (1956)
The Steel Jungle (1956)
The House of Numbers (1957)
Escape From San Quentin (1957)

The One That Got Away (1957)
I Want To Live (1958)
The Last Mile (1959)
Convicts 4 (1962)
Birdman of Alcatraz (1962)
Cool Hand Luke (1967)*
Riot (1969)*
There Was A Crooked Man (1970)
The Big Bird Cage (1972)
The Glass House (1972)
I Escaped From Devil's Island (1973)
Papillon (1973)
The Longest Yard (1974)
Breakout (1975)
Short Eyes (1977)
Midnight Express (1978)
Scared Straight (1978)
Straight Time (1978)**
Escape From Alcatraz (1979)
On the Yard (1979)*
McVicar (1980)
Brubaker (1980)
Rage! (1980)
Bad Boys (1984)
Runaway Train (1985)
Marie (1985)
Hard Choices (1986)
Weeds (1987)
Lock Up (1989)
American Me (1994)
The Shawshank Redemption (1995)
Kiss of the Spider Woman (1995)
Under Lock and Key (1995)
Last Dance (1996)
Dead Man Walking (1996)
He Got Game (1998)
Live! From Death Row (1999)
Brokedown Palace (1999)
The Green Mile (1999)***

*   These movies are based on the inmate-authored novels of the same name referenced in Chapter 2. The result is a double whammy on the part of the inmate trying to influence the public perception of corrections. Inmate words, which often are moving, are translated into powerful visual imagery. The effect is to greatly increase dissemination of the inmate view of corrections and increase the impact of those views on public perception.

**   *Straight Time* is the movie adaptation of Edward Bunker's *No Beast So Fierce*.

*** This is the movie adaptation of Stephen King's 1996 novel.

this manipulation is obvious. Just ask anyone who watched the last five minutes of the classic *Old Yeller* when they were growing up.

Prison Movies and Emotional Arousal. The power of prison movies to influence the public's perception of corrections involves more than good writing and vivid visual imagery. The real source of the power to influence the public's perception is found in the profound ability of talented actors and actresses to bring that imagery to life through the vitality of their on-screen presence and their ability to project the emotions of their characters into the minds of the viewers. Popular movie stars can give a powerful emotional life to a script that will make it memorable long after the movie is over. Even B-class movies can impress themselves on the viewer's mind because there are human beings and aroused emotions associated with the movie's images, no matter how much those images distort reality.

The creative techniques that so effectively can manipulate emotions are thoroughly exercised in the creation of the prison movie. Because of its power to elicit powerful emotions, the prison movie is the most effective means of disseminating the corrections template to the vast audience targeted by the popular culture of corrections.

A Selection of the Top Box Office Serious Prison Movies

Seven movies will be briefly reviewed: *The Big House* (1930); *I Want To Live* (1958); *Cool Hand Luke* (1967); *The Longest Yard* (1974); *Brubaker* (1980); *Runaway Train* (1985); and *The Shawshank Redemption* (1995). These movies have been selected because of the box office power enjoyed by their lead actors.

The Big House (1930). In this movie, the inmate hero (James Cagney) is in prison because of an accident. *The Big House* can be considered one of the seminal movies on prison life because:

> *The Big House* was the source of images and illusions that continue to obscure the contemporary prison. Some of these images and illusions were created by sociologists who began investigating the prison in the 1930s and have since become the authorities on life there. (Even Hollywood, the society's leading image maker, consults sociologists when it makes a new movie about prisons) (Irwin, 1980: 29).

I Want To Live (1958). This is one of the rare prison movies in which a woman stars and is presented in terms other than the blonde stripper stereotype. Susan Hayward plays vivacious party girl Barbara Graham, who was executed in the San Quentin gas chamber for her role in the murder of an elderly woman. According to the movie, Barbara, although involved in various types of crime, was framed for the murder of the elderly woman by an ex-accomplice whose romantic advances she had rejected. Although this movie lacks the senseless brutality of many prison movies, it does present the inmate as a highly sympathetic victim of circumstances and the correctional staff as people who are uncaring and insensitive to the tragedy unfolding before them.

Cool Hand Luke (1967). Paul Newman is the lovable petty criminal Luke, confined to a stereotypical southern work camp for the relatively harmless property crime of light-heartedly cutting the tops off of parking meters after a night of heavy drinking. Handsome, proud, articulate, devil-may-care, Luke's rebel attitude makes him highly attractive to the movie audience, as well as his fellow inmates who look to him for relief from the brutality and mind-numbing monotony of their wretched lives. This relief is provided by Luke through such humorous activities as the famous egg-eating contest which Luke, stomach badly distended, wins. George Kennedy plays Luke's work camp friend, a big, burly, violent, not very bright inmate who nevertheless understands better than Luke that there is no safe way to challenge The Man. The Man is the captain of the work camp, the sadistic Strother Martin who utters the famous line "What we got here is a failure to communicate" after Luke has been beaten by guards.

The most sinister villain in the movie, far more terrifying than any of the inmates, is the gang boss who wears reflecting sunglasses, rarely speaks, and enjoys shooting inmates as much as he enjoys shooting alligators in the swamp where the inmates are forced to labor under brutal conditions. Defiant, unwilling to bend to The Man, Luke escapes three times, is captured each time, and given summary punishment such as long weeks in the camp's sweatbox, or being forced to dig six-by-six foot holes in the blistering summer heat, only to be told to fill them in and start digging again. After the third escape, Luke finally is murdered. The last look the audience has of Luke is his weary face in the window of a prison station wagon. It is obvious that he is dying from a gunshot wound as the gang boss casually decides to take him to a distant hospital, rather than to the closest hospital where his life might be saved. At the end of the movie, the audience knows that a true champion of the underdogs of life has been destroyed by a corrupt and brutal penal system incapable of human dignity and compassion.

The Longest Yard (1974). Rugged, handsome, impulsive Burt Reynolds is an ex-pro quarterback sentenced to a maximum-security prison for stealing his beautiful girlfriend's car and driving it into a lake after a lover's quarrel. Because of his former status as a National Football League quarterback, Reynolds is beaten by the brutal captain of the guards as an incentive to organizing an inmate football team to scrimmage with the guards' semi-pro team. The captain wants his guards to have some quality practice time before the upcoming championship game. The story line of the movie involves the scrimmage between the inmate team, quartered by Burt Reynold's character, and the guard's team.

Eddie Albert is a smooth, sadistic warden who is so desperate for his team to become a semipro conference champion that he cannot stand the thought of his players being beaten by an inmate team. Prior to, and during the scrimmage, he lies, schemes, cheats, and does everything possible to ensure that the inmate team has no chance to embarrass his guards by beating them. There is no deception too low or dirty to pull on the inmates. Albert is an individual so corrupt and devoid of human decency that by the end of the movie the captain of the guards, who has been won over by Reynold's refusal to surrender his dignity during the beating he takes during the scrimmage, ignores Eddie Albert's hysterical orders to murder Reynolds after the inmate team has been declared victorious. Even the warden's brow-beaten, mousey administrative assistant turns his back on the warden because of his admiration for the inmate hero and his disgust at his employer's sleaziness.

Brubaker (1980). Marketed as a fictionalized expose of Arkansas' infamous Tucker prison, this movie presents handsome Robert Redford as a heroic warden whose mission in life is to reform corrections. Improbably, even for the fantasy specialists in Hollywood, Redford enters the prison disguised as an inmate, briefly observes the brutality of his new environment and, after announcing to an incredibly stupid guard that he is the new warden, is escorted without question to the warden's office where he easily and unceremoniously relieves the corrupt warden of his duties and takes command of the institution. Replete with savage guard beatings of sad, helpless inmates; murdered inmates buried in unmarked graves; an incompetent doctor who charges critically injured inmates for emergency medical treatment; a corrupt line staff totally indifferent to inmate suffering; and the attempt of corrupt guards to murder the new warden, *Brubaker* glorifies the virtues of a reform warden by parading every smug hack corrections structural theme in front of the viewing audience.

***Runaway Train* (1985).** Like *Papillon* (1973), *Runaway Train* is the classic prison movie when the subject is the inmate's burning desire for freedom. Jon Voight is Manny, a hardcore inmate "boss" who is so defiant that Renken, warden of the maximum-security prison in which Manny is incarcerated, literally has welded shut the doors of the inmate's cell until a sympathetic judge orders him to be released to the general population. Renken tries to have Manny murdered, so the inmate "boss," along with a younger inmate, escape. The story line concerns Renken's pursuit of Manny. Eventually Manny boards a train heading to Alaska. After a series of mishaps, the train becomes a runaway. The end of the movie shows Manny atop the engine of the runaway train, arms held high, staring straight ahead as the engine heads into a fogbank. The message is clear: Manny will die, but he will die a free man. The visual imagery in *Runaway Train* is stunning, as are the negative stereotypes of brutal guards, the inmate "boss" ablaze with integrity, and the sadistic Warden Renken who will stop at nothing to retain his power over others.

***The Shawshank Redemption* (1995).** In this movie, the handsome inmate-hero, played by Tim Robbins, is an innocent man framed for murder. During his first night in prison, the sadistic guards savagely beat a new, fat, terrified inmate because he is crying for his mother. The warden is grossly corrupt, a master of the art of soliciting a bribe, who exploits his inmates by selling their labor to local business people and farmers who abuse them. The work is hard, unskilled labor. In the prison, there are no educational or training programs. There are no treatment programs or personnel. There are no efforts to counsel or otherwise rehabilitate the inmates. All of the correctional officers are white males. There are no women or minority officers. There is no sense whatsoever of the complexity of a modern prison. There is only senseless brutality and corruption. In fact, the warden is so corrupt that he orders the murder of an inmate who can prove Robbins is innocent. After engaging in such activities as helping the stupid guards fill out their income tax forms, and keeping the warden's books (which document every aspect of his business affairs), Robbins escapes and exposes the warden's corruption. At the end of the movie, the police arrive at the prison to arrest the warden and he, coward to the end, commits suicide by shooting himself in the head with his revolver. In the movie theaters, audiences cheered immediately after the suicide.

All of these movies reinforce the public perception that smug hack corrections is a plausible reality. The popular, highly visible Hollywood acting legends who star in these movies give life to the corrections template by linking powerful emotions with easily remembered faces that will fill in the features of the blank faces that otherwise would exist on the corrections template. The structural themes of stereotypical imagery are given increased power when the movie is based on a true story.

Box 3-2 provides a good example of the true story-based movie featuring an acting legend. Clint Eastwood starred in *Escape from Alcatraz* (1979).

The Worst of the Worst: The B-Class Movies. The movies that have been reviewed up to this point often can be justified on the grounds of literary merit. However, there is a subset of movies that lacks this qualifier. These are the B-class movies. B-class movies present a picture of corrections that is totally negative, often bizarre, and entirely devoid of realism. Even though they very rarely feature acting legends, these movies emphasize the presentation of every correctional stereotype in the most blatant and

Box 3-2 Escape from Alcatraz

Over time, the island prison of Alcatraz on the San Francisco Bay earned itself the nickname "The Rock" because of its tight security and unique location. No inmates were known to have escaped alive until the early 1960s, when three inmates, following an extensive and collaborative plan, left the prison by homemade life rafts, and were never captured. The story of this daring escape is detailed in *Escape from Alcatraz* (1979). Clint Eastwood stars as Frank Morris, an inmate who has spent most of his life being transferred from one institution to another. As Morris and the other inmates are mistreated by the correctional officers, viewers cannot help but cheer on the inmates as their escape plan comes together. Officers, most of the time following orders from the cruel and paranoid warden, are forced to carry out such tasks as hosing down inmates with fire hoses and revoking special privileges, often without reason. Through a lengthy process of digging and mapping their route through the prison corridors, the men finally make it, defying what the warden has emphasized to them during their short stay at the island—no one leaves Alcatraz alive. Although the warden and correctional officers have been made fools of, and in spite of the fact that the escapees are notorious criminals, viewers are glad to see even murderers and thieves escape from such a place as Alcatraz. As in many prison movies, the prison escapees are glamorized as heroes, while correctional officers are the antagonists. A suspenseful action movie is rarely as effective when roles are cast realistically, no matter how factually accurate a story may be (Excerpted from Gursky and Yurkanin, 1989: 95, 98. Reprinted with permission of the American Correctional Association).

lurid form possible. Prominent examples of the B-class movie are *Penitentiary* (1972), *Penitentiary II* (1982), and *Penitentiary III* (1988) in which an inmate named "Too Sweet" Gordon, who has been unjustly convicted of a death in the ring, must contend with a sadistic correctional system. These movies are one reason why:

> . . . the public has such a distorted, stereotyped view of corrections. This is a prison where a live band plays every day in the recreation yard, while inmates do group dances to the music; where winners of the prison boxing tournament receive a conjugal weekend visit with the woman of their choice; and where crowds of wild, screaming male and female inmates are allowed at the boxing matches. The sad part is that this is no comedy. It presumes to show the "reality" of prison life, and that's why it's so disturbing. Overall, *Penitentiary* is a violent, pointless film with blatant racist and sexual overtones. Blacks and whites, staff and inmates alike, are ridiculous, unbelievable characters. The main correctional character is the biggest buffoon of all, a fat, foul-mouthed, cigar-smoking lieutenant who threatens the inmates. *Penitentiary* is basically *Rocky in Prison*, but even the boxing scenes are bad. The plot, as such, boils down to this: The prison's best boxer gets a chance for early parole. For some reason, boxing skill and suitability for release go together. *Penitentiary* is neither entertaining nor informative. From the point of view of corrections and its public image, this film certainly does more harm than good. Even worse, it has spawned two sequels: *Penitentiary II* and *Penitentiary III*, the latest released in 1988. We can only hope that No. 3 will be the last (Excerpted from Gursky and Yurkanin, 1989: 95).

B-Class movies are notorious for their willingness to exaggerate and present people as caricatures and the *Penitentiary* series is only one example of this type of movie.

Bad Girl Movies. Women in prison movies, with remarkably rare exception, fall into the category of B-class movies. Typical of this genre are the following: *Women in Cages* (1971); *Chain Gang Girls* (1972); *Caged Heat* (1974); *Women's Penitentiary VIII* (1974); *Hellhole Women* (1981); *Emanuelle in Prison* (1983); *Chained Heat* (1983); *Chained Heat II* (1984); *Bad Girls' Dormitory* (1984); *Caged Women* (1992); *Caged Heat II: Stripped of Freedom* (1994); *Under Lock and Key* (1995); and *Dykes on Death Row* (1997). These movies have a high level of gratuitous sex (primarily lesbianism and rape) and male officer dominance and sadism. They always present a totally abnormal environment in which anything goes, as long as it is the guards who are the ones engaging in the anything goes behavior. Faith (1993: 55) has noted that:

> The one cinematic arena in which the stereotypes are thoroughly entrenched with little sign of changing is that of the low-budget women's prison movies. Prison movies have been predominately about men, and the stock characters in female prison films are borrowed from the male genre.

These movies are powerful elements of the popular culture of corrections, especially for young males, because they contain a squalid mixture of sex and violence that gives such energy to the stereotypes presented that they will be immediately recalled as soon as the words "women in prison" are heard.

The Occasional Good Prison Movie. In fairness to Hollywood, there occasionally has been a prison movie which has attempted to present a balanced view of prison life and the positive relationship that can develop between correctional employees and inmates. Movies like *My Six Convicts* (1952) and *Carbine Williams* (1952), for example, emphasize the desire of some correctional employees to engage in rehabilitative activities. And correctional officers are not always portrayed in a negative manner. For example, in *Bad Boys* (1984), Sean Penn and Reni Santoni, blood enemies because of their antagonism and acts of violence against each other on the street, are confined to the same juvenile reformatory. The juvenile inmate supervisors (who are never referred to as officers) are presented as individuals who care about the inmates, although they are not very effective in controlling inmate violence.

More recently (1999) Stephen King's *The Green Mile* (set in the 1930s) presents Tom Hanks as Paul Edgecomb, a compassionate correctional officer who cares deeply about other people, including a black inmate named John Coffey who has been convicted of murdering two young white girls and is sentenced to death. The movie is centered on the relationship that develops between Paul Edgecomb and John Coffey. However, as in *Brubaker*, the humanity of Tom Hank's Paul Edgecomb is most effectively demonstrated by contrasting it with the inhumanity of another correctional officer named Percy, who is truly sadistic and malevolent. This is a movie about personal redemption and it has a great deal of artistic merit, but it is set in the 1930s; therefore, it does not present the diversity and complexity of the modern prison.

The Primacy Effect and Rooting for the Underdog

Prison movies are fictionalized accounts of prison experiences that may or may not have actually happened. The viewing public knows that the characters in the movies are actors and actresses playing carefully scripted roles. Given this knowledge, why is it that prison movies, even badly made movies, have such a powerful impact on the public perception of corrections? The answer to this question involves two psychological phenomena which increase the believability and influence of imagery that is provided by actors and actresses during the process of emotional arousal: the primacy effect and rooting for the underdog. These phenomena assist prison movies in influencing the public perception of corrections by establishing a strong association between emotions and imagery. This linkage is often at an unconscious, or subliminal, level.

The Psychology of Popular Culture

The two psychological phenomena that should be considered are the primacy effect and rooting for the underdog.

The Primacy Effect. Psychologists have established that the first information an individual is exposed to about a person or group or organization creates a primacy effect (Belmore, 1987). That is, the first information tends to be given greater weight than later information that is received. If the first information is associated with negative emotions, the unflattering initial impression created by that information will tend to dominate the individual's perception even if later information is positive. This is because people tend to assign a higher weight to negative information than they do to positive information (Hamilton and Zanna, 1972). However, if a great deal of positive information is received subsequently over a period of time (the longer the better), the negative first impression may be modified, especially if the recipient of this positive information involves personal contact (Belmore, 1987).

In the case of corrections, the initial negative emotions and impressions created by viewing the first stereotypical prison movie, or reading the first inmate account of life in prison, are consistently reinforced because Hollywood tends to saturate the public with repeated exposure to the original set of images long after the initial exposure. The most popular movies, such as *Cool Hand Luke*, are shown repeatedly on television and may have been in the TV lineup 90 to 100 times since they first were seen in the theater. There are people who, through frequent viewing of a favorite prison movie, have committed the story line and large sections of the dialog to memory. This movement from the big screen to the TV screen (either through TV programming or videotape rental) ensures that the original imagery of the corrections template will be replayed repeatedly for those individuals who saw the movie in the theater. It also ensures that these movies with their stereotypical imagery and negative emotional tone will be presented periodically to a new generation of viewers who were not yet born at the time of the original screening.

Thus, after many years of viewing stereotypical prison movies, the typical viewers are unlikely to have their negative perception of corrections changed by the single prison movie that presents a balanced, or somewhat positive, view of corrections. The validity of this movie will be discounted because its positive imagery is incongruent with the negative imagery of the popular culture of corrections.

Rooting for the Underdog. This phenomenon involves the tendency of people to cheer for the underdog and display resentment against the powerful oppressor. The typical prison movie has at its core a dramatic role reversal in which the inmate becomes the object of sympathy and the correctional employee (especially the correctional officer) becomes the object of loathing and derision. As one observer has noted:

> What's really bad . . . is that the inmates often end up as more sympathetic characters than the officers. The pervasive attitude is that the crowd should be rooting for the kept, not the keepers (Zaner, 1989: 65).

Hundreds of television cop shows and movies have alarmed audiences by showing criminals to be vicious, brutal, insensitive, sadistic predators of the helpless. Many court movies have shown hard-boiled prosecutors taking on vicious criminals of every type and persuasion, battling sleazy defense attorneys, and eventually being rewarded by the jury's firm assertion of "guilty beyond a reasonable doubt." So how is it that the vicious street criminal, once incarcerated, becomes a likeable, innocent victim of correctional staff who will display the very characteristics attributed to criminals when they are on the street? A suggested answer to this question is as follows:

> The Hollywood portrayal of corrections is best viewed within the context of the Hollywood conceptualization of the criminal justice system as classic melodrama. There is a victim with whom the viewer can identify; a villain who threatens the life, safety, and happiness of that victim; and a rescuer who will, despite much hardship, ultimately prevail and save the victim (Freeman, 1996: 11).

In the Hollywood view of the criminal justice system, the police most frequently are given the enviable role of rescuer. In melodrama after melodrama, innocent citizens menaced by vicious criminals are saved when the police ride to the rescue. But once that vicious criminal has been incarcerated, he (only occasionally she) becomes the victim. Why does this role reversal occur? It occurs because the environment in which the criminal is being viewed has changed, and this change induces audience sympathy.

The Role Reversal of Inmate and the Correctional Officer. In the community, the criminal is free to roam the streets and take advantage of circumstances that favor criminal activity. He (or she) is on home turf and leisurely can stalk victims, waiting for the opportune moment to attack. But this freedom to act independently of the rest of society, to menace that society, ends as soon as the prison gates clang shut and the vicious street predators become confined, no longer able to hunt their prey. The physical act of incarceration automatically transforms predators into prey because physical confinement involves the denial of four valued human desires: control, power, dignity, and freedom:

> Once safely confined behind concrete walls and steel bars, the criminal becomes a victim, a human being capable of compassion, honor, and dignity who is made to endure unconscionable suffering at the hands of sadistic staff operating under the color of law. The criminal becomes a hero. Because heroes are defined in terms of the villain they face, wardens and correctional officers, the counterpart of the police officers and court personnel who have rescued society through the process of arrest and conviction, become the villains (Freeman, 1996: 11).

The resulting role reversal makes good theater for audiences who crave excitement and temporary entry into a forbidden world. The creation of role reversal is particularly effective when the inmate being featured is young and emotions are easily aroused. For example, in *Hard Choices* (1986), a young boy named Bobby grows up in a small town in Tennessee. His dream is to one day fly airplanes. His brother and a friend take him on a joyride, which ends in a murder committed during a botched robbery. Bobby is an unfortunate victim of circumstances, but an indifferent judicial system places him in prison with hardcore criminals. He eventually falls in love with a female social worker. The theme involves a good boy brutalized by an ugly prison system. The movie is a tearjerker that reflects badly on corrections.

However, if the protagonist is a beat down ex-con trying to make it in a harsh world, the emotions that are aroused can be equally as powerful. In *Straight Time*, (1978), Dustin

Hoffman plays a paroled burglar (Max Dembo) who has spent most of his juvenile years institutionalized. This is one of the few prison movies to focus on parole and the alienation and exploitation that ex-cons can experience after release from long-term incarceration. The movie sharply contrasts the sympathetic Max Dembo against an amoral parole officer (Emmett Walsh) whose harassment eventually drives Dembo back into a life of crime and a fatal last heist. The message of the movie is clear: Max Dembo could have become a productive citizen if his parole officer had not been such a morally corrupt member of the correctional system.

Putting a Human Face on Hero and Villain. Because of the universal power of the primacy effect and rooting for the underdog, Hollywood is able to put a human face on people who might otherwise just be words in a book or an article. After Hollywood has done its work, the inmate brutalized by corrupt prison employees is no longer faceless. When we read in the newspaper that a prison guard has brutalized or murdered an inmate, that inmate takes on the face of Paul Newman for the reader who has seen *Cool Hand Luke* or Tim Robbins for the reader who has seen *The Shawshank Redemption*. When we read about a corrupt warden being indicted for embezzlement or bribery that corrupt warden is now Eddie Albert in *The Longest Yard*. The heroes and villains of the corrections template now can be identified because of their emotion-laden association with powerful and attractive Hollywood actors and actresses. This creation of a human face develops a lasting impression guaranteed to reinforce Hollywood stereotypes.

Prison Movies and the Shaping of Public Perception

For those who doubt the power of movies to influence public perception, an August 30, 1998 *60 Minutes* segment on the 1972 Stanford Prison Experiment provides a classic example of that power. To understand the significance of the *60 Minutes* report, it is necessary to briefly review this psychological study.

The Stanford Prison Experiment. In a 1972 experiment designed to simulate the "guard-inmate relationship," Stanford University Professors Haney, Banks, and Zimbardo randomly selected twenty-one male volunteers to play the role of eleven prison "guards" and ten "inmates" in a "prison" located in the basement of the Stanford University psychology building. The guards were issued uniforms, night sticks, and ". . . intentionally given only minimal guidelines for what it meant to be a guard . . ." (Haney et al., 1973: 49). That is, the volunteers selected to play the role of prison guard received no employee orientation, no training, no policy and procedure manuals, no supervision, no explanation of the legal limits of their authority, and no expectation that they were expected to function in a humane manner. All they received was the admonishment to refrain from the use of physical force while maintaining control and order. In other words, they were told to play a role with no knowledge of the legal and ethical context within which that role was to be played.

The result of this lack of a legal and ethical context for behavior should have been easily predicted. As soon as the experiment began, the "guards," operating without supervision, canceled movie and reading opportunities and the reward for positive inmate behavior "became granting approval for prisoners to eat, sleep, go to the toilet, smoke a cigarette, wear sunglasses, or the temporary diminution of harassment" (Haney et al., 1973: 56). Every aspect of the "guard-inmate" interaction was governed by arbitrary and capricious decisions justified by rules made up as the "guards" became increasingly enamored of their authority. The "prisoners" were at the mercy of the "guards" for even the most basic human functions. The procedure for using the toilet, for example, involved an humiliating process that required the inmate to publicly request permission and then, if permission were granted (which was not guaranteed), to be escorted to the toilet while blindfolded and handcuffed. The relationship between "inmate" and "guard" was that of conqueror and oppressed subject. There was no effort on the part of the "guards" to instill any sense of fair play or compassion. The negative consequences of the increasingly arbitrary "guards" behavior were dramatic:

> At the end of six days we had to close down our mock prison because what we saw was frightening. It was no longer apparent to most of the subjects (or to us) where reality ended and the roles began. The majority had indeed become prisoners or guards, no longer able to clearly differentiate between role-playing and self. . . . We were horrified because we saw some boys (guards) treat others as if they were despicable animals, taking pleasure in cruelty, while other boys (prisoners) became servile, dehumanized robots who thought only of escape, of their own individual survival and of their mounting hatred for the guards (Zimbardo, 1972: 4).

This study is frequently presented as a compelling demonstration of the incredibly destructive nature of the prison environment, an environment so corrosive that it transformed good, decent males into inhuman oppressors in a matter of days. However, another interpretation of the meaning of this experiment can be presented.

The Alternative Explanation to the Stanford Prison Experiment Findings. The alternative explanation is that the Stanford Prison Experiment is a compelling example of how individuals can turn to the entertainment media for direction when they must assume a role about which they have no personal knowledge. When questioned after the study about their persistent harassing behavior in the face of rapidly rising prisoner emotional trauma, most "guards" explained that they had been "just playing the role of a tough guard" (Haney et al., 1973: 54). Lacking personal experience, the volunteers had adopted the behavior and attitudes presented in the Hollywood portrayal of correctional officers to which they had been exposed all of their lives. And this adoption of attitudes and behavior was not necessarily unconscious.

Support for this conclusion is provided by the *60 Minutes* segment referenced at the beginning of this section. Interviewed in that segment was a man who had played the role of a prison "guard" in the experiment. Billed as one of the most sadistic of the "guards," this man, when asked about the source of his cruel behavior, calmly stated that the mirrored sunglass wearing gang boss in *Cool Hand Luke* was his inspiration. That movie's imagery led this "guard" to purchase a pair of mirrored sunglasses and treat the "inmates" in precisely the same way as he had seen the guard in *Cool Hand Luke* act. This particular "guard's" performance was so powerful that a former "inmate" stated that for a year after the experiment, he could not look at a pair of mirrored sunglasses. Particularly shocking was the "guard's" lack of any remorse for the negative impact of his role-played behavior.

Television's Contribution to the Popular Culture of Corrections

In addition to running, and rerunning the most popular of the made-for-theater prison movies, television also has produced a very small number of TV series in which a prison setting is featured, most notably: *The Prisoner* (1967); *Within These Walls* (1974); *On The*

Rocks (1975); *Prisoner: Cell Block H* (1979); *Oz* (1997); and *Bad Girls* (1999). Prison-based TV series typically are unsuccessful and short-lived, possibly because they are unable to develop and sustain the intense emotions found in the compressed time frame of the prison movie. However, this does not mean that there has never been a successful television series focused on corrections.

One of the most powerful television series is *Oz*, on HBO. Beginning in 1997, this series presented a stereotyped view of prison life that rivaled any Hollywood movie. Presenting brutal inmates who torture another inmate by defecating into his mouth, this series featured rapes, murders, riots, lockdowns, and gross employee savagery. When asked if *Oz* provided a realistic view of prison life in America, Tom Fontana, the producer of the series candidly responded:

> What I would say is that the best anyone can do in television is approximate the truth. We can't duplicate the truth. I can't say this is exactly the way it is in every prison in every state across America. It's impossible to do that. That's not my job. My job is to say what the things are around the reality so that I can then dramatize and evoke emotional responses like laughter or tears (Quoted in DeGroot and Daley, 1998: 50).

Negative imagery is also available from noncorrections-oriented television series that will occasionally incorporate a corrections segment into the story line. The 1995 episode of *The X-Files* (discussed in Chapter 1) is an excellent example of how an episode of a television series can present a distorted image of corrections to the public. Hollywood has the power to define the social reality of the remote context of corrections for a vast audience that lacks the personal experience necessary to challenge stereotypical messages about that remote context. Members of the general public who accept Hollywood's view of corrections as accurate cannot intelligently participate in debates about correctional issues. They will not even realize that their perception of corrections is inaccurate. Hollywood's power to uncritically define the reality of corrections for the general public is directly reinforced by news media coverage of current correctional employee misconduct.

Points to Consider

1. If Hollywood did not make prison movies, would the constructed image of corrections be as powerful as it is today? Why or why not?

2. Do movies have a greater ability to manipulate emotions than a television series? Defend your answer.

3. What movie that you have seen has presented the most distorted portrayal of corrections? What were the specific elements of this movie that created the distortion?

4. Did the Stanford Prison Experiment create a realistic prison environment? Why or why not?

5. Was the Stanford Prison Experiment conducted in an ethical manner? What is the basis for your answer?

6. If the Stanford Prison Experiment were to be replicated today, what would the researchers have to do to make its conditions accurately reflect today's relationship between inmates and correctional officers?

7. What role does the primacy effect play in the creation of a negative public perception of corrections?

8. What can corrections professionals do to convince Hollywood writers, directors, and producers to present a more balanced view of corrections in their movies?

9. Do you believe that putting a face on the corrections template plays an important role in creating a negative public perception of corrections? Are there other influences that might play a greater role? If so, what are they?

10. If you were a prison superintendent, would you be supportive of a Hollywood producer using your prison as the location for a prison movie? Why or why not? What could you do to influence the movie's characterization of inmates and correctional officers? Do you think the producer and director would be receptive to your advice? Why or why not?

References

Belmore, S. M. 1987. Determinants of Attention During Impression Formation. *Journal of Experimental Psychology: Learning, Memory, and Cognition*.13: 480-489.

Cheatwood, D. 1998. Prison Movies: Films About Adult, Male, Civilian Prisons: 1929-1995. In F. Bailey and D. Hale, eds. *Popular Culture, Crime, and Justice*. Belmont, California: West/Wadsworth Publishing. pp. 209-231.

DeGroot, G. and G. Daley. 1998. An Interview with Tom Fontana: The Producer of *Homicide* and *Oz* Reveals His Perceptions of Life in Prison. *Corrections Today*. (59)1: 50-52.

Faith, K. 1993. Gendered Imaginations: Female Crime and Prison Movies. *The Justice Professional*. 81: 53-69.

Freeman, R. M. 1996. Correctional Staff as the Villain and the Inmate as Hero: The Problem is Bigger Than Hollywood. *American Jails*.(10)3: 9-16.

Gursky, D. and A. Yurkanin.1989. No Rave Reviews for Prison Movies. *Corrections Today*. (51)1: 95, 98.

Hamilton, D. L. and M. P. Zanna.1972. Differential Weighting of Favorable and Unfavorable Attributes in Impressions of Personality. *Journal of Experimental Research in Personality*. 6: 204-212.

Haney, Craig, Curtis Banks, and Philip Zimbardo.1973/77. A Study of Prisoners and Guards in a Simulated Prison. In Elliot Aronson, ed. *Readings About the Social Animal*. San Francisco: W. H. Freeman and Co. pp. 42-59.

Irwin, J. 1980. *Prisons in Turmoil*. Boston: Little, Brown.

Websdale, N. and A. Alvarex. 1998. Forensic Journalism as Patriarchal Ideology: The Newspaper Construction of Homicide-Suicide. In F. Bailey and D. Hale, eds. *Popular Culture, Crime and Justice*. Belmont, California: West/Wadsworth Publishing. pp. 123-141.

Zaner, L. O. 1989. The Screen Test—Has Hollywood Hurt Corrections' Image? *Corrections Today*. (51)1: 64-66, 94-95.

Zimbardo, P. 1972. Pathology of Imprisonment. *Society*. 96: 4.

News Media Documentation of Current Correctional Employee Misconduct:

The Direct Reinforcement of Hollywood Stereotyping

T he news media consists of two powerful mediums that can directly reinforce negative Hollywood stereotypes: the electronic media (television and the Internet) and the print media (newspapers, magazines, and books). Although both mediums can directly reinforce Hollywood stereotyping, we begin with television because that medium has the technology to disseminate powerful sets of visual imagery that can overlap and directly reinforce prison movie stereotypes:

> Television's power to shape politics and meaning is realized through selectively projecting and framing reality, thus creating a sense of the immediate and real and endlessly reproducing it visually (Manning, 1998: 25).

Television's selective "projecting and framing" of correctional reality for the general public involves the broadcast of prison movies, but it also involves newscast segments that spotlight current correctional events and documentaries that feature historical events in corrections. This ability to show both the fictionalized Hollywood account of prison life and actual correctional events (sometimes on the same night of viewing) create an image-reinforcing phenomenon known as a media loop.

Defining the Media Loop. A media loop occurs when "[m]edia images are constantly recycled, reproduced in a new context, and reexperienced" (Manning, 1998: 26). Media loops are particularly effective in influencing public perception when they involve different genre. A genre is "a category of artistic work with a characteristic style, form, or content" (Manning, 1998: 26)—such as television, movies, books, newspapers, and so forth. When different genre are involved, the manner in which the event is shown changes, but the content remains the same. There are a variety of different types of media loops, but one of the most important for our discussion is the linking loop.

The Linking Loop. This involves the linkage of images by a common theme through different electronic broadcasts (Manning, 1998). For example, in September 1989, a television network broadcast the classic prison movie *Riot* with its stark images of inmates rioting and their brutal suppression by correctional officers. In late October 1989, local and national newscasts were filled with the dramatic images of three days of inmate rioting at the State Correctional Institution at Camp Hill in Camp Hill, Pennsylvania. The

53

following January, a television network presented *Weeds*, the 1987 prison movie in which an inmate riot is brutally suppressed by a vicious riot squad of heavily armed correctional officers. The result for the general public over a five-month period included strengthening visual images, which reinforced the public perception that prisons are violent institutions. More importantly, the sandwiching of a riot-related news event between two prison movies featuring prison riots reinforced the validity of correctional officer stereotyping because the viewer watching all three telecasts unconsciously could superimpose the viciousness of the correctional officers in *Riot* and *Weeds* onto the news coverage of the Camp Hill riot with its images of hundreds of heavily armed correctional officers and state police entering the prison to suppress the riots and regain control of the institution.

A similar process can occur in the print media (although the imagery may not be as powerful). For example, someone who reads *In The Belly of the Beast* (Abbott, 1981) and is moved by the scenes of racial prejudice and bias-related violence that inmate Abbott alleged to be encouraged by prison employees subsequently may read a newspaper account of current correctional officers being accused of racial prejudice and discrimination (as was the case at State Correctional Institution-Greene in Pennsylvania, an example that will be presented later in this chapter). The result is a linking loop that ties together a fictionalized account of historical systemic racial prejudice with a news report of current systemic racial prejudice.

If that reader then watches a prison movie containing explicit scenes of racial discrimination by correctional employees, the result can be the strong conviction that racial discrimination in corrections is a current reality. The citizen's perception of race relations in corrections has been framed by the convergence of reinforcing imagery from the entertainment media and the news media. As Lichter, Lichter, and Rothman (1994: 6) have noted: "News used to be the first rough draft of history. Now it is the first (rough draft) of a Hollywood screen play."

The News Media-Corrections Relationship

The news media-corrections relationship is an uneasy one because of the ability of news media professionals to use the written word, visual imagery, and technology to influence the public perception of corrections. The people who work in corrections are individuals who are used to being able to control the activities of other people. But they cannot control the work product of the news media because it is an external organization protected by the U.S. Constitution. Because of the ability of the news media to reach vast audiences around the world, corrections professionals are concerned about news media bias or inaccuracy in the coverage of corrections. If news media reporting is inaccurate or biased, "the public often will view you and your organization as a bunch of buffoons" (Koehler, 1989: 16).

The Issue of News Media Bias. Does the news media have a bias against corrections? This is a difficult question to answer, and it might be more appropriate to rephrase the question: Do some members of the news media have a bias against corrections? It certainly is conceivable that some reporters may have such a bias. Perhaps they have had a negative personal experience with correctional employees, or they may have been influenced by the sociological literature, or perhaps they have seen too many movies about people who are involuntarily confined:

> After a homicide at a psychiatric unit, a radio reporter asked me if our psych unit was like the one from *One Flew Over the Cuckoo's Nest*. He went on almost

gleefully about drugged inmates and all the Hollywood depictions he remembered from the movie (Fairchild, 1998: 31).

Did viewing *One Flew Over the Cuckoo's Nest* influence the reporter's article on a homicide in a prison psychiatric unit? That is not known, but his comments indicate why many corrections professionals are fearful of the news media. They have had similar personal experiences, been misquoted, heard horror stories of misquotes and bias related by their colleagues, or they have read an article slanted in an unflattering direction. For example, Patricia Springer cites the example of a *Fort Worth Star Telegram* article with the headline: "Inmates Feast on Cake." This headline outraged many citizens because it validated the stereotyping of country club corrections. However, the headline was deceptive. Any reader who read only the headline would have missed the fact that the story reported that dozens of inmates had been stricken with vomiting and diarrhea because an employee of a private food services provider had poured dish washing soap in the cake batter (Springer, 1998). The inmates were victims, not coddled wards of the state. Was the headline reflective of a corrections bias or was the reporter just being clever?

Language as a Reflection of Media Bias. A thorough examination of the issue of news media bias is beyond the scope of this book. However, it is easy to find articles in respected news magazines in which the reporter's language appears to reflect a bias against corrections. In many cases, these articles do not even concern corrections, but the descriptive language used to elaborate on the subject of the article does suggest the reporter's acceptance of correctional stereotyping as a valid reflection of correctional reality. Three examples of this apparent bias against corrections are cited from the numerous examples that can be found in upscale news magazines.

A 1994 *Time* magazine article reporting on the career of actor Tim Allen of *Home Improvement* noted his incarceration for cocaine possession and advised that:

> Allen found humor useful in prison. He made the meanest guard laugh by putting pictures of Richard Nixon in the peephole of his cell when they made their rounds. . . . Once, while riding a bus to another prison, he managed to slip out of his handcuffs. The only thing he could think to do was to bum a cigarette off the old bank robber sitting in front of him (Zoglin, 1994: 80).

This article associates the negative descriptor "meanest" with the title "guard," and suggests officer incompetence because Allen was not handcuffed properly. The tone of the article is suggestive of the feats committed by Gene Wilder in *Stir Crazy* as he exploited the stupidity of the correctional officers assigned to supervise him at the prison rodeo.

A 1996 *Time* magazine article about Timothy Leary described the reporter's visit to see Leary in prison:

> So here we were for one more try, in the visitor's tank at the federal pen in San Diego, waiting for the stone-faced warden to decide whether or not to allow our visit (Ressner, 1996: 73).

Stone-faced? Again, this is a negative descriptor because the phrase suggests a lack of humanity and caring. It is a descriptor that also suggests the face of fictional characters such as Eddie Albert's prison warden in *The Longest Yard* or Jon Voight's antagonistic warden in *Runaway Train*.

Finally, a 1999 *Time* magazine article about author Mary Patricia Plangman Highsmith described her as "a recluse with a prison matron's visage" (Corliss, 1999: 159). Of all the occupations in the world, why did the reporter choose that of prison matron when he made his analogy? Is this a reference to the homely prison matrons in *I Want to Live* and the numerous bad girl prison movies presented over the years?

The fact that three highly respected reporters felt free to use this style of phrasing suggests an acceptance of negative correctional stereotyping as well as an expectation that the language will resonate with their readers. This use of derogatory phrasing about corrections suggests that the negative stereotypes of correctional employees in the popular culture of corrections have been fully assimilated into the language of journalism. If these examples do indicate a bias against corrections, a possible source of this bias may be a lack of factual knowledge of corrections that allows the news media to uncritically accept Hollywood stereotypes as reality.

The News Media's Factual Knowledge of Corrections. Although there is a scarcity of research assessing the news media's factual knowledge about corrections, we tentatively can draw some conclusions by returning to the Florida Department of Corrections-commissioned study (Florida Department of Corrections, 1998) referenced in Chapter 1. As part of this study, researchers surveyed general reporters and news directors of daily and weekly newspapers, television/radio stations, and news services located in Florida. The survey responses provide a method of identifying news media perceptions of Florida Department of Corrections' job performance and the accuracy of their factual knowledge about that system.

The Florida News Media Perception of Corrections. The survey yielded 350 Florida Department of Corrections' overall job performance ratings that were distributed as follows:

Excellent	2.0 percent
Good	28.9 percent
Fair	57.4 percent
Poor	11.7 percent

Fewer than a third of the respondents believed the Florida Department of Corrections was doing a good-to-excellent overall job. On a continuum of poor-to-excellent job performance, the Florida Department of Corrections' overall performance was located at the poor-to-fair end of the continuum. In addition, the researchers disaggregated overall job performance by asking respondents to rank department of corrections' performance in different areas of correctional activity. The most relevant areas in terms of the current discussion were preventing escapes, rehabilitating criminals, making criminals pay back their victims, and providing prison drug and alcohol programs to prevent offender substance abuse after release. The following rankings were reported:

Table 4.1 Florida Department of Corrections' Performance

	Preventing Escapes	Rehabilitation	Restitution to Victims	Substance Abuse
Excellent	21.8%	0.6%	0.0%	1.6%
Good	51.7%	7.3%	6.1%	20.3%
Fair	25.1%	42.2%	29.6%	49.8%
Poor	1.4%	49.9%	64.3%	28.3%

Source: Florida Department of Corrections, 1998.

Clearly, the Florida news media perception is that the Department of Corrections' performance is marginal in all areas except in the prevention of escapes. But this determination of perception does not establish the depth of factual knowledge survey respondents have about corrections. This is an important issue because it can be assumed that factual and/or experiential knowledge, or the lack of it, is a critical factor in the formation of perception.

The Florida News Media's Factual Knowledge about Corrections. On the subject of prison crowding, 40.1 percent of the news media (compared to 28.5 percent of the public) thought prison overcrowding was the Department of Corrections' most serious problem; 50.3 percent of the news media (compared to 68.5 percent of the public) thought Florida needed more prisons when the reality is that there are currently enough beds to handle the inmate population.

On a related issue, 87.6 percent of the news media (compared to 95.5 percent of the public) thought inmates were released early due to overcrowding when the reality is that early release due to prison crowding stopped in December 1994. On the always controversial subject of facility air conditioning, 70.3 percent of the news media (compared to 87.7 percent of the public) believe inmates are housed in air-conditioned prisons when the reality is that only seven of Florida's fifty-five state prisons are air-conditioned. Surprisingly, 76.9 percent of the news media (compared to 66.9 percent of the public) did approve of inmates being housed in air-conditioned prisons. Finally, 50.7 percent of the media (compared to 68 percent of the public) think correctional officers working inside of prisons are armed (a popular culture of corrections stereotype) when the reality is that they are not armed.

Clearly, the Florida news media is unclear about some basic facts concerning the most fundamental realities of the Florida Department of Corrections. This lack of knowledge will limit its ability to report accurately on correctional issues and events. To make matters worse, the accuracy of the public's knowledge about corrections was generally lower than that of the news media. This is disturbing because reporters who lack factual knowledge unintentionally can reinforce Hollywood stereotyping when they present factually inaccurate reports to their reading and viewing audiences. When corrections is a remote context to the news media, the public is denied a critical source of factually accurate information.

Although the study focused exclusively on the Florida news media professionals, it is probably safe to say that corrections is a remote context to most news media professionals who infrequently cover corrections, regardless of their state or region. Reporters who do not have corrections "on their beat" are likely to be introduced to this controversial field when there is a breaking news story. This means that the reporter's initial exposure to corrections probably will be a negative event, and the coverage required can be classified as negative-event reporting. Negative-event reporting can be grouped into three subject categories:

1. The failure to achieve a specific mission or goal

2. An inappropriate philosophy defining the mission

3. The corrections horror story

Each of these categories has the potential to create media linking loops, which will reinforce a specific set of correctional stereotyping. The first two categories of negative event reporting reinforce the stereotypes of country club corrections.

The Failure to Achieve a Specific Mission or Goal

The failure to achieve a specific mission or goal most frequently will involve a security failure that results in a threat (or perceived threat) to public safety.

The Failure to Achieve the Mission or Goal of Protecting the Public. An October 22, 1995 newspaper article about a prison escapee had the headline: "He Flunked 1st Grade and Outsmarted the Prison System." The article described how Donald Dillbeck, "a high-school dropout who failed first grade" (Hallinan, 1995: G1), serving twenty-five years to life for killing a Florida police officer, successfully manipulated prison classification staff to transfer him to a minimum-security Florida facility. The article reported that Dillbeck's strategy of manipulation was one of providing false information to classification team members which they could, and should have, easily verified as false. Once Dillbeck was transferred to the minimum-security facility, he was able to casually walk away during an escorted visit to a local elementary school where inmates were providing dinner to a group of senior citizens. Dillbeck then viciously murdered a forty-four-year-old woman by slashing her jugular. The resulting public and political uproar was ferocious and prolonged.

The article emphasized that the detail's "guards had no guns, no walkie-talkies, no handcuffs. They did not even have a key to lock the kitchen door" (Hallinan, 1995: G2). This article presented to the public the image of country club corrections: A vicious cop killer placed into a community situation where he was free to do whatever he wanted, to whomever he wanted, because he was under no control. This article reinforces the imagery of employee incompetence that is created by every prison movie in which a cadre of stupid guards are outwitted by very resourceful inmates who easily exploit the prison's security vulnerabilities.

Accompanying this article was another Hallinan article, "Even Most Negligent of Jail Systems Can't be Sued Over Escapes" (Hallinan, 1995: G3). This article documented the terrifying experiences of victims of prison escapees, including the victim of an inmate who escaped from a prison that had experienced eighty-one escapes in five years. The theme of the article could be summarized in the following paragraph:

> Courts have held that departments of correction have no legal duty to protect individual citizens from escaped inmates. This is true no matter how negligent the prison (Hallinan, 1995: G3).

The implication is clear: Negligence occurs in corrections, but there are no consequences for the system or its employees. This conclusion gives the impression of an injustice that does not reflect well on corrections and does not improve the public perception of its employees. This validates every prison movie in which correctional employees do wrong and are not punished.

The Failure to Achieve the Mission or Goal of Punishing the Criminal: Richard Speck and Partying in Prison. A classic example of the power of television news to damage the public perception of corrections by presenting imagery of country club corrections to the public occurred in Illinois in May 1996 when one of the largest television stations in the state acquired possession of a videotape. It showed notorious mass murderer Richard Speck engaging in "partying" that involved sexual acts, using drugs, and bragging about how much fun he was having in prison. The station aired the tape during "sweeps" week, in the middle of an election year, and it was quickly picked up by the national networks. The public was outraged by the tape and a legislative committee was established to investigate the Illinois Department of Corrections.

More than eighteen months after the incident, the public relations nightmare continued as "the first question you encounter from many members of the public is why the department allows inmates to run its institutions" (Washington, 1998: 34). The Illinois Department of Corrections had experienced a public relations disaster: "The Speck tape rapidly became viewed as irrefutable evidence of the department's failure to manage the state's prison system" (Washington, 1998: 35).

This type of public relations nightmare has a broad range of negative effects:

1. Critics of corrections can use the incident as proof that the current political administration is "soft" on crime and there needs to be a toughening of prison conditions. This may result in political decisions, which make the work of correctional employees even more difficult.

2. Staff morale can be seriously effected. Even if no staff are fired, though such firings frequently happen when elected officials believe a scapegoat must be found, it is difficult to function well when your facility or department is the butt of jokes by Jay Leno and his counterparts as well as being subjected to intense media and legislative scrutiny, often of a hostile nature.

3. One negative event can have a domino effect. That is, it can be media linked to other negative events, such as allegations of employee misconduct, that create the perception that there are a large number of additional problems that need to be fixed. In the case of the Speck tape:

There were allegations of sexual misconduct among staff at the department's primary female facility, and stories of gang influence in the department stemming from the federal drug conspiracy trial of inmate Larry Hoover, which created an atmosphere in which the public was prepared to believe the worst about the administration of the Department of Corrections (Washington, 1998: 35).

This last negative effect is a prime example of how one negative event can be looped to eventually create a simultaneous public focus on the conflicting stereotypes of country club corrections and smug hack corrections.

The Illinois Department of Corrections, by its own admission, had underestimated the controversy which would be created by the TV station's hyping of the tape. They delayed responding to it in an aggressive fashion because they were fearful of overreacting. The result was a high cost in lowered Illinois Department of Corrections' staff morale and damaged public credibility. The Speck tape provided a highly visual piece of "evidence" to the critics of corrections that country club corrections was, indeed, a reality in America.

An Inappropriate Philosophy Defining the Mission

This category of negative event reporting has a much broader focus. It questions the mission's philosophy in terms that strongly suggest that even if the mission has been successfully achieved, that achievement constitutes a failure for society. Chapter 2 referenced a 1994 *Reader's Digest* article titled "Must Our Prisons be Country Clubs?" As previously noted, the author, Robert J. Bidinotto, makes the following assertion about today's prisons in the article:

Hard labor is out, physical fitness is in. From aerobics to strength training to boxing, today's thugs and armed robbers can return to the streets bigger, stronger and faster than ever. When they're tired of working out, they can join theater groups, take music lessons or college courses—all for free. Or they can tune into the latest R-rated movies (Bidinotto, 1994: 66).

Charging that "the overall cost of these amenities . . . take up a huge portion of state correctional budgets, while thousands of violent criminals are released each year for lack of space" (Bidinotto, 1994: 66), Bidinotto uses inflammatory words and phrases such as "residents," and "vast array of recreational and physical-fitness amenities available to convicts," to paint a picture of prisons as resorts. He cites isolated examples of what appear to be luxurious prison conditions without placing those examples in the context of the prison environment. For example,

> At the Dade Correctional Institution near Miami, members of the Inmates' Cultural Club have developed a taste for opera. Prison librarian Rolando Valdes obtained a series of federal grants and purchased a 50-inch television and laser-disc equipment. Each Saturday night, he conducts opera appreciation classes in the prison library. Funded by another government grant, several inmates have even written their own opera, *El Caido*—a tale of a prisoner who rehabilitates himself (Bidinotto, 1994: 68-69).

The bias against corrections of "Must Our Prisons Be Resorts?" is so blatant that Jon Marc Taylor refers to the article as:

> a piece of dangerous distortion, careful omission and false information, reflecting a rigorous one-dimensional point of view. Except for the outright lies, which the quoted experts uttered for him, his article is a classic case of Goebbelian propaganda, a pernicious twist on reality circulated to 28 million homes (1997: 86).

These are strong words, but Taylor backs them up with an excellent analysis of the article in which he demonstrates the validity of his statement. To cite only one example of that analysis:

> The most distorted allegation made in the article was that the 160-year-old Missouri State Prison . . . is a resort. This is a state penal system bulging at 160 percent capacity, where prisoners are forced to sleep in converted kitchens and where portable toilets are trucked in to meet the demand, a system where barely 1 percent of the overall budget is used for education and vocational training. Bidinotto's claim of cushy conditions stemmed from the fact that the prison has an inmate-operated around-the-clock closed circuit TV studio that broadcasts "movies containing sex, horror and violence." But to the prisoners at Jefferson City, who must endure roach-infested cells, barely edible food and a health care system so lacking that prisoners liken a serious illness to a drawn-out death sentence, Bidinotto's focusing solely on the prisoner broadcast system totally misses the mark (Taylor, 1997: 87).

Those members of the general public to whom corrections is a remote context are likely to read the Bidinotto article and accept it as verification that country club corrections is a reality because the article is in a respectable magazine. Why is Bidinotto so vigorously questioning the value of prison rehabilitation programs? Taylor, in his detailed rebuttal of "Must Our Prisons Be Resorts?" reports that Robert James Bidinotto has been mentored by Dr. James Q. Wilson, "the godfather of the get-tough movement advocating judicial restraint, mandatory incarceration, longer sentences and the abolishment of parole boards" (Taylor, 1997: 90). Clearly, a conservative philosophy can influence the way in which a writer presents corrections to the public, just as a liberal philosophy might influence an article about the dangers of supermax prisons.

As troubling as the first two categories of negative-event reporting might be to corrections professionals, the third category is far more disturbing. This category of negative-event reporting effectively reinforces the public perception that smug hack corrections is alive and well in the United States.

The Corrections Horror Story

The news media has the responsibility to report the news, regardless of the personal impact those reports will have on individuals or organizations. As one department of corrections assistant director for communications has noted:

> Some fault the media for reporting official corruption, wrongdoing and incompetence. But it's important to remember that the media doesn't create problems. It only reports them (Kindel, 1998: 22).

The "problems" being reported by the news media frequently involve the misconduct of individual correctional employees. Every correctional organization has a small subset of employees who will choose to engage in criminal or unethical behavior on the job or when off-duty. The reader or viewer exposed to these instances of misconduct easily can be motivated to question the integrity of both the correctional system in which the misconduct occurred and the employee involved in that type of behavior.

Individual Employee Misconduct. Even a cursory check of a newspaper can reveal multiple examples of individual correctional employee misconduct that reinforce the structural themes of smug hack imagery. For example, in the April 2, 1998 edition of *USA Today*, the following events were briefly noted:

1. In Sacramento, California, a judge approved a four million dollar settlement for three state female correctional employees, including an associate warden, who accused their male supervisors of sexual harassment and retaliation.

2. In New London, Connecticut, an ex-deputy warden was sentenced to six months in prison and a correctional officer was sentenced to one year in prison, for having sex with female inmates.

3. In Bismarck, North Dakota, a state correctional officer was sentenced to a year's probation for leaving racial epithets on the answering machine of an African-American he thought was flirting with his girlfriend (*USA Today*, 1998).

These brief accounts often are reinforced by longer articles with sensational titles and image-filled content. For example:

"The Rape Crisis Behind Bars" (Donaldson, 1993: 11A).

"Jail Rocked by Sex, Drugs and Payoff Scandal" (Phillips, 1999).

"Ex-Prison Employee Arrested in Md. Escape" (Lengel and Mishra, 1999: B01).

"Guard Faces Hearing in Sexual Misconduct Case Involving Inmate" (Vidonic, 1999).

"State Hopes Guards Reveal Inmate's Killer" (Silva and Long, 1999).

The first four headlines are self-explanatory. The opening paragraph of the last article is as follows:

> In pursuit of a murderer's murder, investigators say the answer to who killed Death Row inmate Frank Valdez will turn on cracking the loyalty of a close-knit circle of prison guards to find out which ones beat him to death, and which simply watched (Silva and Long, 1999).

The accurate reporting of instances of individual employee misconduct has an impact on the public perception of corrections:

> Most of the public's knowledge of corrections comes from what it sees on television and reads in the newspapers. If all the information is negative . . . public perception of corrections can be negative. . . . the perpetuation of the stereotype that correctional officers and administrators are "disgruntled, alienated hacks prone to violence under pressure" misleads the public, giving it an unrealistic view of the corrections profession (Zaner, 1989: 65).

Defining the Corrections Horror Story. As serious as the reports of individual employee misconduct are, there is a far more serious, and potentially damaging, type of reporting: the corrections horror story. The corrections horror story can be defined as an event (or series of events) which involves a group of correctional employees who use their official position to engage in unethical, corrupt, illegal, or brutal behavior that reinforces one or more of the smug hack corrections structural themes defined in Chapter 2. The corrections horror story has a far greater impact on the public perception of corrections than does individual employee misconduct because the fact that it is an organized group of employees, not a single rogue employee, involved in the misconduct suggests that the offensive employee behavior is systemic and, thus, authorized, or at least condoned, as flogging was once systemic and authorized. A limited sampling of recent corrections horror stories includes:

Georgia. Under the heading of the provocative title "Prison Scandal in Georgia: Guards Traded Favors for Sex," reporter Mark Curriden reported that a 1984 class action lawsuit alleging that more than 1,600 women in the Georgia Department of Corrections were being mistreated physically and psychologically was updated to include the sexual abuse allegations of 150 female inmates. More than 200 women eventually filed affidavits claiming that they and other female inmates over a period of years had been coerced into having sexual relations with officers, maintenance workers, teachers, and a prison chaplain, in exchange for cigarettes, candy, or soft drinks or any other favor that would make doing time a little more comfortable. Reportedly, female inmates who refused sex were retaliated against through the use of disciplinary segregation, hog tying, and parole denials. Pregnant inmates in halfway houses refusing to have an abortion said they would be punished by being sent back to prison and losing good time. One inmate who refused to have an abortion stated that she was denied medical treatment until she miscarried.

The imagery in this article resonates strongly with the imagery contained in the bad girl prison movies cited in Chapter 3 as well as the sociological literature documentation of the history of sexual abuses against female inmates that have bedeviled corrections since the first male prison received a female inmate. It is this type of media linking loop that embeds a host of negative correctional stereotypes into the human psyche.

The Curriden article supported the smug hack corrections structural theme of employee incompetence, corruption, and cruelty by reporting that the Department of Corrections' management response to the allegations of employee misconduct was slow and unproductive. Internal investigations failed to find evidence of employee misconduct. It was only after some very intense political and media pressure that the Department of Corrections dismissed fourteen line staff: eleven men and three women. A deputy commissioner was also fired after it became apparent he knew of the allegations but had taken no actions to prevent the staff misconduct. The dismissals were upheld by an administrative law judge (Curriden, 1993). Although only a minority of Georgia Department of Corrections' employees were involved, this corrections horror story badly tainted the public perception of Georgia corrections and, when picked up by the national news services, the public perception of corrections in general.

Pennsylvania. The Pennsylvania Department of Corrections' supermax prison, State Correctional Institution-Greene, was shaken by scandal in May 1998 when four correctional officers were fired and twenty-one others were demoted, suspended, or reprimanded because of their treatment of inmates. An internal investigation revealed that the correctional officers were ordered by their superiors "to 'adjust the attitudes' of some inmates by roughing them up" (Bucsko and Dvorchak, 1998: 2). In addition, there were allegations of:

- racial discrimination and racial taunting of black inmates that involved beatings, references to the Klu Klux Klan written in inmate blood, and dehumanizing treatment such as tobacco juice being spit into inmate food

- strip searches of female visitors and a practice of forcing women, including attorneys, to remove their bras before being allowed to pass through a metal detector

- restricted housing unit correctional officers ordered by superior officers to beat inmates outside the view of video cameras as part of an ongoing policy of "attitude adjustment"

- a practice of falsifying misconduct reports against inmates

- confiscation of inmates' legal documents and attorney correspondence

After a Department of Corrections' investigation, the superintendent and one of his deputies was transferred to another state prison. Any Hollywood writer or director looking for sensational material for a stereotypical prison movie has only to read these reports and interview a few ex-inmates, to have enough material for two movies. This kind of behavior reinforces the corrections template and resonates with the comments of inmate Victor Hassine in the description of the Pennsylvania Department of Corrections he presented in *Life Without Parole: Living in Prison Today* (1996).

California. In the California Department of Corrections, twelve inmates were killed and thirty-two inmates seriously injured between 1994 and 1998 by correctional officers firing assault rifles to break up inmate fights. In many of those fights, there were no inmate weapons involved and no staff were at threat of death or injury. During the same period, in the rest of the nation, only six inmates were fatally shot. All of these inmates were trying to escape (Arax and Gladstone, 1998: 1).

In 1998, a number of correctional officers at California Department of Corrections'

State Correctional Institution-Corcoran were accused, by fellow officers, of placing rival inmate gang members together in exercise yards for the purpose of physical combat. After a period of fighting, the correctional officers would fire assault rifles to break up the fights. The result: seven inmates killed and forty-three wounded between 1989 and 1994. The resulting intensive FBI investigation led to the indictment of five correctional officers, one lieutenant, and two sergeants for conspiring to deprive inmates of their civil rights "by setting them up to fight each other in the recreation yard" (*The Corrections Professional*, 1998a: 10). The California Department of Corrections, after an investigation of the secure housing unit, fired two correctional officers, suspended four officers, demoted one officer, and had actions pending against six other officers. In his report on the indictments, the FBI agent in charge stated:

> It appears the fights were staged, and even provoked, for the amusement of correctional officers or as retribution against inmates. That this activity could be allowed to occur, and did occur, with the knowledge and participation of prison management personnel is particularly troubling (*The Corrections Professional*, 1998a: 10.)

In addition to FBI and media scrutiny, the courts also became involved in the situation. In 1999, the California Department of Corrections agreed to pay $2.5 million to the widow and mother of Mark Adams, who was shot to death by a San Quentin correctional officer in March 1994 while he was fighting with another inmate (*The Philadelphia Inquirer*, 1999). Undoubtedly, there will be other large cash settlements to follow as public awareness of the Corcoran situation and the FBI investigation grows.

In November 1998, the California Department of Corrections announced a policy change after intense media coverage and a public outcry. The new policy, similar to the policies in most other department of corrections, mandates that "the use of deadly force will be allowed only if an armed inmate is inflicting serious injury on another prisoner or prison employee" (*The Corrections Professional*, 1998b: 7).

The accusations about the State Correctional Institution-Corcoran are particularly damaging when viewed within the context of movies such as *Penitentiary I, II*, and *III*, in which sadistic guards force "Too Sweet" Gordon to fight other inmates to the death. Compounding the public perception problem for the California Department of Corrections was the fact that in October, 1999 four correctional officers went on trial for allegedly "setting up a prison-cell rape to punish an inmate" (*The Corrections Professional*, 1999: 4) for kicking a female correctional officer. The inmate accused of the rape was known as the "Booty Bandit" and a former correctional officer who reportedly confirmed that the incident did occur as the inmate victim stated was Roscoe "Bonecrusher" Pondexter. Just imagine what a Hollywood writer could do with this event and these names. (Note: the correctional officers were found not guilty by a jury on November 8, 1999).

News media coverage of current employee misconduct brings that offensive behavior into the conscious awareness of millions of citizens who otherwise would be ignorant of it. The result is a bright visibility that directly reinforces negative Hollywood stereotyping and increases the negative public perception of corrections. The most abhorrent misconduct is quite likely to be incorporated into a new prison movie or a television series which needs a prison segment. As a result, the power of the popular culture of corrections to influence public perception will increase, and there will be additional material for the creation of dramatic media linking loops. The reinforcement of popular culture of corrections stereotypes also can be achieved through the news media's accurate coverage of a high-profile correctional employee whose controversial philosophy and management style clearly resonates with managerial stereotypes firmly embedded in the popular culture of corrections.

The High-profile Controversial Corrections Manager

In recent years, considerable news media coverage has been given to Sheriff Joseph Arpaio of Maricopa County, Arizona: "In a crime-obsessed society that tends to believe that criminals are coddled, Maricopa County Sheriff Joseph Arpaio is a beacon for people who want prisoners punished, not rehabilitated" (Banisky, 1996: 18). Arpaio is a favorite of reporters because he always can be counted on to provide interesting film footage and colorful sound bites and quotes. He also can be counted on to present his brand of no-nonsense corrections as the alternative to country club corrections. His alternative emphasizes "myriad schemes for saving money and humiliating criminals—schemes that roll out roughly every three months and might have been designed for the evening news" (Whittell, 1996). As a result, the news media have dubbed Sheriff Arpaio "America's Toughest Sheriff."

Sheriff Joseph Arpaio and the Media. Reporters like snappy headlines and sharp sound bites. Joseph Arpaio is a natural for both. A February 19, 1996 article in *The Patriot-News* in Harrisburg, Pennsylvania titled "The Grumpier the Inmates, the More Happy the Sheriff" presents a sampling of Arpaio's jail management activities: The banning of *Playboy*; the removal of commercial television and substitution of C-SPAN and the weather channel; and, above the jail, on a light tower, is a neon vacancy sign. When asked why he has substituted the weather channel for commercial television, Sheriff Arpaio provides another made-for-the-media sound bite: "The chain gang ought to know if it's going to be 120 degrees" (Banisky, 1996: A1).

In a November 30, 1996 article, a reporter captures Arpaio's philosophy of corrections in the following headline: "Treat 'Em Mean, Keep 'Em Clean" (Whittell, 1996). This article develops a more detailed outline of the Arpaio crime control strategy:

An official slogan: "So much crime, not enough punishment"

Nine hundred inmates living in surplus army tents in the Estrella Jail yard

A ban on coffee and cigarettes

No hot lunches, only sandwiches made of green spam

A daily food cost of 34 cents per inmate

Jail underwear dyed pink to prevent theft

A male chain gang

A female chain gang

A 2,500-member Citizen's Posse to fight street crime (1,000 of the members have purchased their own guns and uniforms.)

A second slogan: "I'm an equal opportunity incarcerator."

The policies of Sheriff Arpaio provide the news media a golden opportunity to present to the public attention-getting film footage. The sound bites arouse public interest.

A May 31, 1998 article in the *Boston Globe* titled "Chain of Pain" reinforces the Joe

Arpaio contribution to the popular culture of corrections. The article describes America's first female chain gang. It also notes that when it comes to Sheriff Arpaio and the media:

> The inmates deride his penchant for performing before the cameras; when they spot two sheriff's photographers tagging along with Arpaio, one of them mutters, "Uh-oh, looks like a Joe show" (Grossfeld, 1998: 15).

The article details the work of the chain gang—painting curbs, removing graffiti, picking up trash, and burying deceased babies in a paupers' graveyard twenty miles outside of Phoenix, Arizona. It also contains typical Arpaio quotes such as: "I'm not here to do what criminals want me to do."

To the public, Arpaio typifies every tough-talking warden they have ever seen in a prison movie. And, if he exists, then maybe the other correctional stereotypes also exist.

Negative-event reporting and controversial high-profile correctional managers create a powerful confirmation for the general public that the image of corrections presented by Hollywood is, indeed, an accurate representation of corrections as it exists in America. Negative correctional stereotypes are reinforced directly by media linking loops that merge Hollywood imagery with news media imagery and are indirectly reinforced through the appearance of credibility bestowed by correctional silence.

Points to Consider

1. If you were a corrections superintendent, what actions would you take to discourage employee misconduct?

2. If a news reporter calls with a question about a specific employee's criminal behavior, how should you respond?

3. If a member of the news media makes allegations about employee misconduct which you know to be false, how should you respond?

4. Is the news media, in general, biased against corrections? Defend your answer.

5. What do you think a commissioner or superintendent of corrections can do to educate news media professionals about the reality of modern corrections?

6. If a scandal occurs in your organization, what steps can you take to reduce damage to the organization's reputation?

7. If your institution was featured in an article like "Must Our Prisons Be Resorts?" what actions would you take to educate the public to the reality of your institution? How would you publicly challenge the inaccuracies in the article?

8. What can a corrections professional do if a member of the news media is only interested in sensationalizing the negative aspects of corrections and does not want to report a balanced story?

9. What correctional initiatives have a "horror story" potential? What actions should correctional managers take to reduce the possibility of a horror story involving those initiatives?

10. What strategy could a pro-rehabilitation correctional manager develop to generate the type of news media coverage Sheriff Arpaio has been receiving?

11. Identify ten corrections horror stories that have occurred over the past decade and determine which smug hack corrections structural themes have been reinforced.

References

Abbott, J. H. 1981. *In the Belly of the Beast: Letters from Prison*. New York: Vintage Books.

Arax, M. and M. Gladstone. 1998. Only California Uses Deadly Force in Inmate Fights. *Los Angeles Times*. October 18. Part A, Page 1.

Banisky, S. 1996. The Grumpier The Inmates, The More Happy The Sheriff. *The Patriot-News*. Harrisburg, Pennsylvania. February 19, A1.

Bidinotto, R. J. 1994. Must Our Prisons Be Resorts? *Reader's Digest*. November: 65-71.

Bucsko, M. and B. Dvorchak. 1998. Firings, Charges Shake Up SCI-Greene: Maximum Security. *Pittsburgh Post-Gazette*. August 9.

The Corrections Professional. 1998a. Correctional Officers Indicted for Civil Rights Violations at California Prison. April 3. 314: 10.

———. 1998b. Prison Shootings in California Spur Stricter Deadly Force Policy. 45: 7.

———. 1999. Four Correctional Officers on Trial for Arranging Inmate Rape. 55: 4.

Corliss, R. 1999. Ripley's Creator: The Talented Ms. Highsmith. *Time*. 154, 26: 159.

Curriden, Mark. 1993. Prison Scandal in Georgia: Guards Traded Favors For Sex. *The National Law Journal*.163: 8.

Donaldson, S. 1993. The Rape Crisis Behind Bars. *The New York Times*. December 29. 11A.

Fairchild, B. 1998. Corrections' Public Relations Dilemma: A Good PR Plan Can Effectively Counter Negative Public Perceptions. *Corrections Today*. (59)1: 30-31.

Florida Department of Corrections. 1998. *Corrections in Florida: What the Public, News Media and DC Staff Think*. Tallahassee, Florida: Florida Department of Corrections.

Grossfeld, Stan. 1998. Chain of Pain. *Boston Globe*. May 31.

Hallinan, Joe. 1995. He Flunked 1st Grade and Outsmarted the Prison System. *Sunday Patriot News*. Harrisburg, Pennsylvania. October 22. G1, G2.

———. 1995a. Even Most Negligent of Jail Systems Can't Be Sued Over Escapes. *Sunday Patriot News*. Harrisburg, Pennsylvania. October 22. G3.

Kindel, Tip 1998. Media Access: Where Should You Draw the Line. *Corrections Today*. (59)1: 22-24.

Koehler, Richard J. 1989. Like It or Not: We Are News. *Corrections Today*. (51)1: 16-17.

Lengel, A. and R. Mishra.1999. Ex-Prison Employee Arrested in Md. Escape. *Washington Post*. May 26. B01.

Lichter, S. R., L. S. Lichter, and S. Rothman.1994. *Prime Time: How TV Portrays American Culture*. Washington, D.C.: Regnery.

Manning, P. K. 1998. Media Loops. In F. Bailey and D. Hale, eds. *Popular Culture, Crime and Justice*. Belmont, California: West/Wadsworth Publishing. pp. 25-39.

The Philadelphia Inquirer. 1999. No title. January 2.

Phillips, R. A.1999. Jail Rocked by Sex, Drugs, and Payoff Scandal. *APB News*. November 22.

Ressner, J. 1996. Dr. Tim's Last Trip. *Time*. 147:18: 72-73.

Silva, M. and P. Long. 1999. State Hopes Guards Reveal Inmate's Killer. *The Miami Herald*. July 22.

Springer, P. 1998. The Influence of the Media on Our Perception of Crime. In Claudia Whitman, Julie Zimmerman, and Tekla Miller, eds. *Frontiers of Justice, Volume 2: Coddling or Common Sense?* Brunswick, Maine: Biddle Publishing Co. pp. 46-47.

Taylor, J. M. 1997. Prisons Do Not Coddle Inmates. In *America's Prisons: Opposing Viewpoints*. San Diego, California: Greenhaven Press. pp. 85-93.

USA Today. 1998. No Title. April 2.

Vidonic, B. 1999. Guard Faces Hearing in Sexual Misconduct Case Involving Inmate. *Beaver County Times*. November 23.

Washington, Odie. 1998. Sex, Lies and Videotape. *Corrections Today*. (59)1: 34-36.

Whittell, G. 1996. Treat 'Em Mean, Keep 'Em Clean. *The Times*. November 30.

Zaner, Laura O. 1989. The Screen Test: Has Hollywood Hurt Corrections' Image? *Corrections Today*. (51)1: 64-66, 94-98.

Zoglin, R. 1994. Tim at the Top. *Time*. 144-24: 76-81.

Correctional Silence During Public Crime Control Policy Debates:

The Need for a Community Education Strategy to "Legitimize" Corrections

There are ways to challenge the influence of the popular culture of corrections on the public perception of corrections. One way requires decertifying its negative stereotyping through the liberal dissemination of contextual information. *Contextual information* is that combination of factual and experiential information that is presented to a specific target audience to confront, contradict, and invalidate stereotypical imagery (in other words, to decertify the popular culture of corrections). Contextual information provides a standard of validity against which prison movies, inmate novels, and news media accounts of correctional events can be measured. The importance of mounting this challenge has been summarized by Ray Surette (1998):

> If you influence the symbol-creating and symbol-defining engine of a society, you create the social reality of that society. And if a particular perspective of social reality gains control of a social construction engine, other constructions will never be competitive. . . . For in crime and justice, perceptions have a nasty habit of becoming reality (Surette, 1998: xxiii-xxiv).

The "particular perspective of social reality" that is of most concern in this chapter is country club corrections. We will examine the proposition that corrections' executive managers fail to publicly participate in crime control policy debates in which "get tough on crime" political rhetoric and legislation reinforce the stereotypes of country club corrections. This failure "to influence the symbol-creating and symbol-defining engine" of the popular culture of corrections is identified in the literature as correctional silence.

For our purposes, *correctional silence* will be defined as the withholding of contextual information that can inform crime control policy debates, change the outcome of those debates, and educate the general public. This is a topic of interest because of a widely held perception that correctional silence unintentionally provides credibility to allegations that country club corrections is a reality. Thus, the unintended negative consequence of correctional silence is the indirect reinforcement of stereotypes of country club corrections.

Correctional Silence:
The Failure to Speak Out on Crime Control Policy Debates

During the 1988 presidential campaign conducted by George Bush, the country was saturated with campaign ads that featured the face of Willie Horton, an African-American serving a life sentence for murder who raped a white woman during one of his furloughs from a Massachusetts Department of Corrections' prison. The violent racial imagery associated with this crime was used to exploit the racial fears of white voters and convince them that Massachusetts Governor Dukakis was too soft on crime to be allowed in the White House. Bush's get tough on crime campaign rhetoric eventually expanded to include proposals to eliminate community-based corrections programs. The campaign rhetoric was effective and Bush was elected President.

The 1988 presidential campaign challenged the firm belief of many of corrections' executive managers that community-based programs are a valuable component of correctional programming. Slick campaign ads and carefully worded rhetoric successfully presented Willie Horton and community corrections to the electorate as accurate illustrations of country club corrections. As recognized experts on rehabilitation programs, corrections' executive managers possessed the knowledge needed to challenge the powerful stereotypes being reinforced through the Willie Horton ads. They could have argued publicly that furloughs are a proven tool of rehabilitation that very rarely present a threat to public safety. They easily could have supported that argument with a host of studies that established the effectiveness of furlough programs. But this challenge did not occur:

> Most correctional professionals knew the furlough ads were inaccurate and intentionally misleading. Most knew the majority of states have furlough programs. Most knew there had been tragedies with offenders on parole, on probation, and on work release as well as on furlough. And most correctional professionals believe these community-based programs are among the more progressive directions in corrections. They recognized that closing these release valves can have catastrophic consequences for population levels inside our institutions. Finally, most correctional professionals quickly recognized the broad emotional attack on furlough programs would have a long-term negative effect on the field of corrections as a whole. What, then, was the response from the corrections field? A deafening silence! (Schwartz, 1989: 38).

In Massachusetts, the impact of the Willie Horton scandal was far reaching. In addition to those correctional employees who lost their jobs during the political fallout from the scandal, the negative impact on system behavior was disastrous:

> Today, Massachusetts' prison system holds 9,400 inmates, and less than 1 percent participate in furloughs. In a prison system releasing nearly 4,000 inmates each year, only 5 percent have had a furlough, only 16 percent leave through community-based programs and only 57 percent are paroled. In a parole system touting 92 percent success, 60 percent of the inmates requesting consideration are denied. The system's goal now is no risk and no failure. It is a system that operates under the fear that an offender will falter and the subsequent fallout will take down the corrections professional. But it should not have to be that way (Larivee, 1993: 24, 26).

More recently, similar instances of correctional silence occurred across the country as elected officials advocated a broad spectrum of "get tough on crime" proposals. For example, in 1997, the Oklahoma legislature passed a truth-in-sentencing bill requiring the majority of convicted felons to serve 85 percent of their sentences. Although it was estimated that the incarceration of the 788 felons who would be adversely effected by this piece of legislation would cost the taxpayers an additional $12 million dollars a year, sheriffs and prosecutors went on record as agreeing that the offenders who met the guidelines for community sanctions instead should be incarcerated. Another adverse result would be a significant increase in prison crowding with all of the problems that are created by jamming too many inmates into too small a physical environment. Corrections' executive managers were witnessing a debate over legislation that they were certain would have a negative impact on their facilities. Although the imagery of country club corrections was displayed throughout the public debates on this proposal:

> Curiously absent in the entire debate were the corrections professionals, whose jobs it is to fulfill the mandates handed down by the Legislature and other governing bodies. Many of them were on the sidelines, praying that with the mandate would come the dollars it will take to manage them (Cowley, 1998: 38).

In both cases, the executive managers of corrections did not enter into a public debate that structured its propositions and arguments in terms of the need to replace a system of country club corrections with a system based on a "get tough on crime" philosophy. In his 1993 keynote address at the January American Correctional Association conference, ACA President Perry M. Johnson made the argument that the draconian mandatory minimum sentencing structures developed over the past twenty years have had the unintended consequences of creating massive prison crowding and the expenditure of billions of dollars for a policy of incarceration that is unfair and has had little impact on the crime rate. During his speech, Johnson noted the failure of corrections professionals to attempt to speak out about the disastrous results of mandatory minimum sentencing practices:

> But what I am afraid we have not done is questioned or challenged, in any fundamental way, the policies that caused that crowding. Put another way, we have long accepted the responsibility for dealing with offenders sentenced under criminal law. But we have focused on the individuals and said little about the law or the sentences. Some explain this by saying these are matters for courts and legislators to decide. Ultimately that is true. But we, better than anyone else, directly see and understand the real effects of criminal sanctions. We know what these sanctions cost in human and economic terms, and we see firsthand when they fail and when they succeed. If we do not apply our collective wisdom to the shaping of public policy, no one will do it for us (Johnson, 1993: 52).

The perspective shared by Schwartz, Larivee, Cowley, and Johnson is supported by empirical evidence.

Research Support for the Existence of Correctional Silence. Freeman (1996) conducted a content analysis of 1,546 newspaper articles on corrections appearing in the United States during the period of September 8, 1994 and November 24, 1995. The purpose of this study was to catalog the crime control policy issues that could have an impact on corrections and identify the participants in the public debate over those policy issues. Two hundred and seven articles focused on crime control policy proposals that could effect corrections. There were 137 articles on the death penalty; the remaining 70 articles covered: Megan's Law (9); "get tough on crime" legislation, including three strikes and you're out (24); various parole reorganization strategies (31); and victim's rights legislation (6).

Freeman found that the public policy debates over these issues involved a wide spectrum of citizens, politicians, and editorial writers, but corrections was not represented in the debates (Freeman, 1996: 16). These findings were similar to the findings of Chermak (1998) in a similar content analysis study, which examined 2,500 crime stories collected from newspapers and television stations in Dallas, Detroit, Cleveland, San Francisco, Albany, and Buffalo. Chermak found that only 17 percent of the crime stories covered corrections. In his analysis of the data, Chermak made some interesting observations about the infrequency of correctional news coverage:

> Reporters do not have relationships with officials from correctional organizations. These officials were the least likely of all sources considered . . . to be presented as providing comments in news stories, accounting for less than 1 percent of the total number of sources mentioned. Correction officials do not make an effort to legitimize their activities because public interest is limited. . . . The closed environment of correctional programs shields officials from scrutiny (Chermak, 1998: 97).

Both studies support the perception that corrections' executive managers remain silent during crime control policy debates and that silence can affect corrections negatively.

Correctional Silence as Credibility for Country Club Stereotypes

Previously, we noted that correctional silence is of concern because it gives credibility to stereotyping of country club corrections. The problem with giving credibility to any element of popular culture is as follows:

> . . . people forget or do not realize that popular culture is an extract of reality.
> . . . Like candy to cavities, a diet heavy on popular culture will rot one's perception of reality (Surette, 1998: xv).

When corrections' executive managers remain silent and do not challenge Willie Horton-type political ads and the attendant attacks on community-based programming, they are allowing the public to continue to uncritically accept the seductive imagery of country club corrections. This acceptance fuels a public anger against corrections that gives a green light to both conservative and liberal elected officials to promote "get tough on crime" legislation that increases the harshness of sentencing, abolishes inmate furlough programs, restricts inmate parole eligibility or eliminates parole, and greatly reduces the availability of in-house and community-based rehabilitation programs.

The Unintended Consequences of Accepting Country Club Corrections

The public and political revulsion against country club corrections that results in "get tough on crime" legislation has unintended consequences. First, it creates the twin conditions of gross prison crowding and a reduction in the quality of institutional life, which can produce the riots and escapes that so frequently symbolize the reality of corrections to the general public. Second, as both correctional employees and inmates "stress out" under the increasingly harsh conditions of confinement, some employees will be encouraged or provoked to engage in acts of brutality or corruption that shock the public conscience. These acts will be dutifully reported by the news media and provide new script material for Hollywood. The result of these unintended consequences is reinforcement of the smug hack imagery. It is one of the paradoxes of public perception that the imagery of country club corrections and smug hack corrections can coexist without creating cognitive dissonance for the members of the general public. That is, the public rarely, if ever, asks the question: If inmates have it so good in prison, why do we constantly read about guard abuse and brutality?

Why don't correctional managers participate in the public discussion of crime control policy issues? Arguably, it is in their professional interest to publicly protest draconian crime control policies. So, why are they silent? The simplest answer is found in a historical public/media avoidance strategy known as *fortress corrections*.

Fortress Corrections

Schwartz argues that the history of corrections in America is a history of fortress corrections:

> Historically, "fortress corrections" has been both a mentality and a philosophy in the field. Prisons . . . were built far from populated areas partly because those places wanted no more public scrutiny than absolutely necessary. Too many staff . . . do not understand the public's right to know or disagree with the concept and work actively to thwart efforts to open up corrections to the public (Schwartz, 1989: 40).

Fortress corrections represents a calculated policy borne of an isolationism characterized by rigid adherence to a centuries-old tradition of actively segregating prisons from community life because of a fundamental distrust of the public. The basis for this distrust is located in the compelling belief that the public never truly can understand the unique nature of corrections. What the public does not fully understand, it may criticize and try to change and corrections, historically, has been resistant to change, especially change imposed by the external environment. Therefore, corrections as a remote context may be in the best interests of correctional managers and line staff alike if public knowledge of their activities would result in an unwanted political scrutiny and externally generated changes in the fundamental policies and procedures that have served them so well.

Herein lies the dilemma when the issue is the public perception of corrections. Those institutional and/or system policies and procedures that create and maintain the isolation of fortress corrections may shield corrections from unwanted public scrutiny. Yet, at the same time, they inadvertently increase the power of the popular culture of corrections to present the stereotypical imagery that creates a negative public perception of corrections.

However, the traditional fear of public scrutiny embodied in fortress corrections provides only a partial explanation of correctional silence. The full explanation is considerably more complex. The decision to maintain their silence during public crime control policy debates is not a matter of corrections' executive managers possessing the prerogative of exercising individual discretion in making that decision. Instead, it is a decision mandated by four organizational constraints that those managers are expected to respect. These organizational constraints are political, ethical, legal, and operational in nature. The first organizational constraint is rooted in the political reality surrounding executive managers.

Vulnerability to Career Termination

Executive managers in corrections are aware of the potential for career termination created by the power differential between themselves and the elected officials who appoint them. They are classified as at-will employees who can be dismissed from their positions without cause or explanation at any time by the appointing elected official unless they are protected by strong political allies. Commissioners of corrections historically have had a very short tenure because of their political vulnerability. Currently, the average length of service for a department of corrections commissioner is only 3.6 years (Camp and Camp, 1998: 128).

State department of corrections superintendents also have the unenviable distinction of having a high attrition rate (Benton et al., 1982: 18). Lunden (1957) studied the careers of 612 prison superintendents in 43 states over a 50 year period. He found that 61 percent of the superintendents served a term of office that was less than four years. Today, the term of service as a superintendent ranges from 2.5 to 26.1 years with the average term being 13.5 years (Camp and Camp, 1998: 129). This average is clearly an improvement over the findings cited by Lunden; however, in many states tenure is still quite short. Therefore, correctional silence can be partially defined as a self-protective response to the executive manager's marked vulnerability to career termination for political reasons.

The Ethical Requirements of Professionalism

The elected officials who appoint the executive managers in corrections expect those individuals to accept the appointment with the clear understanding that it is the responsibility of elected officials to define the mission of corrections and the responsibility of executive managers to achieve that mission in the most effective manner possible, regardless of their personal views about the policies shaping that mission. It would be highly unethical for an individual to accept an executive level appointment, then actively strive to undermine the crime control policy created by the elected officials who have made the appointment by publicly challenging that policy. An executive manager who cannot tolerate the negative consequences of a specific crime control policy (such as the mandatory minimum sentencing that has created prison crowding) has an ethical obligation to resign prior to publicly speaking out against the policy. To do otherwise is to act in an unprofessional manner.

This does not mean that corrections' executive managers are to consider themselves muzzled. The ethical standards inherent in professionalism also require them to express frankly their opinion of any crime control policy that has a negative impact on corrections during their private sessions with governors and other powerful elected officials when they believe those officials are not aware of all the facts. Ethical executive managers will say what they believe must be said if elected officials are to make an informed policy decision. Chase Riveland, the former secretary of the Washington Department of Corrections, in an article entitled "Being a Director of Corrections in the 1990's," succinctly describes the ethical dilemma that confronts executive managers in corrections:

Governors, legislators, and other officials have all learned the political lesson of Willie Horton well. Few around the country have been willing to challenge the perceived public feeling that "tough on crime" is an essential political corner-stone. Therefore, the correctional administrator remains caught between the pragmatic knowledge that many persons in our prisons can safely be dealt with elsewhere, and the requirement to remain politically consistent and loyal to an administration's desires (Riveland, 1991: 11).

Correctional managers, especially those at the highest levels, also have an ethical obligation to win public trust and confidence in the organization, its employees, and the mission they are expected to accomplish.

The Need to Speak with a Unified Voice. The ability of an organization to win public confidence and trust is limited if there is open conflict between organization members and elected officials. The chain of command in correctional organizations mandates that executive managers, or their designated press officers, are to be the only official spokespersons for the institution or system. Line staff and subordinate managers are prohibited from making public statements, especially to the news media. Otherwise, the public will be confused if every correctional employee can speak out and present messages that may contradict the statements of elected officials and the executive managers appointed to implement their agendas. In addition, any attempt to educate the public about corrections will fail if too many contradictory voices are heard.

The Constraints of the Law

There are two types of legal constraints controlling the public voices of corrections' executive managers.

The Role of the Civil Servant. Executive managers are civil servants. In many cases, the law prohibits them from using their position to lobby for specific crime control policies or procedures. The rationale for this prohibition is that civil servants have the legal responsibility of ensuring the efficient management of government organizations, but they are expected to be subservient to, and actively assist, the elected officials who represent the will of the majority of the voters. Executive managers are not elected officials. They have not been put into power by the people to advance, or oppose, a specific agenda. That responsibility falls to those elected officials whose platforms have been endorsed by the electorate. Civil servants who publicly advocate alternative crime control policies will create conflict that can divert the political time and energy needed to implement the will of the people. Conflict between the elected representatives of the people and the appointed managers of corrections is self-defeating, divisive, and can be viewed as self-serving, three conditions that ill-serve the electorate.

Civil Litigation. The constant possibility of civil litigation filed by inmates or community special interest groups plays a role in the decision not to express publicly personal beliefs about specific crime control policy issues. One of the perennial annoyances associated with the high-profile position of executive leadership in corrections is the tendency of plaintiffs to automatically name the highest ranking correctional manager in the organization as a defendant in civil litigation filed against any employee(s) during that manager's term of office. The danger of participation in public discussions about specific crime control policies is that the executive manager's statements may provide ammunition to the plaintiff in a lawsuit that challenges that crime control policy or the administrative procedures that the policy has required the executive manager to implement. An executive manager who publicly has espoused a point of view that is congruent with the views of the plaintiff in a lawsuit may be called into court and find himself or herself listed as a witness against the state. This is personally embarrassing as well as politically risky.

Operational Priorities

The challenge of hands-on management of the daily operation of the correctional institution or system leaves little time for executive managers to enter into public debates about crime control policy. In a comprehensive survey of 487 superintendents, McShane and Williams (1993) found that the 276 superintendents who responded had an internal environmental focus, not an external environment focus. Their most important priorities were defined in terms of maintaining the operational stability of their facilities. Influencing crime control policy formulation was not a priority. Superintendents spent most of their time on pragmatic institution-oriented matters: personnel issues, resource management, inmate management, meetings with security staff, and a variety of routine and long-term planning activities:

> Wardens, then, do not appear to occupy much of their time in meetings with those external to the institution. In an average month, wardens spend most of their time on internal programmatic and people issues. When custody levels were examined, there were no significant differences in estimates of time consumption across the various activities (McShane and Williams, 1993: 39).

The superintendents who responded to the survey were quick to express their grave concern about the external influences that directly affected the day-to-day management of their prisons. They were especially sensitive to the externally imposed issues of inadequate budgets; staff management problems (high turnover rates, chronic shortages of employees, and low quality employees) that are frequently the result of the low salary structures set by elected officials; prison crowding with all of its attendant ills; and a variety of legislative decisions that made their jobs more difficult. All of these issues are strongly influenced by crime control policy decisions.

However, while the superintendents decried the negative impact of current crime control policy on their ability to run their prisons, they were quick to affirm that their primary priority was the maintenance of organizational efficiency. Typifying this philosophy is Ronald Hutchinson, the warden of the Maryland House of Correction in Jessup, Maryland:

> Hutchinson has a distaste for theoretical policy debates, dismissing them as "for politicians." He likens his job to that of a corporate manager with a single bottom line: maintaining order in the sprawling, castle-like prison built in the 19th century (Mishra, 1999: B1).

Simply put, the complexity of running a modern prison leaves little time or energy for executive managers to publicly participate in complicated crime control policy debates.

Correctional Silence: Only a Partial Truth

The fact that corrections' executive managers cannot publicly challenge ill-conceived crime control policies because of organizational constraints does not mean that they are expected to be, or want to be, silent about the daily operations of their organizations and the responsibilities and accomplishments of correctional employees. The constraints that limit participation in public crime control debates do not prohibit interaction with the general public. To put it in Chermak's (1998) words, organizational constraints do not prevent corrections' executive managers from working to "legitimize their activities." They do not prohibit development of a unified strategy of community education designed to decertify negative stereotyping.

Community Education:
The Decertification of the Popular Culture of Corrections

Corrections professionals (Koehler, 1989; Fairchild, 1998) frequently define the negative public perception of corrections in terms of the failure of correctional organizations to have an effective public relations strategy. They make the argument that what corrections needs to do to change public perception is to develop a good public relations campaign. When they use the term public relations campaign they mean:

> . . . doing whatever is necessary to create and maintain good relations and to avoid or remove bad relations. If bad relations are due to ignorance or misunderstanding by the public concerned, an education or informational campaign may be indicated (Brody, 1992: 355).

Or, as Brian Fairchild, public information officer of the Illinois Department of Corrections put it:

> Good PR strategies are long-term programs aimed at identifying negative perceptions or inaccurate stereotypes of an organization and designing communications efforts to balance criticism, outline decision-making and accurately describe the situations or policies in question (Fairchild, 1998: 31).

In other words, public relations is a calculated strategy of confronting negative stereotypes with a steady flow of contextual information. When discussing how to develop an effective public relations campaign, many corrections professionals employ the phrase "managing the news" to refer to this process of providing accurate information about corrections.

Unfortunately, "public relations" and "managing the news" may not be the best phrases to use when discussing solutions to corrections' image problem. The use of these phrases can be counterproductive because citizens are increasingly likely to interpret them as code speak for "spinning the story," a highly specialized form of information manipulation performed by public information officers and other communication specialists known in slang terms as "spin doctors."

During the 1990s, the term spin doctor became closely associated with a series of controversial events occurring on the political scene. Because of this negative association with politics, public information officers and press secretaries both inside and outside of the political arena can be viewed as manipulative individuals whose job it is to con the public into uncritically accepting a false interpretation of a particular story or event because the truth would do harm to the reputation of their boss or their organization. As a result, corrections' use of the phrase public relations may be perceived in negative terms, in other words, the clever manipulation of the facts to protect a reputation chronically tarnished by employee misconduct and inmate abuses. Given the distinct possibility that the term public relations can carry a negative connotation, it is suggested that corrections professionals avoid its use and employ the term *community education*.

Defining Community Education. Chermack (1998) stresses that a major problem for corrections is a general lack of public interest in correctional events, unless they are sensational, such as a riot or an escape. As a result, news media professionals perceive that the public is not interested in the daily routine of correctional organizations, especially those that are outside of the local market. In addition, the news media has only a limited access to correctional stories because "correctional sources have greater opportunities to control news images because media access to inmates is limited by law" (Chermak, 1998: 97). These three issues can be addressed through a systemic process of community education that increases public interest in routine correctional activities, encourages news media professionals to document those activities, and opens channels of communication between corrections and the news media:

> Correctional administrators would better serve their interests if they embarked on high-profile, clearly articulated, well-organized education programs targeted at both the public and legislative bodies (Wittenberg, 1996: 46).

Community education can be defined as a proactive communication strategy with the goal of decertification of correctional stereotypes through the dissemination of high levels of contextual information to the general public. As a proactive strategy, community education has the distinct advantage of not currently being burdened with the baggage associated with the concept of spin doctors and spinning the story.

Structuring a Community Education Strategy. A community education strategy must be designed to make corrections less of a remote context for the general public. The greater the amount of contextual information members of the general public have about corrections, the higher the probability that those individuals will be able to see the fallacy of correctional stereotypes when they are encountered in the entertainment and news media. To promote decertification effectively, community education must be structured to provide a steady flow of contextual information about the following things:

- the mission of corrections
- professional activities of correctional organizations and correctional employees
- challenges facing corrections
- resources needed to meet those challenges
- successful efforts to manage those challenges
- constraints affecting the challenges to management
- the full range of contributions correctional organizations make to the community
- the role members of the community can play in correctional programs and activities

The skillful delivery of contextual information will provide the consumers of the "popular arts" with the foundation necessary for a more positive perception of corrections by challenging the thematic structure of smug hack corrections, especially the powerful stereotypes of the sadistic guard, the incompetent/corrupt warden, and the inability of correctional employees to do more than warehouse inmates in conditions of brutal confinement. It also will expose the fallacies of country club corrections.

Effective Implementation. To be effective, a community education strategy cannot assume that the general public is a monolithic social entity. Instead, the general public can be more usefully thought of as a social entity that is composed of a number of different publics, each of which is a subset of the larger society. The most important publics to be targeted by community education are defined by those individuals who:

- have the authority to create the mission of corrections and allocate resources to it (elected officials)

- help shape public perception (the news media, Hollywood, and the academic community)

- are members of that social collective known as the consumers of popular culture (the community or general public)

- possess resources that can be used by corrections (technology industries, private corrections, correctional watchdog organizations, and victims rights' groups)

Community education strives to provide contextual knowledge to these publics through the process of active communication. The approach to each public will be tailored to take into account the unique qualities of that specific public.

The Core of Community Education: Active Communication

Active communication can be defined as a consistent, honest, long-term commitment to an aggressive policy of contextual information dissemination that emphasizes the accomplishments and successes of corrections before a crisis situation erupts into news media headlines. Active communication provides a baseline perspective from which the various publics can view corrections and its events, including those that are negative.

Principles of Active Communication. Chapters 6 through 10 present a random sampling of the range of community education strategies currently being used by corrections' executive managers to "legitimize the activities" of corrections and decertify negative correctional stereotypes. The fundamental dynamic of the majority of these strategies is face-to-face verbal interaction. The success of any community education program depends on strict adherence to basic principles of active communication during these interactions. These principles are presented in Box 5-1.

Body language is also important in any face-to-face communication. Glosser (1998: 10-11) talks about "the expressive you." That is, the physical presence you project during a public speaking engagement. She suggests that the good speaker will gesture while talking if that is a natural form of expression. Moving while talking is also a positive act because standing behind a desk or podium erects a psychological barrier between the speaker and the audience. Eye contact with members of the audience for five or six seconds is a good way of engaging individual members of the audience.

However, there are a number of physical motions which Glosser refers to as "power-robbing nonverbals" (Glosser, 1998: 10). Power-robbing nonverbals are types of body language that distract the audience or offend them: pacing, scratching, fidgeting, slouching, using rocking motions, excessive smiling, excessively crossing your arms as you speak, holding your hands in a prayer position, or repeatedly wetting your lips (Glosser, 1998: 10-11).

Community education is an ongoing process that presents contextual information about corrections to different publics and strives to refute the stereotypes of the popular culture of corrections. The strategies of community education that will be presented in the remaining chapters of this book are not presented as magic bullets. There is no

Box 5-1 Principles of Active Communication

Every correctional employee should be taught the following guidelines for verbal interactions:

- Don't bluff. If you don't know the answer, then say so.
- Don't use profanity.
- Don't ridicule members of your audience or groups of people used in examples or stories.
- Don't patronize your listeners.
- Don't lose your patience.
- Don't hide behind a podium or table.
- Don't exaggerate.
- Don't make excuses (Glosser, 1998:11).

The reason for each of these items is self-explanatory, but the list is not yet complete. In addition to the guidelines set forth by Glosser, we suggest the following:

- Avoid jargon. If it must be used, define it, especially loaded terms like "segregation."
- Do not use slang or racially loaded terms.
- Dress in a professional manner.
- Actively listen to questions and do not become defensive.
- Answer questions courteously, but do not let challenges go unanswered.
- Do not end the discussion until every question has been answered.
- Consciously avoid any behavior that will reinforce stereotypes.

In illustration of the final point, do not make the mistake of a county jail warden this author once knew who used to carry a Number 10 coffee can into which he loudly and frequently spit tobacco juice while talking to visitors about staff professionalism. This warden's constant use of profanity also was unsettling.

guarantee that any of these decertification efforts will significantly change the current negative public perception of corrections. They certainly will not do so overnight. But, they do have the potential to help influence the public perception of corrections. The remainder of this book documents the decertification strategies currently being used in correctional community education programs throughout the United States.

Points to Consider

1. What compelling reasons justify correctional silence?
2. Is the threat of career termination as great a threat to corrections' executive managers as the author seems to think it is? Justify your answer.

3. What are the most important accomplishments to bring to the attention of the general public? What should be the priority ranking of these accomplishments?

4. Do you think each of the publics noted in this chapter really want to be presented with a more positive view of corrections? Defend your answer.

5. What are the risks involved in educating the community?

6. Is it really possible to change the negative public perception of corrections through community education? Defend your answer.

7. How can you reduce the risks identified in question number 6?

8. Are there any publics other than those defined by the author that should be considered in community education? If so, who are they?

References

Benton, F. W., Ellen Rosen, and Judy Peters. 1982. *National Survey of Correctional Institution Employee Attrition*. New York: Center for Public Productivity.

Brody, E. W. 1992. The Domain of Public Relations. *Public Relations Review*. 184: 349-363.

Camp, C. G. and G. M. Camp. 1998. *The Corrections Yearbook 1998*. Middletown, Connecticut: Criminal Justice Institute, Inc.

Chermak, S. M. 1998. Police, Courts, and Corrections in the Media. In F. Bailey and D. Hale, eds. *Popular Culture, Crime and Justice*. Belmont, California: West/Wadsworth Publishing. pp. 87-99.

Cowley, J. 1998. Changing Public Opinion. *Corrections Today*. (59)1: 38-40.

Fairchild, B. 1998. Corrections' Public Relations Dilemma: A Good PR Plan Can Effectively Counter Negative Public Perceptions. *Corrections Today*. (59)1: 30-31.

Freeman, Robert M. 1996. Correctional Staff as the Villain and the Inmate as Hero: The Problem is Bigger Than Hollywood. *American Jails*. (10)3: 9-16.

Glosser, S. 1998. How to Add Pizzazz to Your Community Presentation. *Community Links: Progress Through Partnerships*. 13: 10-11.

Johnson, P. M. 1993. Corrections Should Take the Lead in Changing Sentencing Practices. *Corrections Today*. (55)2: 52-56.

Koehler, R. J. 1989. Like It Or Not: We Are News. *Corrections Today*. (51)1: 16-17.

Larivee, J. L. 1993. Community Programs—A Risky Business. *Corections Today*. (55)6: 20-26.

Lunden, Walter. 1957. The Tenure and Turnover of State Prison Wardens. *American Journal of Correction*. November/December: 14.

McShane, Marilyn D. and Frank P. Williams, III. 1993. *The Management of Correctional Institutions*. New York: Garland Publishing, Inc.

Meddis, S. 1989. A Reporter's Notebook: Forming Partnerships with the Press. *Corrections Today*. (51)1: 22-26.

Mishra, R. 1999. New Warden in Jessup Lets Prisoners Know Who's Boss. *Washington Post*. November 22. B1.

Riveland, Chase. 1991. Being a Director of Corrections in the 1990s. *Federal Probation*. (55)2: 10-11.

Schwartz, Jeffrey A. 1989. Promoting a Good Public Image: Effective Leadership, Sound Practices Makes the Difference. *Corrections Today*. (51)1: 38-42.

Surette, R. 1998. Some Unpopular Thoughts About Popular Culture. In F. Bailey and D. Hale, eds. *Popular Culture, Crime and Justice*. Belmont, California: West/Wadsworth Publishing. pp. xiv-xxiv.

Wittenberg, P. M. 1996. Power, Influence, and the Development of Correctional Policy. *Federal Probation*. (60)2: 43-48.

The Education of Elected Officials:

Mitigating the Indirect Political Reinforcement of Country Club Corrections

A fundamental tenet in communications theory is "that attitudes and beliefs develop gradually in response to significant trends in media representation" (Barak, 1994: 23). One of those significant trends has been the news media's reporting of sensational crimes committed by hard-core criminals and their coverage of the subsequent demands by elected officials and special interest groups for "get tough on crime" sentencing legislation and collateral legislation designed to make prison life harsher for inmates. Variations on this theme have been replayed over the past thirty years, forming an increasingly persuasive media loop. The result is an impact on the political environment in which corrections functions:

> . . . the most important effect of media loops and the creation of media events is that the events become political reality. Simulation or hyperreality lurks inevitably when media loops are involved (Manning, 1998: 36).

Political rhetoric focused on getting tough on criminals through mandatory sentencing, the abolition of parole, and the elimination of weight lifting from prison recreation yards reflects a "political reality" based on the news media-generated imagery of country club corrections. This imagery resonates with citizens, especially crime victims and their friends.

The Perception of Country Club Corrections as Reality. The fact that many citizens suspect prisons of being too posh an environment for inmates is reflected in the 1994 Florida Department of Corrections-commissioned poll of public attitudes. For example, 43.8 percent of the general public respondents answered "No" to the question "Do you think the typical inmate is required to work in prison?" The reality is that as of June 30, 1997, 83 percent of Florida Department of Corrections' inmates worked, participated in academic or vocational programs, or were involved in a combination of work and programs (Florida Department of Corrections, 1998: 30). In addition, 95.5 percent of the general public respondents believed that inmates are released from prison early because of crowding, despite that fact that the early-release policy was eliminated in December 1994 (Florida Department of Corrections, 1998: 23).

The public disapproval of country club corrections is reflected in three survey areas. In the case of inmates having access to television, 50.6 percent of the general public respondents disapproved of that access; 51.2 percent disapproved of inmate access to weight lifting equipment; and 33.1 percent disapproved of inmates having air conditioning (Florida Department of Corrections, 1998: 33-35). The view of corrections as country club corrections, created in large part by political rhetoric, arouses public fear and anger, which is communicated to elected officials in the form of a demand for "get tough on crime" policy.

Corrections as a Remote Context for Elected Officials. Elected officials rarely come from the ranks of corrections. Therefore, for the vast majority of crime control policymakers, corrections is a remote context. This suggests that their personal perceptions of corrections may be influenced by the stereotypes of the popular culture of corrections in much the same manner as the electorate's perception. Because this misperception can generate support for the passage of ill-conceived crime control legislation, community education requires a commitment to the education of elected officials. Such a commitment requires the exercise of correctional leadership.

Asserting Correctional Leadership. There is a growing consensus in corrections that its executive managers need to take a more active role in the process of shaping crime control policy:

> Today, corrections directors must spend large amounts of their time in the public policy arena. The political process a few years ago adopted the credo of ". . . Tough on crime . . ." As sentencing policy became more politicized, we once again experienced overcrowded prisons and jails. The corrections director must, at a minimum, enter the political arena as a harbinger projecting the resources that will be required and, preferably, as one who can shape a course of sound public policy through the political process (Riveland 1991: 10).

Attempting to play a more active role in the formulation of crime control policy is in the best interests of corrections and, therefore, should be a goal in the efforts to educate elected officials:

> Corrections professionals can benefit from recognized leadership—leadership that is attentive to public opinion but not captured by it; leadership that is able to speak with authority on what corrections can and cannot do. . . . (Larivee, 1993: 24).

The formal core of the elected official's component of community education is a formal communication structure that: (1) presents a broad array of contextual information to elected officials; (2) provides corrections' executive managers with the capability to effectively monitor the legislative process; and (3) facilitates advisory assistance to the elected officials formulating crime control policy. An effective communication structure uses both written and verbal strategies. These strategies include: (1) written documentation in the form of an annual report and supplemental documents; (2) periodic scheduling of formal and informal personal interactions between corrections' executive managers and elected officials; and (3) creation of a central office legislative liaison officer and a legislative liaison team.

The Annual Report and Supplemental Documents

The Federal Bureau of Prisons, the majority of state departments of corrections, and an increasing number of large county correctional organizations issue an annual report. An annual report typically begins with a mission statement and an overview of the status of the organization. This provides the initial opportunity to educate elected officials to the challenges of corrections. For example, the issue of crowding has been prominently displayed in some annual reports for the past two decades:

> While we have maximized our existing resources through double bunking of prisoners and stressed better use of alternative punishments like boot camp, probation and other programs funded through our Office of Community Corrections, the fact remains that our prison beds are rapidly filling up. This Department continues to look forward to working with the Legislature and other policy makers on long term solutions to Michigan's prison population problems (McGinnis, 1996: foreword).

While the size, contents, and use of sophisticated graphics may vary, the most effective design layout for an annual report is one that is unified. A unified layout effectively links three key areas—correctional issues, organizational structure, and statistical information—together to create a comprehensive, readily accessible source of contextual information. Typical of this unified layout is the structure of the Arizona Department of Corrections' annual report (Arizona Department of Corrections, 1999) in Box 6-1.

One of the most useful sections of a unified annual report, and a relatively recent innovation, is the "Misconceptions, Frequently Asked Questions" section. This section is designed to decertify country club corrections stereotypes. Box 6-2 provides an example of this useful approach to stereotype debunking.

The written answers provided by the Florida Department of Corrections in its annual report give elected officials accurate answers to the questions most likely to be raised by constituents for whom corrections is a remote context. This approach has a double benefit for corrections. The elected official and his or her staff learn facts about corrections that may influence their thinking about the field and the constituent receives factual information, not speculation or assumptions fueled by the popular culture of corrections.

The Ineffective Annual Report. Annual reports generally have a wide distribution and are sent automatically to elected officials within the state. They also should be sent to the state's elected representatives in Washington because of the impact federal decisions can have on state corrections. The purpose of an annual report is to call attention to critical areas of correctional achievement and need. However, not all annual reports are equally useful in educating elected officials.

The quality of annual reports varies. Some fail to communicate the contextual information elected officials need to hear. An ineffective annual report has no table of contents, provides a boring description of the facilities within the system, does not address critical challenges and issues, and presents reams of statistical data without any explanation or linkage between the statistics and important issues. The least useful annual reports are those that consist only of statistical tables. Unless the reader is a statistician, stand-alone statistical tables are boring. They will not be read by the vast majority of elected officials. Nor will they confront negative stereotyping.

Annual reports that leave it up to the reader to try and ferret out the critical challenges facing corrections, or interpret complicated statistical data, have little value when the goal of the report is the education of elected officials, nor are they useful in educating the other members of the community that corrections professionals should be trying to educate. The most useful annual report is the one (like Arizona's and Florida's) that is both comprehensive and easily read and understood by a community composed of diverse populations that range from the average citizen to the academic researcher.

Box 6-1 Arizona Department of Corrections' Annual Report for Fiscal Year 1998

This sixty-two-page document has eighteen sections. The table of contents of the Arizona Department of Corrections' Annual Report is organized to efficiently take the reader through a complex correctional environment:

Sections one through sixteen provide a comprehensive description of the organizational structure of the Arizona Department of Corrections, its goals and challenges, and provides a wealth of information about how those challenges are being managed. The contributions of specific employees are noted and the use of private corrections providers documented. Important corrections-specific legislation is discussed in detail. The statistical information section is organized to complement the descriptive sections of the report by providing:

Box 6-1 Arizona Department of Corrections' Annual Report for Fiscal Year 1998 (continued)

The directory concludes the annual report by providing a listing of the phone numbers and addresses of key personnel and facilities. The website for the Arizona Department of Corrections is also listed:

Supplementing the Annual Report. An increasing number of correctional organizations are supplementing their annual reports with the publication of special reports documenting a specific issue of interest. The Minnesota Department of Corrections, for example, periodically publishes a special report entitled *Backgrounder*. Typical of the quality of *Backgrounder* reports were the January 9, 10, and 13, 1997, issues, which presented an excellent overview of three challenging issues: capital punishment, sex offenders, and juveniles certified as adults (Minnesota Department of Corrections, 1997). The writing was professional, the facts were accurate, and illustrations were effectively used to highlight key information. A list of popular misconceptions surrounding these politically hot subjects was confronted by factual information presented in a readable format.

This type of document does not have to be presented in the traditional hard copy format. Increasingly, correctional organizations, especially the state departments of corrections, are using the Internet to make contextual information available to the general public.

The Corrections Newsletter. There are very few department of corrections that do not publish a monthly or bimonthly newsletter. These vary in quality, but the best of the newsletters provide a variety of contextual information that is of both professional and personal interest. One of the best newsletters is *The Communicator*, published by the Ohio Department of Rehabilitation and Correction. This newsletter always contains a blend of information. The Spring 1998 issue, for example, provided information about the following items: Ohio's community justice cabinet; the experiences of Ohio Department of Rehabilitation and Correction employees returning to college to earn a degree; Ohio Department of Rehabilitation and Correction training opportunities; restorative justice; community justice councils in action; victim and offender meetings; the achievements of the department's community service program; minutes from the Ohio Department of Rehabilitation and Correction executive retreat; a message on community justice from a warden; "A Look Across the Country" section that contained information about community service activities in which other departments of corrections are engaged; and an article about local community justice activities (Ohio Department of Rehabilitation and Correction, 1998).

This type of newsletter can be particularly effective in decertifying negative stereotypes because it presents corrections professionals in a range of positive activities, professional and personal. It presents them as regular people, not stereotypes.

Box 6-2 Misconceptions, Frequently Asked Questions

In the Florida Department of Corrections' Annual Report for 1997-98, the "Misconceptions" section presents stereotype-based misconceptions about corrections as statements or questions and debunks them by presenting the facts. These statements and questions include:

1. Inmates don't work.
2. Inmates have cable television and satellite dishes.
3. Most inmates are released early because of prison crowding.
4. Why don't inmates grow their own food?
5. The department of corrections determines how long inmates serve in prison.
6. Inmates still aren't serving most of their sentences.
7. Prisons are air conditioned.
8. Inmates who get life sentences don't really stay in prison for life (Florida Department of Corrections, 1998: 21-22).

The misconceptions section is followed by a "frequently asked questions" section:

1. Where can I get some information about privatizing prisons?
2. I read recently that some inmates were executed on the first warrant. Isn't that unusual? I thought an inmate had an average of three warrants signed before he or she was executed.
3. My elderly aunt has a prison pen pal who asks for money for various reasons, and I'm suspicious of him. How can I check out what he says he's in for, when he'll be released, and so forth?
4. I am a crime victim and my family and I wish to be notified when a certain inmate is released. Whom do I contact and how?
5. To whom can I talk about my family member's transfer, gaintime, discipline, release, and so forth?
6. How much does it cost to incarcerate an inmate for a year?
7. What is the current recidivism rate?
8. How many prisons does Florida have?
9. What's the difference between a jail and a prison?
10. How many inmates are in Florida prisons? On death row? On community supervision like probation?
11. What is the web address for information on released inmates?
12. How can I find out more about gangs in prison?
13. My son is being harassed in prison, and I fear for him. To whom can I report this?
14. I am interested in a career with the Florida Department of Corrections. Where can I get more information? (Florida Department of Corrections, 1998: 22-23).

The Facts Brochure. An increasingly popular form of information dissemination, especially at the department of corrections' level, is the facts brochure. The Arkansas Department of Corrections, for example, puts out *Facts Brochure 1998*, a well-written forty-seven page brochure that provides easily understood information about the department of corrections' organizational chart, management structure, history, and programs, as well as a directory of facilities (Arkansas Department of Corrections, 1998). Any individual wanting to know about the Arkansas Department of Corrections can obtain a thumbnail sketch in less than an hour.

Unfortunately, there has been a trend in recent years for government budget cutters to target correctional publications in their zeal to reduce the cost of government. A number of department of corrections, including some of the largest in the country, have had their ability to present contextual information to elected officials and the public restricted because of the perceived need for fiscal conservatism. However, even when an agency retains the ability to fund this element of community education, another problem arises. No matter how well-designed, and fact-filled these documents are, they are of no value if they are not read. And it is always possible that some information, especially statistical information, will be open to controversial differential interpretation by recipients. Therefore, the human touch is needed. The formal communication structure also must include a strong verbal element that presents opportunities for face-to-face interaction that is designed to increase the contextual information available to those elected officials who do not know corrections.

Face-to-face Interaction with Elected Officials

Corrections' executive managers must engage in face-to-face interactions with elected officials, whenever possible. The range of opportunities for these interactions include: giving personal testimony before legislative bodies, holding formal membership in the governor's cabinet, participating in national conferences focusing on crime control policy, and engaging in informal meetings.

Testimony before Legislative Bodies. When legislation with the potential to affect corrections is pending, executive managers must personally testify before the legislative bodies considering that legislation, especially if they anticipate a negative impact on corrections. The organization's position on the legislation should be clearly and professionally articulated with appropriate history, research, and statistics cited. Short, but fact-filled handouts should be provided to reinforce key points. The executive manager always should be ready for hostile and/or pointed questions. When appearing in front of a legislative body, the executive manager always should begin his or her testimony by presenting a prepared opening statement. Failure to present a prepared opening statement will cost the organization a valuable education opportunity.

This author once attended a session of a state House Judiciary Committee meeting convened to discuss legislation designed to reduce the number of offenders absconding while on state parole. Several key provisions of the proposed legislation had the potential to severely reduce the number of inmates being paroled on their minimum. The negative impact of this reduction on a severely crowded system was obvious to everyone working in corrections. All of the witnesses called by the committee, except one, arrived with prepared opening statements. The executive manager representing the department of corrections had no prepared statement. When called to testify, he simply stated "I don't have a prepared opening statement, but I'm ready to answer any questions the committee might have."

There were no questions and the legislation subsequently passed. The resulting impact on crowding in the department of corrections was as substantial and negative as corrections professionals had predicted behind closed doors. The refusal to present a prepared opening statement also costs the organization a valuable opportunity to educate any members of the general public and the news media present during the testimony.

Membership in the Cabinet. Commissioners of corrections are usually members of the governor's cabinet and have access to their counterparts in other state agencies. This provides an excellent opportunity to educate those powerful individuals about corrections and debunk any stereotype-based misconceptions they might have. Commissioners of corrections who are not members of the governor's cabinet certainly should advocate for their inclusion in that group.

Participation in National Crime Control Policy Seminars. The active participation of corrections' executive managers in the workshops and panels of national conferences dedicated to discussions of crime control policy can do a great deal to present a positive image of corrections.

For example, in December 1999, Delaware Department of Corrections Commissioner Stan Taylor led a discussion on the importance of in-prison substance abuse treatment at the National Assembly on Drugs, Alcohol Abuse, and the Criminal Offender in Washington, D.C. This provided Commissioner Taylor the opportunity to present information about Delaware's KEY and Crest substance abuse programs as well as exchange views with National Drug Czar, General Barry McCaffrey; Attorney General Janet Reno; and Department of Health and Human Services Secretary, Donna Shalala. The purpose of the three-day conference was to "bring together key state and local policy makers from across the country to examine opportunities to reduce crime and implement smarter drug policies for criminal offenders" (Welch, 1999: 1). The individuals invited to the conference included governors; state attorneys general; legislative, judicial, corrections, and health officials. Commissioner Taylor's involvement in this conference created an opportunity for increasing the contextual knowledge bases for those program participants for whom corrections was a remote context.

Informal Interaction with Elected Officials. Corrections' executive managers must do more than attend cabinet meetings. They must establish as broad a base of political support as possible by periodically having face-to-face meetings with:

- the leadership of the key house and senate committees (such as the judiciary committee and the budget committee), which have the most direct impact on corrections
- the representatives and senators who have correctional facilities in their districts
- those elected officials who are the most hostile to corrections. It is a mistake to avoid meetings with hostile elected officials. They are the ones who are most in need of education.
- those elected officials who are in their first term of office and have no experience with corrections. Education of the first-timers is important because some of them eventually will become the political leadership.
- former elected officials who are now functioning as lobbyists and retain a measure of political influence

Private meetings with elected officials undoubtedly have educational value. But the amount of legislation affecting corrections during any given year can be large. Frequently, it is not possible for executive managers to meet with elected officials about all relevant legislation. One effective method of compensating for this time deficiency is to modify the organizational structure to create a managerial substitute.

The Central Office Legislative Liaison Officer/Team

The correctional employee who is assigned the task of educating elected officials frequently is referred to as the legislative liaison officer. Because of the importance of the legislative liaison officer's role, that individual should report directly to the top executive manager of the organization. Depending on the size of the organization, the legislative liaison officer may be an individual working alone or as the director of a group of support staff dedicated to working with elected officials. In either case, the role is varied and time-consuming. Take, for example, the expectations for the Office of Intergovernmental Relations of the Illinois Department of Corrections. Defined as the "link between the agency, the General Assembly and the Governor's Office," (Illinois Department of Corrections, 1997: 13), the Illinois Department of Corrections Office of Intergovernmental Relations:

> . . . contains the legislative liaison and staff. It oversees all legislative matters of interest to the department. In doing so, the office alerts executive staff and division heads to newly introduced bills, arranges sponsorship and passage of agency proposed legislation, and, more often, attempts to stop or amend legislation harmful to the department. This involves working with House and Senate staff, interest groups and organizations as well as the sponsors or legislators themselves in order to amend legislation when deemed necessary or draft new legislation if needed. The liaisons also arrange for the department to be represented when testimony on a bill is required. The Office . . . also assists legislators on corrections-related problems and questions from their constituents (Illinois Department of Corrections, 1997: 9).

Legislative liaison officers must possess the broad range of verbal and written communication skills that are essential to working with a broad range of legislators (some of whom are openly hostile to corrections) on a variety of issues that require a thorough knowledge of corrections in general, and the liaison's agency, in particular. The most effective legislative liaison officer will be the intelligent extrovert who is genuinely comfortable interacting with a wide range of individuals, many of whom are strangers. A legislative liaison officer who is an introvert, who has difficulty initiating an interaction with a stranger, or responding to hostile statements, will be ineffective. Prior experience working with elected officials and/or the news media also will improve the ability of the legislative liaison officer to effectively communicate corrections' messages. A broad background in journalism and communication (both academic and experiential) will be extremely helpful to the legislative liaison officer.

The Legislative Liaison Team. Given the amount of crime control and corrections-specific legislation that might be in the legislative pipeline at any given moment, it is often beneficial to develop a broad-based legislative liaison team. The team approach is especially critical because correctional organizations cannot afford to be passive when legislative bodies are busily formulating crime control policy. The correctional organization best suited for gathering political support and surviving in a highly volatile political environment is the agency that not only monitors relevant legislation, but that develops and seeks sponsorship for corrections-friendly legislation. The old saying that the best defense is a good offense comes to mind.

A particularly well-defined example of using this strategy is the team approach developed by the Oklahoma Department of Corrections (See Box 6-3).

Face-to-face interaction with elected officials is not limited to formal political meetings. It also can occur in other settings, including the correctional facility.

Associating Elected Officials with Corrections

An effective community education strategy will attempt to associate elected officials with positive correctional events. For example, elected officials can be invited to attend the opening day ceremonies for new correctional facilities, in-prison treatment programs, special community corrections programs, and inmate community service programs. Associating an elected official with a specific correctional event guarantees positive news media coverage and provides an opportunity to educate that official about some aspect of corrections. The participation of elected officials in correctional events raises public awareness of these programs and suggests political support.

One of the public events to which elected officials are invited most frequently is the ceremony acknowledging Correctional Officers Week, a form of recognition traditionally held during the first full week in May. At the state level, the governor attends a public ceremony where an official proclamation lauding the efforts of corrections professionals is read. The department of corrections will issue a press release highlighting the accomplishments of the department and, in many instances, emphasize the accomplishments of specific correctional employees. At the national level, the President will attend a similar ceremony and read a similar proclamation.

Bringing the Elected Official into Corrections. Elected officials must be physically exposed to the prison environment if they truly are to understand the complexity of corrections and the impact "get tough on crime" policy has on the ability of corrections professionals to effectively do their job. One of the best methods of creating this exposure is the legislative tour.

The Legislative Tour

Every elected official can benefit from a personal tour of the prison(s) or community corrections agencies in the area he or she represents. A tour of a prison or community corrections agency provides a contextual framework for all subsequent agency discussions about crime control and corrections that paperwork and meetings in the capitol cannot provide. Elected officials can read a report about the consequences of prison crowding but for that official to actually spend several hours in a crowded prison where the human misery is readily apparent conveys a very different reality. It is one thing for an elected official to read about an effective drug rehabilitation program that is now requesting a continuation of funding. It is quite another thing for that elected official to actually talk to program counselors and clients in the setting where the treatment occurs.

The Hostile Elected Official. One of the most difficult challenges faced by corrections professionals is the elected official who has a preconceived opinion about corrections even though he or she has never set foot inside a correctional facility. Because the elected official is as vulnerable to the seductions of the popular culture of corrections as the next citizen, these preconceptions will be congruent with either smug hack corrections or country club corrections. The elected official who presents the greatest challenge to community education strategists is the hostile official. That is the politician who uses the power of the office to directly attack corrections as either repressive and

Box 6-3 Oklahoma Department of Corrections' Legislative Monitoring Process

Politics is not a dirty word. Politics includes the allocation of scarce resources. One of the primary tasks of the director and his staff is to secure sufficient resources to incarcerate and supervise as many inmates and clients as the courts sentence to the department. As a large state agency much legislation has an effect on operations, not just "corrections" or "criminal justice" legislation.

The director appoints a legislative team to formulate department initiatives, secure authors and sponsors, and monitor progress of initiatives and other legislation that might affect the department. The team members attend assigned legislative committee meetings and visit with legislators about bills important to the department.

The Department of Corrections 1998 Legislative Team includes:

- James L. Saffle, Director
- David C. Miller, Chief of Population Management and Fiscal Operations
- Kathy Waters, Deputy Director, Probation and Parole/Community Corrections
- Justin Jones, Deputy Director, Community Sentencing
- J'me Scruggs, Deputy Director, Administrative Services
- Vincent Knight, General Counsel
- Dennis Cotner, Director, Medical and Inmate Services
- Debbie Boyer, Administrator, Human Resources
- Debbie Winterstein, Administrator, Personnel

This team is staffed by Bob Zapffe, Executive Assistant, Research and Evaluation.

The legislative team begins the legislative monitoring effort with a request for suggested department initiatives from the department's administrative and field unit employees, through the unit heads. Bob Zapffe compiles these for team review.

The team selects initiatives from those submitted and may add others. A refined list of initiatives is compiled and a team member volunteers or is appointed to promote and monitor each one, including securing an author. A request for legislation, submitted to the Office of the Cabinet Secretary, Safety and Security, is completed for each initiative by the team member appointed to that initiative. They are collected and forwarded to the cabinet secretary's legislative liaison.

The initiatives list is updated throughout the session. The list is also posted to the department website. A commercial legislative service is employed to deliver a daily electronic download of committee hearing agendas, bill actions, and full bill text. This information is then used to update a software package called *Legislative Information Agent*.

Bill assignments are made in this package according to the subject matter of the bill and whether it might be important to the department by the executive assistant, research and evaluation. A monitoring level from one to three, with one being the most important, is assigned initially. The assigned bill monitor is notified,

continued

Box 6-3 Department of Corrections' Legislative Monitoring Process (continued)

with a request for bill analysis and a bill caption, author, and current status. Depending upon the monitor's assessment of the bill, the priority may be changed.

Bill analyses are forwarded through the responsible team member to the executive assistant, research and evaluation. He or other staff enter that information into the *Legislative Information Agent* software to produce reports. As bills pass through evaluation by committees and legislative staff, copies of bill analyses are faxed or delivered to Capitol staff and the cabinet secretary. The governor's office also receives copies of analyses on important bills.

The legislative team normally meets each Friday morning to review the status of bills and discuss strategy. Reports are issued at least weekly, sorted by bill number and another report is sorted by author. Each team member receives a report of the bills they are assigned and a complete report on all priority bills.

As bills progress through the session, are amended, or fail to pass, bill analyses and reports are revised. Reports are posted to the website, along with links to full text of bills important to the department of corrections. A Legislative Information Newsgroup e-mail list also is alerted to important press releases and crucial committee meeting agendas. During the session, there are links on the legislation page of the website to house and senate committee agendas on their respective sites.

The Department of Corrections' legislative web page also provides links to contact legislators by mail, e-mail, or phone. At the end of the session, team members write thank you letters to all authors and sponsors of their initiatives. These legislators also are listed on the department of corrections' legislative initiatives web page so everyone can know who authored our initiatives.

Links to session highlights and interim studies are added to the web page as available between sessions. After elections, information on members and committee leadership is updated for the next session (Zapffe, 1999:1-2). (Reprinted by Permission).

Author's Note: The Oklahoma Department of Corrections website referenced throughout this article is http: //www.doc.state.ok.us.

brutal or too soft on criminals. Frequently, there is a tendency to try and ignore these elected officials through a strategy of silently suffering through their hostile press conferences, letters to the editor, and commentary during corrections-related legislative debates. However, avoidance, as a strategy, is counterproductive.

While a priority of executive level management should be to persuade every elected official to tour a prison, the highest priority should be assigned to persuading hostile elected officials to tour the facility about which they have been most critical. This may take quite a bit of persuasion, but frequently the elected officials can be persuaded to make the tour. This tour has been dubbed by a seasoned, and very cynical, superintendent as "The Political Enemy Tour." It is vital that the tour guide and the staff not display a negative attitude during the tour. The results of a political tour can be very rewarding, as demonstrated in the August 27, 1998, letter presented in Box 6-4.

The letter of Representative Lawless is everything a corrections professional could desire: support for both the department and the secretary from a long-time critic;

Box 6-4 Letter Based on a Political Tour

House of Representatives
Commonwealth of Pennsylvania
Harrisburg

Susan McNaughton, Editor
NEWSFRONT
Pa Department of Corrections
P.O. Box 598
Camp Hill, Pa. 17011

Dear Ms. McNaughton,

On August 4, 1998, I was invited by Secretary of Corrections Martin Horn to tour Graterford State Correctional Institution (SCI).

In the past, I have been extremely critical of the lavish lifestyle enjoyed by Pennsylvania inmates—three square meals, weight benches, handball courts, baseball fields, in addition to lower cable television rates, which, as you may know, I have recently been questioning.

At the urging of many inmates, I accepted Secretary Horn's invitation. The result is that my views have changed dramatically. While I continue to believe that inmates should not have luxuries that law-abiding citizens cannot afford, I have learned that Graterford SCI is no country club.

My visit to Graterford SCI was perhaps the most informative, yet frightening, day in my eight years as a member of the General Assembly.

Year after year, we legislators vote to appropriate hundreds of millions of dollars to our state correctional system with little or no knowledge as to what actually takes place at those facilities. I learned that Graterford SCI is just what it is supposed to be—a top-notch, maximum security facility that is managed and operated by personnel who are second to none—even to those who are employed in private industry. My hat goes off to those guards and other staff who must be prepared to deal with difficult situations at a moment's notice.

In closing, I want to particularly acknowledge the courtesy displayed by Secretary Horn to his Department employees. During our visit, Secretary Horn made a point to greet and speak with prison personnel as we moved throughout the facility. Martin Horn is not some Harrisburg bureaucrat; rather, he is someone who cares and recognizes the importance of every individual employee at Graterford SCI.

I urge each and every one of my colleagues to visit one of our state correctional facilities.

Thank you to Secretary Horn, and thank you to the entire Graterford staff for the important role you all play in the security of our communities.

Sincerely,

John A. Lawless
State Representative
150th Legislative District

(Source: Pennsylvania Department of Corrections (1998). *Newsfront*, Fall.

a positive comparison of department of corrections employees to private sector employees; a stated appreciation of the challenges successfully being met by corrections; and an urging of other elected officials to tour correctional facilities. It also suggests that in the future this elected official may place less faith in stereotypes of correctional employees than was the case before the personal experience.

We have focused on elected officials during the discussion of crime control policy. However, there is another group of powerful officials (although some of these individuals are appointed to office, not elected) who also have a profound influence on crime control policy. These individuals are the trial and appellate court judges. Judges influence crime control policy because they have the responsibility of judicial review: reviewing laws created by legislatures to determine if they are constitutional. They also review the behavior of correctional employees and correctional systems to determine if they will allow certain behavior to continue. Judges also must be exposed to the correctional environment and its professionals because they, and other officers of the court, can influence both elected officials and public opinion about the state of corrections.

The Judicial Tour. The positive exposure of judges and other officers of the court to the correctional environment can be accomplished through a specialized tour known appropriately enough as the judicial tour (or open house). The Federal Bureau of Prisons excels in providing an effective judicial tour. For example, on July 2 and 8, 1999, 6 federal judges and 120 staff (including law clerks, deputy clerks, interns, and the public defender's staff) from the U.S. District Courts in Eastern Pennsylvania and New Jersey toured the Federal Correctional Institution Fairton (Federal Bureau of Prisons, 1999).

An effective judicial tour will include a short videotape of the history of the prison (and the department of corrections in which it is located), the opportunity to see all of the prison; the opportunity to talk in private to both employees and inmates; and a question and answer period in which executive and second level managers candidly respond to the visitors' questions. Particular attention should be paid to extending judicial tour invitations to those judges and attorneys who are most hostile to corrections, or most ignorant of its complexity.

Structuring the Legislative and Judicial Tour. If these types of tours are to be effective, it is important that elected officials and judges be allowed to see every part of the facility. There is no area that can be designated as being off limits. To attempt to prevent any elected official or judge, especially one who is hostile in the first place, from going into a particular part of the facility, or talking to specific inmates, will only arouse suspicion and distrust. In addition, the superintendent and key staff always should take an active part in conducting the tour. A good technique is to introduce elected officials and officers of the court to employees as they are encountered during the tour and encourage these visitors to ask questions about the employee's specific responsibilities.

If elected officials want to talk to inmates, they should be allowed to randomly select the inmates with whom they can talk. If they wish these conversations to be private, that request should be accommodated. Arrangements always can be made to allow private conversations in an area where the individuals can be observed (for security purposes), but not overheard. The length of the tour should be the prerogative of the official visitor. If a question is asked that cannot be answered immediately , a staff member should be sent to obtain the information while the tour continues. Every effort should be made to create a climate of "We have nothing to hide; the facility and its staff are at your disposal." A positive first impression on a political tour can go a long way toward gathering political support in the future.

To be effective, the open house must be highly structured and organized to present specific clusters of information. It is not enough to simply take official visitors on a tour, cite a few statistics, and then have a brief question and answer period after the tour. An excellent example of how to effectively conduct a legislative (and judicial) tour is the approach used by the Oregon Department of Corrections (Box 6-5).

Although the information presented in Box 6-5 is designed to educate elected officials and news media management representatives, this type of approach easily could be (and should be) adapted to help structure the education provided during the community open houses that will be discussed in Chapter 8.

The creation of contextual information for elected officials should not be considered the sole responsibility of corrections managers. There are community resources to which they can turn for assistance if they are willing to form alliances.

Forming Alliances

Current corrections' executive managers can form alliances with three groups: retired corrections managers, employee unions, and professional organizations.

Retired Corrections Managers. Correctional organizations can identify and enlist the services of retired corrections managers who have the credibility to educate elected officials. These individuals may be well suited to using the strength of their former relationship with elected officials as a springboard to influence their position in current debates about crime control policy. These retired individuals may be even more persuasive than they could be when they were part of the system because they no longer have a career that has to be protected. They can speak their minds more freely and make the arguments that a fear of career termination may have prevented them from making during their tenure. Current correctional leaders can use retired leaders as a surrogate to speak for them and the entire system.

Correctional Employee Unions. Correctional leaders can take the initiative to form alliances with the leadership of employee unions and agree to speak out on issues of mutual concern. Many correctional managers and union leaders view each other as the enemy because their respective agendas and loyalties create tension and conflict. The major obstacle to an alliance with correctional employee unions is economic. Many union leaders may be reluctant to lobby against mandatory sentencing legislation because the subsequent massive prison construction programs result in more correctional officers being hired. And more correctional officers translates into increased union growth in political power, prestige, and wealth. However, this does not mean that union and management cannot find areas of mutual concern such as dangerous working conditions, inadequate pay levels, and the growing number of special needs inmates to be managed. Certainly both groups are concerned about the negative public perception of corrections and should be willing to work together to promote the workforce professionalism and commitment to employee ethical behavior that will be discussed in Chapter 9. Both groups can benefit from pooling their resources and reaching agreement on the most effective strategy for educating elected officials about the negative impact of crime control policy on corrections. They also can work together to devise ways to confront negative stereotyping. Many of the community education strategies presented in Chapter 8 involve this type of joint participation.

National Correctional Organizations. Corrections' executive managers can educate legislators for national correctional organizations such as the American Correctional

Box 6-5 The Legislative/Media Management Tour Approach
of the Oregon Department of Corrections

The envelope containing the material describing the legislative and media management open houses offered by the Oregon Department of Corrections has, underneath the return address of the department, the following list of statements:

- "Prisons are country clubs."
- "Everyone gets out of prison early."
- "No one completes their sentence."
- "Probation is a copout."
- **"Anybody can run a prison."**
- "What's so complicated about executing someone?"
- "They are just guards."
- "I can't believe they don't have all the inmates working."
- "They ought to be in chain gangs."
- "Escapes are at an all time high."
- "Only bad people go to prison."
- "Inmates are coddled."
- "Inmates are lazy."
- "Once a crook always a crook."
- **"Prisons and jails are the same thing."**
- "Drugs are rampant in prison."
- "Prison is a deterrent."
- "Prisons make bad neighbors."
- "Why do inmates use the Internet?"
- "If you work in a prison, you must be a sadist."
- "If you work in a prison, you must be a masochist."
- "OREGON IS SOFT ON CRIME."
- "Private prisons are just as good as state prisons."
- "Put them all out in the middle of nowhere."
- **"INMATES ARE STUPID OR THEY WOULDN'T BE IN PRISON."**
- "Probation, parole, they're both the same thing."
- "Lock 'em up and throw away the key!"

The envelope with these stereotype-based statements contains a packet of cards, each of which describes a specific open house available to elected officials, candidates running for office, and media management representatives. On the outside of the packet is the challenge:

If you agree with any of the statements listed on the envelope, the Oregon Department of Corrections challenges you to put your beliefs on

Box 6-5 (continued)

the line! No excuses! Spend just a few hours with us and you can learn firsthand about the facts and fiction of corrections today. In exchange for your time, we promise a bounty of information that will help you in your job or on the campaign trail.

The cards in the packet describe the tours to be conducted at the Oregon State Penitentiary, community corrections facilities, a boot camp, the Eastern Oregon Correctional Institution at Pendleton, and the Powder River Correctional Facility, which specializes in drug offenders. Legislators, legislative candidates, news organization management, and editorial board members also can meet and talk to correctional managers involved in carrying out executions and siting new prisons.

(Source: Oregon Department of Corrections, 1999).

Association and the American Jail Association and develop formal alliances with other criminal justice organizations, such as the Academy of Criminal Justice Sciences and the American Society of Criminology. The purpose of these alliances would be the creation of a coalition of practitioners and academicians who could jointly promote crime control policy proposals that are based on the most recent, and rigorous, research on crime control policy and its impact on the crime rate and ability of corrections to operate safely and humanely. Both practitioners and academicians have a stake in creating a rational crime control policy. There is no reason why they cannot work together to achieve this goal, if both groups are willing to make the commitment to an arduous task that requires a long-term commitment of time and financial resources.

Elected officials who receive contextual information about corrections may be less inclined to support ill-conceived crime control policy. They also may be less inclined to indirectly reinforce the negative stereotypes of the popular culture of corrections through the use of heated political rhetoric based on those stereotypes. In a best-case scenario, the overall effect of the education of elected officials will be a reduction in their contribution to the hyperreality created by media loops.

Points to Consider

1. What other types of information could correctional organizations publish to supplement the documents discussed in this chapter? Who would be the recipients of this information?

2. If you were writing a job description for a legislative liaison officer, what duties would you include? What qualifications would you require for the position?

3. Are there any risks associated with having face-to-face interactions with elected officials? If so, what are they?

4. What actions can be taken to minimize these risks?

5. Are there any risks associated with legislative and judicial tours? If so, what are they?

6. What actions can be taken to minimize the probability of the occurrence of these risks?

7. Do legislative and judicial tours create political support for corrections? Defend your answer.

References

Arizona Department of Corrections. 1999. *Annual Report: Fiscal Year 1998.* Phoenix, Arizona: Arizona Department of Corrections.

Arkansas Department of Corrections. 1998. *Facts Brochure 1998.* Pine Bluff, Arkansas: Arkansas Department of Corrections.

Barak, G. 1994. *Media, Process and the Social Construction of Crime: Studies in Newsmaking Criminology.* New York: Garland.

Federal Bureau of Prisons. 1999. USP Florence Staff Speak With At-Risk Youths. *Monday Morning Highlights.* January 11. Washington, D.C.: Federal Bureau of Prisons.

Florida Department of Corrections. 1998. *Corrections in Florida: What the Public, News Media, and DC Staff Think.* Tallahassee, Florida: Florida Department of Corrections.

————. 1998. *1997-98 Annual Report: The Guidebook to Corrections in Florida.* Tallahassee, Florida: Florida Department of Corrections.

Illinois Department of Corrections. 1997. *Insight Into Corrections: Illinois Department of Corrections: Fiscal Year 1996 Annual Report.* Springfield, Illinois: Illinois Department of Corrections.

Larivee, John J. 1993. Community Programs—A Risky Business. *Corrections Today.* (55)6: 20-26.

Manning, P. K. 1998. Media Loops. In F. Bailey and D. Hale, eds. *Popular Culture, Crime and Justice.* Belmont, California: West/Wadsworth Publishing. pp. 25-39.

McGinnis, K. L. 1996. *Michigan Department of Corrections 1995 Statistical Report.* Lansing, Michigan: Michigan Department of Corrections.

Minnesota Department of Corrections. 1997. *Backgrounder: Capital Punishment; Sex Offender Facts; Juveniles Certified As Adults.* January 9, 10, 13. St. Paul, Minnesota: Minnesota Department of Corrections.

Ohio Department of Rehabilitation and Correction. 1998. *The Communicator.* Spring. Columbus, Ohio: Ohio Department of Rehabilitation and Correction.

Oregon Department of Corrections. 1999. Information Packet on Open Houses. Salem, Oregon: Oregon Department of Corrections.

Pennsylvania Department of Corrections. 1998. *Newsfront.* Fall. Camp Hill, Pennsylvania: Pennsylvania Department of Corrections.

Riveland, C. 1991. Being a Director of Corrections in the1990s. *Federal Probation.* (55)2: 10-11.

Welch, B. 1999. DOC Commissioner to Lead National Debate on In-prison Drug Treatment. Delaware Department of Corrections Press Release, December 2. Smyrna, Delaware.

Zapffe, B. 1999. DOC Legislative Monitoring Process. *Oklahoma Department of Corrections: Inside Corrections.* Oklahoma City, Oklahoma. 111: 1-2.

Getting the Facts Straight:

Educating the News Media and Hollywood

The relationship between corrections and the news media is often a difficult one because of the ability of the news media to shine a negative light on corrections. There are four news media activities that can damage the image of corrections. First, reporters can sensationalize negative events (such as the Willie Horton incident) by not framing them in a context that will give the audience an accurate perspective on the issue. Second, reporters can write articles such as the Georgia sex scandal story cited in Chapter 4 that damage the image of corrections no matter how much context is provided. Third, journalists can write well-researched and accurate books about isolated correctional events that reinforce the stereotypes of smug hack corrections.

Roger Morris' *The Devil's Butcher Shop: The New Mexico Prison Uprising* (1983/1988) presents a fascinating and factual accounting of the deplorable prison conditions and mismanagement that produced one of America's most savage prison riots. A more balanced book (because it does not focus on one tragic incident) is Peter Earley's *The Hot House: Life Inside Leavenworth Prison* (1992). This book provides negative imagery, but it also includes the voices of correctional officers in its examination of life in a maximum security prison.

Fourth, news media documentaries often look to corrections for examples to illustrate the issue(s) that are the focus of the production. In many cases, the aspects of correctional life they choose to emphasize are negative. For example, *Cruel and Unusual*, a 1995 Insight Media video, which examines a range of philosophical issues involved in the confinement of violent criminals, "portrays the dungeons at the U.S. Penitentiary at Alcatraz, beatings by the guards, and horrible deaths during botched executions" (Rafter and Stanley, 1999: 191-192). A video from the University of California Extension, *From One Prison* (1996), documents the lives of four women inmates serving sentences for their self-defense killings of abusive partners. During the filming, the women "reflect on their prison experiences, discussing the issues of sexual harassment and prison rape, overcrowded living conditions, poor medical care, unhealthy food. . . ." (Rafter and Stanley, 1999: 196).

Media Avoidance. Because they do not want to run the risk of being spotlighted by the news media, many corrections managers refuse to talk to reporters unless they have no other choice or they limit their contact to prepared statements at a press conference that provide no opportunity for follow-up questions. This phenomenon is known as *media avoidance*. It is an attitude rooted in the natural tendency for individuals to dislike other individuals who have the power to make them look bad. Media avoidance is a negative strategy that does more harm than good. It denies contextual information to the media, precludes use of the news media as a community education resource, and creates reporter hostility or indifference to the positive corrections story when it does occur. A policy of media avoidance ensures that corrections will remain a remote context for the general public. Media avoidance is based on the perception of threat. But is there empirical evidence to justify such a perception?

The News Media's Current Perception of Corrections

Princeton sociologist John DiIulio reports that the news media often portray correctional staff as "stupid ogres and inmates as their victims . . . underplay the difficulty of their work and portray those who work in prisons as sadistic or sub-human" (DiIulio, 1987: 254). Is this really the perception today's news media professionals have of corrections? To answer this question, we turn to a more recent source of information.

The 1998 Florida Attitude Survey. The 1998 survey commissioned by the Florida Department of Corrections asked members of Florida's public, news media, and the department of corrections to list the ten most common words they would use to describe correctional officers. When compared to the public and department of corrections' staff responses, the news media responses yielded some interesting information about their perception of correctional officers:

Table 7.1 Descriptions of Correctional Officers

General Public	News Media	Department of Corrections' Employees
tough	tough	dedicated
brave	brave	professional
underpaid	dedicated	underpaid
dedicated	stressed	brave
strong	underpaid	hardworking
mean	undereducated	overworked
big	guard	stressed
honest	crazy	good
patient	employed	courageous
fair	frustrated	fair
		security

Source: Florida Department of Corrections, 1998.

Clearly, the public and Department of Corrections' employees have a more positive perception of correctional officers than the news media although the public does view them as "mean." News media representatives used more negative descriptive terms and tended to use the term "guard" which, in and of itself, carries a negative connotation to the corrections professional. Many corrections professionals lament the fact that years of effort have failed to persuade most news reporters and editors to replace "guard" with the more acceptable "correctional officer." It is difficult to believe that this perception of correctional officers as "crazy," "frustrated," "stressed," and "undereducated" does not influence the news media's coverage of corrections. However, on the positive side, the responses certainly do not rise to the negative level suggested by DiIulio. And there was a perception of correctional officers being "tough," brave," "dedicated," and "under-paid." Those descriptive terms suggest that the news media is receptive to viewing corrections in a more positive light than may have been the case in the past. It also suggests an incentive to reject media avoidance and work to educate the news media.

Rejecting the Strategy of Media Avoidance

James A. Gondles, Jr., CAE, executive director of the American Correctional Association has noted:

> The media in 1998 is a powerful tool, weapon, provider—choose your word. It can cause the masses to change their personal habits; it can raise politicians from the dead; and it can make old enemies become new-found friends. Radio, television, the World Wide Web and print media influence public perceptions tremendously. Corrections professionals can suffer or be appreciated and ad-mired. The media leads the way and public perceptions follow. Each of us has an important role and stake in ensuring that the media knows what a good job we do for our citizens, how very difficult our jobs are, and how important corrections is to society. Make one of your professional goals this year to educate a reporter, a writer, or even a neighbor about what you do, how you do it and how it helps us all. Corrections professionals will benefit and society will respond kindly (Gondles, 1998: 6).

This approach addresses a critical problem identified by Chermak (1998) in his study of news coverage content. Chermak found that a major reason for the lack of news media coverage of corrections was the fact that "News media do not have a corrections' beat that fulfills the same function as a police or court beat" (Chermak, 1998: 97). In essence, Gondles is saying that it is up to corrections professionals to create a "corrections beat" for the news media.

The first step in creating a "corrections beat" is to establish a positive working relationship with individual news media professionals that encourages them to view correctional employees as individuals, not stereotypes. The development of a positive working relationship requires the introduction of news reporters, editors, and directors to the complex challenges confronting corrections. Conversely, corrections professionals must understand the deadline-driven challenges faced by news media professionals.

The Challenges of the News Media Professional. News media professionals have stressful jobs with tight daily deadlines and demanding time and space requirements. A TV anchor has to fill up a specific number of minutes of air time, a job that has been made more difficult by the trend in the 1990s toward replacing thirty-minute evening news broadcasts with sixty- or ninety-minute broadcasts. The proliferation in the 1990s of prime time news shows modeled on the highly successful *60 Minutes* has increased the pressure to bring exciting stories to the public's attention. And a newspaper reporter or magazine feature writer must fill up a set number of columns or pages with the written word.

Regardless of the news format, there is little margin for time delays. All news media professionals have tight deadlines. Information needed for a specific story must be received sufficiently in advance of the deadline to allow reporters and editors to prepare and edit the material. Because of the time pressures these individuals face, they cannot struggle to research a new story from scratch every day. They learn to rely on established sources of readily available information. It is in the best interests of corrections to achieve the status of being defined as an established source of information:

> Think of the mass media as a free distribution system to reach your community. Providing the news media with story ideas is in your agency's best interest. Don't be afraid to brag about what has been done and what is planned. Seek out reporters who show an interest in your work and keep them informed (Kidd and Braziel, 1999: 197).

Understanding the Needs of the News Media. If correctional organizations succeed in becoming an established source of information for the news media, they have a powerful channel for the presentation of contextual information to the general public. As Tip Kindel, assistant director of communications for the California Department of Corrections notes:

> Here's a practical example to consider. Tonight's television news is going to broadcast a story on complaints about your high-security housing unit. With or without you, the story is going to run. If you help the public see how the housing unit looks and is operated, that will shape its impressions of whether you or your critics are right. The public's impressions also will be influenced by a "no comment" and your refusal to cooperate. Ask yourself which response you'd accept as a taxpayer (Kindel, 1998: 22).

The ability to present contextual information is increased by understanding the specific needs of television, radio, and the print media. Television requires visual images, especially those involving action and executive managers willing to appear on camera to offer short (ten to twenty seconds) sound bites that summarize a situation or position on a controversial issue. TV camera operators seek shots of uniformed employees, prison guard towers, exterior gates, perimeter fences and walls, groups of inmates engaging in activities (especially work or athletic), cell blocks, and exercise yards. Radio producers want short sound bites by people in positions of authority who are willing to verbally go on the record about a specific issue or situation. The print media wants background information, statistics, photographs, and any form of supporting documentation that can be verified by reporters. Education of the news media must be a proactive process that is coordinated by the public information officer.

The Public Information Officer

To work more effectively with the news media, most large correctional organizations employ public information officers. Although the job description of public information officers initially emphasized reactive responses to routine and crisis-generated requests for information from reporters, legislators, and judges, the 1990s witnessed a growing recognition that corrections can benefit from a proactive interaction with the news media.

Background for the Position. Chermak (1998: 99) notes that "Reporters are not motivated to develop relationships with correctional sources because there is little public interest in these type of stories. . . ." For this reason, the most qualified public information officer is an individual who previously has been employed by the news media in a professional capacity, knows the challenges that have to be confronted on a daily basis, has mastered the techniques of meeting those challenges, and knows that correctional stories can be of interest to the general public if they are properly presented. The more varied the personal news media experience, the greater the likelihood that the public information officer will be able to establish a positive working relationship with news media professionals. In fact, the public information officer may have previously worked with the local news agencies and maintained a relationship with their employees.

Communication Skills. Skillfully honed writing and verbal communication skills are essential to effective performance. These skills can be developed through a combination of formal education (at least a bachelor's degree, preferably a master's, in communication/journalism) and professional experience. The ability to use verbal skills to make a positive first impression, whether it is when using the phone or lecturing to a group, is a critical skill. Equally as important is the ability to write a lead paragraph that immediately grabs readers' attention and makes them eager to continue to read.

Emotional Makeup. A public information officer must be gregarious by nature and enjoy working with people from different backgrounds and with different interests. A clear speaking style and a high degree of comfort talking to large groups, sometimes under conditions of duress, such as during a prison riot, is essential. The ability to think clearly and react creatively when under time pressure is vital, as is the capacity to routinely process large amounts of information rapidly and effectively.

Emotional maturity is also mandatory. The public information officer is frequently the individual delegated to receive angry calls from victims, legislators, judges, and members of the general public when the organization is engaging in behavior those individuals wish to protest. The public information officer can expect to work long, emotionally draining days when the organization is confronting a crisis and the news media is howling for information. Being an effective public information officer involves a great deal more than answering the phone and writing copy.

Privacy Statutes. Public information officers also must understand that they are constrained by legal privacy statutes that prevent them from providing information to the public about employees who are the target of news media interest. This is why they respond to news media questions about employees under investigation, or who have received administrative action, or have been convicted of a job-related crime, with the statement that "Confidentiality laws prohibit me from making a statement" or "That's a personnel matter and I can't comment on it." Unfortunately, when public information officers are asked about the details of corrections' horror stories (such as those that occurred in Georgia, Pennsylvania, and California) and respond with the comment "I cannot discuss personnel issues," they are unintentionally reinforcing the imagery of smug hack corrections. The public will hear the allegations of staff misconduct, but will not see the actions the agency previously has taken to prevent employee misconduct or actions they currently are taking. In fact, the public is likely to view the press officer's refusal to discuss the matter as evidence that the organization is trying to cover up the situation.

Public information officers can contribute to news media education in two ways. First, they can engage in frequent face-to-face interaction with news media professionals. Second, they can create a constant flow of news media press releases and supporting documentation.

Face-to-face Interaction with the News Media

The public information officer should develop a system for scheduling face-to-face meetings with individual news media representatives. These meetings will eliminate what has been called the "faceless voice" syndrome (Phillips, 1993: 8). That is, the public information officer is just a voice on the phone because there has been no prior personal interaction with the individual being called. The value of emphasizing face-to-face interactions cannot be overemphasized. A new public information officer always should make it a priority to initiate contact with as many news media professionals in the community as possible. During this initial contact, the public information officer should extend a gracious invitation to have them visit the correctional facility and make a request to visit the news agency. Reporters who know a public information officer as an individual, not a title, are more likely to request corrections' side of the story when a controversial event has occurred. They are also more likely to actually read the press releases sent to them by public information officers.

A positive initial meeting lays the foundation for a productive working relationship with the news media. The good will created by that initial meeting needs to be nurtured by the public information officer's adherence to a specific set of inviolate rules.

The Rules for a Productive Relationship with the News Media. An important goal for every public information officer is to establish a relationship of trust with as many news media professionals as possible before a correctional crisis occurs. Key to establishing a relationship of trust is a fundamental inviolate rule: Never lie! Whether reporters are developing a routine story to be aired or printed in the near future or frantically demanding immediate information about a full-scale correctional emergency that has just erupted, the public information officer (and every other correctional employee being interviewed or issuing an official statement) always must remember that reporters will discover the truth if they want to dig deep enough.

If public information officers lie, stonewall, or issue "No comment" statements, the typical reporter will seek out other readily available information sources: employees, ex-employees, inmate relatives, ex-inmates, and any group with an ax to grind against corrections. So, if the public information officer does not know a specific answer, that individual should say so and promise to find the answer and communicate it as quickly as possible. No matter how painful the truth, being caught in a lie is even more painful. And the first lie, once it is detected, may permanently poison the relationship between that correctional organization and the news media.

Box 7-1 contains a set of rules for nurturing a positive relationship with the news media during normal circumstances.

In addition to adherence to these fundamental rules, public information officers can facilitate news media education by sponsoring two-day seminars with reporters, editors, and directors for a frank exchange of ideas and information; continually educating new reporters as they begin their careers; holding news organizations accountable when they sensationalize the news about corrections; and making openness a long-term commitment (Jarvis, 1998: 20).

Periodically, public information officers should visit editors, producers, and reporters at their agency and attend press association conferences. The press association conferences provide the public information officer an excellent opportunity to meet a variety of news media professionals in a social setting, participate in their professional seminars, and understand their viewpoint of corrections and the challenges coverage of the field presents. All of these recommendations fall under the heading of nurturing a productive

Box 7-1 Do's and Don't's of Interaction with the
News Media During Normal Circumstances

DO have pertinent facts concerning the area to be discussed prior to giving a media interview.

DO require inmates to stipulate in writing whether they do or do not agree to be interviewed by a requesting reporter.

DO be careful about giving statements to the news media that might affect the outcome of a trial.

DO give the news media and the public the information that they are entitled to have under the Freedom of Information Act without requiring them to file a formal request.

DO regard reporters as professionals who are trying to do a job.

DO respond to a reporter's request for information as quickly as possible.

DO be responsive to media needs.

DO be responsive to reporters' questions.

DO try to give inquiring reporters as much information as possible about transfers, releases, or furloughs without jeopardizing security or the inmate's privacy rights.

DO prepare a release, if there is time, on important happenings.

DO treat reporters fairly on breaking news stories.

DO respect the law and agency policy surrounding release of information.

DO NOT use the phrase, "No comment." If you are unable to release information, explain why.

DO NOT give reporters information, such as medical or treatment information, about individual inmates that privacy statutes bar them from having.

DO NOT give a reporter's request such a low priority that he or she misses the deadline.

DO NOT report routine events that don't help the media or public better understand the facility's operation or mission.

DO NOT withhold information sought by, or of interest to, some reporters in your area so that you can give a break to a reporter you like.

DO NOT regard reporters as enemies or friends.

DO NOT hide behind laws and regulations out of laziness or lack of knowledge.

DO NOT quarrel with the courts or with other government agencies in the newspapers or on the air.

DO NOT volunteer information about such matters in advance; wait until the reporter comes to you.

DO NOT issue information on the death of an inmate until after notification of the inmate's family.

DO NOT criticize or comment on another agency's policies or procedures, especially if the other agency is in a crisis or emergency situation.

DO NOT criticize your peers in other correctional agencies.

DO NOT get into a debate, fueled by the media, as to whether you would have handled an event differently or about the quality of another facility or its staff or program.

(Source: Quoted from Phillips, 1993: 43-45. Reprinted by permission of the American Correctional Association).

interaction with the news media during the good times, in other words, when there is no crisis. But what happens when there is a correctional crisis? What is the role of the public information officer?

Assisting the News Media During a Correctional Crisis. When a crisis occurs in corrections, the time pressure for news media professionals increases dramatically as they rush to be the first with the breaking story. At this point, corrections is most vulnerable to sensational stories that only present one side of an issue. But corrections does not have to be a victim of news media deadlines. If a positive relationship has been created with reporters, editors, and directors, they should be receptive to receiving background information from the public information officer that will put the current crisis into the proper perspective. The problem for the public information officer is having readily accessible and accurate background information that can be given to the news media on very short notice. Freeman (1999: 33) has suggested:

> To meet this need, top correctional managers should develop and maintain a current statistical database for controversial issues such as furloughs, community corrections centers, escapes, prison violence, and parole violations so they will have available current facts and figures to give perspective to stories about those issues. Research and Planning units can identify a wide range of programs that are likely to arouse controversy and develop a periodically updated database.

A public information officer's data bank of potential crises background information requires work to develop, but the payoff in deflating a negative news story approaching crisis proportions can be invaluable. In addition, the public information officer must make every attempt to provide the news media with updated information about the current crisis as soon as the approval to release newly acquired information is received from executive-level managers. As much as possible, updated information should be released in conjunction with contextual information that will provide a proper perspective.

Box 7-2 provides a set of guidelines for interaction with the news media during their coverage of a correctional emergency.

The correctional emergency can create an enormous strain between corrections and the news media because of the time pressures and emotional intensity that characterize these events. However, it would be folly to rupture a productive relationship that may have been nurtured for years by failing to follow the basic guidelines contained in Box 7-2.

Face-to-face interactions are an excellent method for initiating the process of news media education. However, the location of these interactions must not be limited to the public information officer's office or the offices of the news agency. Reporters, editors, and directors actively must be encouraged to enter and observe the internal environment of corrections.

Making the News Media Welcome in the Correctional Environment

A fundamental principle of news media education is that reporters, editors, and directors must be given the message that they are welcome to enter and observe the internal correctional environment, whether it is a maximum-security prison, supermax, or a community corrections center. There are a variety of solid approaches that can be used to deliver this message.

The News Media Open House. This event should be held on a regularly scheduled basis, at least once a year. The day's activities should be structured to provide ample

BOX 7-2 Do's and Don't's of Interaction with the
News Media During Correctional Emergencies

DO arrange for a media liaison person to give regular briefings to reporters.

DO have a relief media liaison person, should the emergency last more than twelve hours.

DO arrange for the facility head to meet at least once a day with reporters.

DO consider the physical and technical needs of reporters by arranging to provide them with a media center, if at all possible.

DO arrange to tape news conferences and radio and television newscasts.

DO monitor newspaper and wire service reports.

DO be prepared to provide background information on the institution's history, programs, and policies.

DO be cautious about making statements that may be libelous or that could affect the future course of events.

DO give specific information about inmates killed, following notification of the next of kin.

DO caution staff about making statements to reporters during an emergency.

DO keep reporters away from fires that are not under control.

DO have liaisons with other official spokespersons for the armed forces, police, or other agencies assisting in the resolution of the crisis.

DO provide updated reports for staff as well as reporters (shift change might be a convenient time).

DO return media requests for information in the order they were received.

DO NOT guess if you do not know the answer to a question. Say you do not know and then attempt to find out.

DO NOT grant inmates interviews with the media during an emergency.

DO NOT identify victims until their families have been notified.

DO NOT give out too many details of negotiations; this may prolong the emergency and endanger lives.

DO NOT give any reporter an exclusive on an important development.

DO NOT make off-the-record statements.

DO NOT deny reporters news about a fire.

DO NOT name suspects, use words like "arson," or make any other statements that could affect the future course of an event.

DO NOT use confusing terminology, abbreviations, or acronyms.

(Source: Quoted from Phillips, 1993: 45-46. Reprinted by permission of the American Correctional Association).

opportunity for news media professionals to freely talk to both managerial and line staff. The news media open house can be structured in much the same way as the legislative and judicial tours/open houses discussed in Chapter 6.

Increasing access to the internal environment of corrections will help reporters develop the experiential background necessary to correctly interpret subsequent correctional events and activities that they are covering. In essence, they will be able to provide their own background information about events that become of interest to their audiences. A reporter who has focused on a controversy about the effectiveness of drug treatment programs, for instance, can do a more accurate, and positive, story if he or she has had prior personal experience with these types of programs, their clients, and the treatment staff providing the services. Editors and directors also may be more likely to allocate limited resources to report on significant organizational achievements such as a prison or community corrections center attaining American Correctional Association accreditation. A positive visit to a correctional facility can provide the impetus for important stories that ordinarily would not have been considered. The television news media periodically can offer a serious look at corrections when they are invited into correctional facilities.

News Media Prison Documentaries. Ted Koppel's *Crime and Punishment* series in the summer of 1998 presented an objective view of incarceration, the use of supermax units, prison gangs, and the death penalty. Although some of the events presented were disturbing, such as the strip search of a recalcitrant inmate being taken to supermax, and the segment showing fat, middle-aged correctional officer trainees gracelessly going through the motions during ten hours of self-defense training, there was an obvious effort made to present a balanced view of modern corrections.

A similar effort was evident in *The Farm: Life Inside Angola Prison* (1998, A & E Home Video) in which the stark reality of inmate and staff life in a mammoth operation like Angola was presented in a nonstereotypical manner that focused on the reality of serving a heavy sentence in one of the largest prisons in the world. While the viewer might feel sorry for the inmates, it was a sorrow based on their decision to throw away their lives by engaging in crime, not a sorrow based on system mistreatment of them.

Other corrections-assisted documentaries include *Shakedown at Santa Fe* (1988, PBS Video), which examines postriot conditions at the New Mexico State Penitentiary; *Doing Time* (1990, Ellis Productions, Inc.), which also examines conditions at the New Mexico State Penitentiary ten years after the 1980 riot; *Women Doing Time* (1992, Ambrose Video), which examines the lives of four female inmates at the New York Bedford Hills Correctional Facility; and *CCI: Case Study of a Southern Prison* (1993, Films for the Humanities and Sciences), which examines rehabilitation issues at the Central Correctional Institution in South Carolina. Although all of these productions showed some negative imagery during their broadcast, the corrections professionals featured had the opportunity to present themselves to the general public in a manner that could help decertify negative correctional stereotyping.

However, making the news media feel welcome in corrections involves more than periodically hosting an open house or allowing the filming of a prison documentary. It also involves the difficult challenge of assisting news media professionals in their coverage of controversial events, such as executions.

News Media Interest in Executions. Historically, prison executives have opposed reporters being present at executions because of concern that a solemn event would be turned into a media circus. They also were concerned that grotesque mistakes made by the execution team (such as an inmate taking twelve minutes to strangle to death because the hangman did not properly knot the noose to cleanly break the neck, or an inmate catching on fire in the electric chair) would be reported to the public and lead to scathing derision and caustic editorials. But the news media legally cannot be barred from attending executions. Therefore, correctional managers must develop a policy that allows reporters to cover executions without complicating the process.

The California Department of Corrections has adopted the wise policy that "the public interest would be served best by the widest news coverage possible" (Kindel, 1993: 66).

To accomplish this goal, in 1992 the Department of Corrections established a news media center in a one-story building inside San Quentin's east gate. After evaluating space limitations, the Department of Corrections decided to allow 125 reporters and 125 photographers, engineers, producers, and videotape editors to set up in this building. Reporters are allowed to station twenty-six large broadcast vans in an adjacent parking lot. A pass system to limit access to the media center and the parking lot has been established. Eighteen journalists are allowed to actually witness an execution.

The distribution of news media witnesses is as follows: two from national wire services; eight from radio and TV stations; and eight from newspapers. Three witnesses are to come from the city where the crime occurred. The Associated Press and United Press International are allowed to send representatives. The remainder of the witness slots are determined by the radio and television organizations themselves, in accordance with a system of random selection that is acceptable to all parties. The newspapers have been unable to work cooperatively and the Department of Corrections has developed objective criteria for providing the widest possible coverage: one reporter from the largest papers in San Francisco, San Diego, Los Angeles, and Sacramento; two from a random drawing of papers with a circulation greater than 1,000; and one from a newspaper in the community where San Quentin is located.

After witnessing the execution, the eighteen news media representatives brief their colleagues in the media center. The advantage of this procedure to corrections is obvious: "Now the spotlight was on 18 news reporters—not prison officials—to interpret the execution. No one had to wait for the next newspaper edition" (Kindel, 1993: 69).

Executions are not the only events that the news media is interested in covering. Periodically, prisons receive high-profile inmates who are of interest to the public because of the sensational nature of their crimes. Serial killers, in particular, fascinate the public. These individuals may or may not be scheduled for execution. News media interest in high-profile inmates also presents a challenge to corrections.

The High-profile Inmate and the News Media. When a high-profile inmate is received by a correctional facility, staff may be taken by surprise by the news media onslaught that follows. For example, African-American Mumia Abu-Jamal, convicted of the murder of a white Philadelphia police officer in 1982 and sentenced to Death Row, has mobilized a large number of death penalty foes in America as well as other countries through his ability to articulate his perceptions of criminal justice system racism. His book *Live From Death Row* (Abu-Jamal, 1995) has contributed significantly to the prison literature and the popular culture of corrections perception of corrections as systemically racist. The news media demand for interviews with Abu-Jamal have been relentless: he is very good copy.

Abu-Jamal's predecessor, George Jackson, an African-American convicted in the 1960s of robbery, was equally successful in arousing news media interest in corrections and criminal justice system racism in general. His book *Soledad Brother: The Prison Letters of George Jackson* (Jackson, 1970/1994) was a powerful indictment of American racism and is considered a significant contribution to the prison literature. Jackson died in 1971 in a botched escape attempt from San Quentin Prison.

The Debate over News Media Access to Inmates. The issue of how much access the news media should have to any given inmate always has been controversial. The concerns of correctional managers have been clearly articulated by Florida Department of Corrections Public Affairs Director, C. J. Drake. These fears center on the potential for media interviews to be:

- disruptive to the orderly operation of an institution that depends on order
- compromising to the safety of corrections officers and other inmates
- sometimes glorifying to prisoners
- often hurtful to their victims
- a propellant to violence by other inmates against the one interviewed
- burdensome to supervising staff
- a hindrance to prisoners' rehabilitation (*The Corrections Professional*, 1999: 7).

For these reasons, correctional managers often restrict the access of news reporters to inmates. However, the news media forcefully expresses opposition whenever corrections attempts to restrict access to inmates. In 1999, the Michigan Department of Corrections developed a proposal to ban news cameras and recording devices from state prisons and limit reporter access to inmates by restricting them to telephone interviews and the normal visitation schedule. The response from the news media sharply defined the risk to the public perception of corrections:

> . . . a proposal to limit prisoner interviews would violate the public trust and allow abuses to go unchecked. . . . News representatives testified that the media have a vital role in showing taxpayers the conditions in prisons. Several gave examples of conditions brought to light in newspaper and TV reports that resulted in changes in the system. . . . "One result of a refusal to allow reporters broad access to inmates may be the perception, if not the reality, that prison officials have something to hide," Walters wrote in an affidavit given to the department. "That, in turn, undermines the confidence in the entire criminal justice system" (Pickler, 1999).

The perception that "prison officials have something to hide" is powerful and pervasive. In his 1989 book *Doing Time in American Prisons*, Dennis Massey, in discussing the constraints on the development of the prison novel, casually notes:

> A system with so much to hide and such control over its inmates can make it difficult indeed for anything to be written or sent out that might expose these conditions, however indirectly (Massey, 1989: 41).

This statement is given credibility by Massey's statement in the preface to his book that he was "director of a large college program at a state prison in Ohio for over ten years" (Masey, 1989: Preface). This suggests that he was certainly in a position to report that corrections has "so much to hide."

Working It Out with the Media. A blanket denial of access to inmates will only make news media professionals suspicious. More importantly, correctional managers will lose the opportunity to provide contextual information by not being available to respond to questions raised by the reporter after the interview. A more productive strategy is to invite representatives of the news media to meet with correctional managers in an effort to develop mutually a news media access policy that will address the concerns and needs of all concerned. The need of corrections to maintain security must be recognized by the news media. Conversely, corrections must recognize the right of the public to know what is going on in America's prisons and the obligation of the news media to report on correctional activities. Policy should recognize the obligations and perspectives of both groups.

Making the news media welcome in the correctional environment is a positive action, but the information and positive impressions reporters, editors, and directors gather during their visits must be reinforced. One effective way for a public information officer to continually reinforce a positive impression of corrections is to offer a steady flow of press releases that provide the basis for future articles, editorials, or television news segments.

The Press Release as an Educational Tool

The press release is an excellent tool for disseminating contextual information. There are five basic types of press releases that the public information officer can issue.

The Event-oriented Press Release. Any event that casts the organization in a positive light can be the subject of a news release. For example, on May 5, 1999, the Delaware Department of Correction issued the following press release:

> An elite unit of emergency response officers with the Delaware Department of Correction has made history. The Department's Correctional Emergency Response Team (CERT) graduated 10 officers Tuesday; including its first-ever female member. Benyette Rodriquez of Dover joins the team and is assigned to the Delaware Correctional Center. The Department's CERT team is responsible for handling major disturbances in facilities and institutions across the state. The CERT has responded to inmate escapes, riots and hostage and barricade situations. Officers volunteer for CERT duty and must complete 136 hours of training in areas that include the use of chemical agents, riot control, building assaults and repelling (Delaware Department of Correction, 1999a).

The message is clear. The Delaware Department of Correction has recognized that female officers can be trusted to engage in the most hazardous of correctional activities: emergency management. The press release also details the demanding responsibilities involved in CERT duty and the many skills required by team members.

The Heroic Employee Press Release. An example of this type of press release is provided in Box 7-3.

The press release on Lieutenant Heverin demonstrates that correctional employees are members of the community who commute to and from work—just like everybody else and also are willing to unselfishly give of their time and energy to serve the community. If a correctional employee has performed an outstanding service to the community, the agency should make every effort to publicly recognize and honor that service.

The Trojan Horse Press Release. This type of press release provides notification of a negative event of interest to the public, but also uses the opportunity to educate the public. For example, when the Delaware Department of Correction publicly released its Public/Media Notification of Work Release Escapes policy, it included in that notification the following statement:

> The press and public must be mindful that these notifications do not indicate an escape from a secured correctional facility. These are instances that can include an offender's failure to report back from a work assignment, failure to report back from a treatment appointment or failure to abide by an imposed curfew. These are individuals whose sentence allows them to go into the community daily. Some offenders will take advantage of the restricted liberty afforded to them. As such, it is possible that such incidents may occur several times a week

Box 7-3 The Heroic Employee Press Release

For Immediate Release, February 26, 1999

DOVER—It started out as a normal drive home from work last October for Lieutenant Ralph Heverin. He planned on traveling the same route he'd taken for several years; south on Route 13 from the Delaware Correctional Center in Smyrna to his Felton home. It was October 27, 1998 and it would turn out to be anything but a normal ride home for the 22-year Delaware Department of Correction veteran. In fact, the action he'd soon take in what would turn out to be a life or death situation would win him honors. As Lt. Heverin traveled south on the busy roadway, he saw the rush hour traffic slowing and coming to a stop at the Court Street intersection in Dover. As he approached the intersection, Lt. Heverin realized there had been a terrible traffic accident. In fact, five passenger cars had collided. Lt. Heverin realized it was a serious accident. At least 6 people lay injured in and around the wreckage. Heverin, certified in CPR (cardio-pulmonary resuscitation), jumped from his car to see if he could help. "There were injured people everywhere," says Heverin. "I acted on instinct. I wanted to know if I could help anybody." He realized paramedics had the injured well tended to but he noticed another danger. Traffic was backing up. He feared another accident from motorists straining for a better look at the crash scene. Working with the Dover Police Department, Lt. Heverin directed rush hour traffic traveling in 5 different directions. This allowed rescue personnel to quickly enter and exit the accident scene. His actions also kept hundreds of cars moving smoothly and without further incident. For his efforts, Lt. Heverin recently received a commendation from the Dover Police Department in recognition of his assistance on October 27, 1998. Dover Police officials say Lt. Heverin displayed the teamwork which is necessary in order for law enforcement to be successful. Congratulations Lt. Heverin. Note: Photos of Lt. Heverin are available (Delaware Department of Correction, 1999b. Reprinted by permission of the Delaware Department of Correction).

across the state. In a majority of cases, offenders return on their own to their assigned work release facility (Welch, 1999).

This is a strong proactive statement that is more effective if it is made prior to news media coverage of a work release walkaway than after a walkaway has occurred. The routine inclusion of contextual information in organizational policy press releases can be an effective element of community education.

The Outstanding Employee Award Press Release. A favorite activity designed to promote a positive public image of corrections is the Employee of the Month Award Ceremony, which typically involves a plaque or certificate presented to a staff member in an official ceremony. The ceremony is documented in a press release, which the public information officer sends to local and employee home town newspapers. Employee of the Month and other types of press releases highlighting specific corrections professionals should contain information that encourages the reader to identify with the employee. An example of an article that humanizes a correctional employee being honored for her achievements appears in Box 7-4.

The article cited in Box 7-4 continues for three more columns, each column revealing a very personal picture of Officer Connor that stands in stark contrast to the bull-necked smug hack imagery so prevalent in the prison movies.

Box 7-4 Outstanding Employee Press Release

Professionalism Key to Officer's Success

Becky Connor leads a double life. In the evenings and on weekends, she is a loving mother and wife, spending time caring for her husband and her two daughters. Just like most females, she likes to look nice and spends extra time fixing her hair and putting on makeup. Sometimes she even wears perfume. But when it comes time for Connor to report to work as a correctional officer at Davidson Correctional Center, a minimum security prison for adult males, all that changes. Gone are the makeup, perfume and perfectly styled hair. While at work, Connor abandons her role as mother, wife and female and becomes, strictly, a professional, correctional officer. "I come to work looking very professional," she said. "I don't wear makeup or nail polish. I wear starched uniforms with military creases. This causes the inmates to have respect for me. They see me as an officer, not as a female."

Connor even goes so far as to wear uniforms a size larger than her normal size to ensure that she does not come to work wearing clothes that are too tight. She feels her professional demeanor has helped her be successful in a field where women are in the minority. "I have been here (at Davidson) coming on five years, and during that time, I have seen 17 females come and leave," she said. "Some of these female officers would come in here wearing tight uniforms, lots of makeup and perfume which would lead to problems with the inmates. To me, to work here, you have to have a positive attitude, but you must also have a very professional demeanor" (Hardee, 1998: 1-2. Reprinted by permission of the North Carolina Department of Corrections).

Recognizing the Diversity of Corrections Press Releases. The general public needs to be aware that correctional organizations have employees other than correctional officers. One method of creating this awareness is the press release that highlights the achievements of staff who are not correctional officers. For example, on June 22, 1999, the Delaware Department of Correction issued a press release about Kay Wood Bailey, Prison Arts Administrator for the department. Kay Bailey was named Delaware Art Educator of the Year by the Art Educators of Delaware (AED), a nonprofit statewide arts organization that made the selection from a group of highly qualified candidates. Bailey was cited for her professional achievements in bringing "art, music, dance and cultural classes into the state's adult correctional institutions and facilities." The press release ended with the advisement that "In 1997, Kay Wood Bailey was honored as Delaware Mother of the Year" (Delaware Department of Correction, 1999c).

This type of press release effectively challenges the smug hack imagery of corrections because it presents a woman working in corrections, but outside of the traditional officer role. She is engaging in activities which most members of the general community have experienced themselves during their school years. While some might argue that this type of press release will reinforce the imagery of country club corrections, the more important point is that the general public is provided an image of a correctional employee as a regular human being.

Rules for the Dissemination of Press Releases to the News Media. When developing press releases (or any other type of written documentation), the public information officer should try to avoid the following basic mistakes:

- failing to tailor a communication to the specific interests of the target audience
- failing to follow up on a press release with a phone call
- continually sending reporters, writers, editors, or producers information in which they have no interest
- canceling advertising in a major publication because of negative publicity
- Causing the audience to think, "Why are you telling me all this?" (Benn, 1982).

Press releases are useful, but whether or not their content is presented to the general public by the news media is a decision made by editors and producers, not corrections. Therefore, corrections needs a way to disseminate information to the general public without having it filtered through the bureaucracy of the news media. Corrections needs to use the Internet.

The Internet and Community Education

The Internet provides corrections with a golden opportunity to disseminate accurate information that remains accurate because it has not been filtered through the media. This is an opportunity corrections cannot afford to overlook because the critics of corrections are already on the Internet and using its access to the public to denounce correctional policies and practices.

The Internet can be used in any way a creative public information officer can develop. A growing number of department of corrections are using their web sites to provide a wealth of information about the organization's history, mission, challenges, and activities. To cite one example, the California Department of Corrections has an enormous web site (http://www.cdc.state.ca.us) that provides information about such topics as: current job opportunities and personnel examinations; capital punishment; California Department of Corrections facility descriptions and history; inmate programs and services; and statistics about California inmates and parolees. Numerous photographs, as well as maps and statistical charts and graphs, are used to illustrate the information provided (California Department of Corrections, 1999).

An innovative approach to community education has been created by the Maryland Division of Correction. This agency uses the Internet, radio, and cable television to educate the general public. Both radio and the Internet provide viewers a look at corrections through a radio program called *Crimeline*. In 1998, programs included: *Central Booking; Crime Investigations in Prison; Crime Investigations in Prison, Part II; National Consensus on Correctional Issues; National Consensus on Correctional Issues, Part II; Training Seeing Eye Dogs in Prison; Training Seeing Eye Dogs in Prison, Part II; Supermax: Maryland's Toughest Prison; Supermax: Maryland's Toughest Prison, Part II; Parole and Probation; and Parole and Probation, Part II* (Maryland Division of Correction, 1998).

As of September 10, 1998, *Crimeline* was being aired by fifteen different radio stations throughout Maryland. Seven shows were using the program as back-up or filler and the other eight stations aired the show on a regular basis—giving it air time approximately sixty times a month. Another department program, *Public Safety Today*, was aired on fourteen cable stations throughout the state approximately 170 times a month (Piepenbring, 1998: 1). The response to the tapes provided to television stations for *Public Safety Today* show they have been well received by local television programmers and the public.

The Internet provides benefits to corrections other than community education. It can also assist in increasing the safety of the public and help law enforcement. For example, the North Carolina Department of Corrections, in 1998, expanded their web site by adding a list of prison escapees. A photograph and description of the escapee provides information and viewers are encouraged to report any information they have about the escapee to their local police or the Division of Corrections (Poston, 1998: 3).

It takes time, effort, and computer expertise to construct a department of corrections web site; however, assistance in constructing a web site is readily available in the community. For example, the Delaware Department of Correction's web site was designed by two high school students working under the guidance of their school's librarian (Delaware Department of Correction, 1999d). The Delaware Department of Correction's web site contains information about its nationally acclaimed substance abuse programs; boot camp; employment opportunities; prisons; and probation and parole divisions. There is also a section on the most frequently asked questions about the Delaware Department of Correction.

However, despite the best efforts of public information officers and correctional managers, inevitably there will be news media coverage that is inaccurate or misleading because all of the facts have not been presented. Confronting inaccurate news coverage requires a carefully prepared response.

Responding to Inaccurate News Media Coverage

Corrections professionals need to respond aggressively to articles, editorials, or television segments that are presenting inaccurate information. However, this response must be professional. Under no circumstances should the response be insulting, whiny, hostile, bitter, angry, or confrontational.

The Michigan Department of Corrections has developed an excellent strategy for responding to what the department believes is inaccurate information. The strategy uses a press release. Box 7-5 provides an example of this approach to responding to attacks on organizational integrity.

The press release reproduced in Box 7-5 is professionally written and edited. It honestly presents statistics and is not afraid to acknowledge that instances of sexual misconduct have occurred. This article tries to set the record straight by outlining the Michigan Department of Corrections' response to a serious situation. It is factual, but not defensive, although it does contain a hint of sarcasm that might be deemed inappropriate by some readers.

An effective public information officer can create a positive working relationship with the news media. There will be exceptions, but, in general, reporters, editors, and directors are like everyone else: they appreciate the people who make their job easier.

Educating Entertainment Media Professionals

To educate entertainment media professionals, corrections must enter the world of Hollywood. How does an individual working in corrections become part of such an alien environment? There are a number of useful approaches to try.

Becoming an Author. One option is to write a book or screenplay that is dynamic, emotional, and has the potential to make a profit. This can be done without resorting to the distortion typically seen in Hollywood productions or inmate-authored novels.

Box 7-5 from The Insider: A Public Service of the Michigan Department of Corrections

No True Amnesty: International Organization Not Letting Facts Get In Its Way

For the past four years, the Michigan Department of Corrections has faced claims, made by the U.S. Department of Justice, that it was not providing humane treatment for female offenders. Perhaps unwittingly, the once-renowned human rights group Amnesty International has recently made the same claims—but offered little new evidence or insight into what is now a legal issue between the state and federal governments.

Had officials at the organization, which once was honored with the Nobel Peace Prize, bothered to simply call the department and ask, they would have been provided with detailed information that documents Michigan's commitment to providing humane treatment to prisoners and protecting them from sexual misconduct. For example, as proof that the department takes seriously allegations of sexual misconduct, Amnesty officials might have wanted to know that:

Michigan—unlike most other states—has an extensive training program for corrections staff who will supervise female offenders. In addition to the 16 weeks of training that new custody personnel receive—among the most elaborate training for new employees in the country—Michigan has a mandatory 40-hour course that covers the special needs of female offenders. The course is so thorough and highly regarded that the Federal Bureau of Prisons (BOP), which is a branch of the Department of Justice, has adopted the same curriculum for training its staff.

Michigan also has an exhaustive prisoner-complaint procedure. The process is even certified by the Department of Justice and "substantially complies with Department of Justice standards," according to DOJ.

The Michigan Department of Corrections aggressively investigates allegations of unprofessional behavior between staff and offenders. The department takes appropriate disciplinary action against employees when warranted, up to and including dismissal.

In 1996, there were 13 allegations of sexual misconduct at Michigan's two prisons for women (the Scott Correctional Facility in Plymouth and the Crane Correctional facility in Coldwater). Each of the allegations resulted in an investigation; of those, two were sustained and resulted in disciplinary action and one is still pending, although the employee has resigned.

In 1997, there were 19 such allegations and investigations at the two facilities; of those, five were sustained and resulted in disciplinary action and nine are still pending.

To date in 1998, there have been 24 such allegations and investigations at the two facilities; of those, five were sustained and resulted in disciplinary action and nine are still pending.

Those numbers clearly show that sexual misconduct not only is prohibited, it is also aggressively investigated. Far more chilling than Amnesty's officials' reluctance to seek information is what appears to be an acceptance of allegations as fact. It is precisely that method of conviction by kangaroo courts and nefarious governments that Amnesty was originally formed to oppose. By foregoing rigorous pursuit of facts and simply reiterating existing claims, Amnesty appears to be denying to the hard-working men and women of the Michigan Department of Corrections the same due process that it would demand from governments who were holding people against their will.

(Source: Michigan Department of Corrections, 1998. Reprinted by Permission of the Michigan Department of Corrections).

Correctional work is full of intense emotional conflicts and situations that can be presented accurately to the public. Human drama can be found at every level of corrections. A fact-based, but dynamic, novel can be published. All the corrections professional has to do is write it.

Corrections professionals do not have to limit their literary efforts to novels. Biographical books also can influence the public perception of corrections. This author, as a teenager, read the memoirs authored by Clinton T. Duffy, a former warden of San Quentin (*The Story of San Quentin*, 1950). Duffy's words about his decades of experience made a powerful impact that ultimately helped influence this author's decision to enter corrections. And Duffy's book would have made a good movie. Good books about corrections can be made into good movies.

Entertainment Media Consulting. If authorship is not a possibility because of a lack of talent, or interest, then corrections professionals can offer their services to Hollywood as consultants. Every state has a unit of government that attempts to entice Hollywood producers and directors to film in their state. The commissioner of corrections should go on record that a condition of filming a prison movie, especially if an existing facility is to be a site for filming, is that the producer consult with a corrections representative who can advise on the factual accuracy of the production. This may not always be acceptable to either producers or the state's governor, but the value of technical accuracy to the quality of the production should be stressed to the producer.

Of course, there is a powerful economic reality created by the decision of a producer or director to film in a specific state. During the 1990s, a number of states recognized Hollywood as an important source of additional revenue that was needed by governors struggling to balance their budgets without increasing state taxes. Although a very small number of prison movies (in comparison to police movies) are produced every year, governors eager to bring entertainment-based revenue into the state may not be receptive to the image concerns of corrections. However, this lack of political support does not mean that corrections must remain silent. Corrections professionals should be quick to point out to their elected officials that a negative prison picture set in an identifiable state will not present an image of the state that its elected officials will appreciate. A governor trying to promote the state as progressive and ready to meet the challenges of the twenty-first century head-on does not politically benefit from the bitter images created by the *The Shawshank Redemption* or *Cool Hand Luke*.

Letter Writing Campaigns. If a stereotypical prison movie does hit the screen, regardless of the state in which it was filmed, corrections professionals should coordinate national letter writing campaigns that denounce the production in the strongest possible terms (although within the bounds of professionalism). Specifically, the letters should identify the practices depicted, which are no longer supported by corrections professionals. Letter writing campaigns can be tricky because they inadvertently may increase public interest in an otherwise mediocre production. However, remaining silent may be even worse because silence suggests approval.

On the other hand, if there is a documentary that does provide a balanced view of corrections, then corrections professionals should publicly express their support of that production and try to increase public interest in viewing it. If a producer expresses an interest in using an existing prison for a prison movie, or documentary, correctional staff should be assigned to research that producer's previous movies. This will help executive managers decide if they want to support the request.

Creating Videos. Finally, correctional organizations have the media resources necessary to produce professional quality videotapes about corrections that accurately present the full range of challenges faced on a daily basis by corrections professionals at both the line and management level. These productions can be distributed to the news and entertainment media, secondary and postsecondary educational systems, community service organizations such as the Lions and Kiwanis, youth organizations such as the Cub Scouts and Boy Scout and Girl Scout organizations, and any other community organizations interested in learning about corrections. A skilled public information officer can write the video scripts, select the staff to be profiled, and identify the locations for filming without difficulty. Given the state of technology available to corrections, there are no significant barriers to the ability of correctional organizations to create and distribute professionally produced videotapes as an element of their efforts to educate the community.

The American Correctional Association, as an advocate of corrections, has been particularly prolific in producing films with a high level of factual content. For example: *The American Prison: A Video History* (1990); *Men, Women, and Respect: Stopping Sexual Harassment in Correctional Facilities* (1993); *Boot Camps in Corrections* (1995); and *Correctional Perspective: Inmates* (1996) are just a few of the films available from the American Correctional Association. The association also sponsors an annual film festival at its national conference every August during which awards are presented for the best correctional films of the year.

Nobody will claim that an individual department of corrections or the American Correctional Association truly can rival Hollywood when it comes to the quality of the production, and the size of the audience that can be reached. And whether the American Correctional Association's and department of corrections' productions have the emotional impact of such HBO specials as *Lock-up: The Prisoners of Rikers Island* (1994) with its disturbing cell block search by correctional officers or *Against the Wall* (1994), which presents the failure of correctional management to prepare for, and properly respond to the 1971 Attica riot or the Cinema Guide production of *Through the Wire* (1990) whose powerful footage resulted in a special unit at a federal prison in Lexington, Kentucky being shut down (Rafter and Stanley, 1999: 203) is obviously open to question. However, there is certainly no harm in corrections documenting its successes and accomplishments on film. After all, community education is an integrated strategy and every element plays a role in achieving its goals.

Points to Consider

1. Are there any circumstances when media avoidance would be in the best interests of corrections? If so, what are they? Why do these circumstances justify media avoidance?

2. How can one lie permanently ruin the relationship between the public information officer and news reporters?

3. Are there any circumstances when lying to a reporter would be in the best interests of corrections? If so, what are they? Why do these circumstances justify lying?

4. What potential correctional crises would you include in a public information officer data bank?

5. Are there any potential problems that can be created by face-to-face interaction with news reporters? What might they be? How can that potential be reduced?

6. What types of positive employee behavior would you include in a press release?

7. Is it really necessary to let news media professionals into the prison? Defend your answer?

8. How receptive will Hollywood be to the advice that can be provided by corrections professionals?

References

Abu-Jamal, M. 1995. *Live From Death Row*. Reading, Massachusetts: Addison-Wesley.

Barak, G. 1994. *Media, Process and the Social Construction of Crime: Studies in Newsmaking Criminology*. New York: Garland.

Benn, A. 1982. *The 23 Most Common Mistakes in Public Relations*. New York: American Management Association.

California Department of Corrections. 1999. *Corrections: Public Safety, Public Service*. Sacramento, California: California Department of Corrections.

CCI: Case Study of a Southern Prison. 1993. Princeton, New Jersey: Films for the Humanities and Sciences.

Chermak, S. M. 1998. Police, Courts, and Corrections in the Media. In F. Bailey and D. Hale, eds. *Popular Culture, Crime and Justice*. Belmont, California: West/Wadsworth Publishing. pp. 87-99.

The Corrections Professional. 1999. Access to Inmates Under Intense Scrutiny in Florida. November. 19: 7.

Delaware Department of Correction. 1999a. Emergency Response Team Welcomes First Female Member. Press Release. May 5.

———. 1999b. No title. February 26.

———. 1999c. DOC Prison Arts Administrator Named Art Educator of the Year. June 22.

———. 1999d. 2 High School Students Design Dept. Of Correction's New Web Site. Press Release. May 19.

DiIulio, John, J. Jr. 1987. *Governing Prisons*. New York: The Free Press.

Doing Time. 1990. New York: Ellis Productions.

Duffy, C. T. with A. Jennings. 1950. *The Story of San Quentin*. New York: Macmillan.

Earley, P. 1992. *The Hot House: Life Inside Leavenworth Prison*. New York: Bantam Books.

Florida Department of Corrections. 1998. *Corrections in Florida: What the Public, News Media, and DC Staff Think*. Tallahassee, Florida: Florida Department of Corrections.

The Farm: Life Inside Angola Prison. 1998. Video. Arts and Entertainment, Investigative Network.

Freeman, R. M. 1999. *Correctional Organization and Management: Public Policy Challenges, Behavior and Structure*. Woburn, Massachusetts: Butterworth-Heinemann.

Gondles, J. A., Jr. 1998. Influencing Public Perception. *Corrections Today*. (59)1: 6.

Hardee, C. 1998. Professionalism Key to Officer's Success. *Correction News*. July. North Carolina Department of Correction.

Jackson, G. 1970/1994. *Soledad Brothers: The Prison Letters of George Jackson*. New York: Bantam Books.

Jarvis, J. 1998. Openness Is the Best Policy. *Corrections Today*. (59)1: 20.

Kidd, V. and R. Braziel. 1999. *Cop Talk: Essential Communication Skills For Community Policing*. San Francisco, California: Acada Books.

Kindel, T. C. 1993. Planning Is the Key to Handling Media Interest in an Execution. *Corrections Today*. (55)4: 65-69.

―――. 1998. Media Access: Where Should You Draw The Line? *Corrections Today*. (59)1: 22-24.

Koppel, Ted. 1998. *Crime and Punishment*. ABC Television. Summer.

Manning, P. K. 1998. Media Loops. In F. Bailey and D. Hale, eds. *Popular Culture, Crime and Justice*. Belmont, California: West/Wadsworth Publishing. pp. 25-39.

Maryland Division of Correction. 1998. *Crimeline*. Baltimore, Maryland: Maryland Division of Correction.

Massey, D. 1989. *Doing Time in American Prisons: A Study of Modern Novels*. New York: Greenwood Press.

Michigan Department of Corrections. 1998. No True Amnesty: International Organization Not Letting Facts Get in its Way. *The Insider*. November 20: 1-2.

Morris, R. 1983/1988. *The Devil's Butcher Shop: The New Mexico Prison Uprising*. Albuquerque, New Mexico: University of New Mexico Press.

Phillips, R., ed. 1993. *Improving Media Relations: A Handbook for Corrections*. Lanham, Maryland: American Correctional Association.

Pickler, N. 1999. Michigan May Limit Media Access to Prisoners. *Associated Press*. November 16.

Piepenbring, P. 1998. Annual Survey of Radio and Cable Television Shows. September 10 Memorandum. Maryland Department of Public Safety and Correctional Services.

Poston, B. 1998. Improvements Made to DOC Web Site. *Correction News*. March.

Rafter, N. H. and D. L. Stanley. 1999. *Prisons in America: A Reference Handbook*. Santa Barbara, California: ABC-CLIO.

Shakedown at Santa Fe. 1988. PBS Video.

University of California Extension. 1996. *From One Prison*. Video.

Welch, B. 1999. Public/Media Notification of Work Release Escapes. Press Release. Delaware Department of Correction.

Women Doing Time. 1992. New York: Ambrose Video.

Educating the Consumers of the Popular Culture of Corrections:

The Creation of an Alternative Set of Images

Graber (1989) has reported that mass media information has the power to reinforce existing stereotypes even if the receiver of that information cannot accurately recall the media format in which the stereotypes were presented. The creation of mass media-based stereotypes is accomplished through a multilayered process known as *a mediated spiral*: a process in which "we are watching not only images but images of images" (Ferrell, 1998: 76). Or, as Austin H. MacCormick noted during his Presidential Address at the Congress of Correction in New York City in 1939:

> The newspaper reader turns from the murder on page one to the rape on page two and then to the armed robbery on page three and, his paper finished, goes to his neighborhood movie house and sees a film of prison life in which riots and violent escapes are made to appear a daily occurrence. Before going to bed he tunes in the radio and listens to a news flash in which it is reported that Elmer Zilch, on parole from State prison, has been arrested in connection with the hold-up of the Tip-Top Bar and Grill last Thursday (American Prison Association, 1939).

For corrections, the final product of this mediated spiral is a definition of the "typical" correctional employee that is framed in terms of the types of images presented in this 1998 *Time* magazine article about Sheriff Joe Arpaio:

> Picture the bullnecked jailer in *Cool Hand Luke*, throw in some of former Philadelphia mayor Frank Rizzo, add a touch of Yosemite Sam and you get Sheriff Joe. And right now the boss hog, who averages a speech a day and makes Madonna look like a media wallflower, is wowing the retirees with lines about how he'd hate to be in a top bunk tonight (Lopez, 1998).

The goal of community education is to ensure that the consumers of the popular culture of corrections have an alternative set of images that define correctional employees as dedicated, hard-working professionals who support family and community:

> Officer Amsdill is family oriented and is active in his community with the organization and development of youth activities. He is considered a team player

who is well respected by supervisors, co-workers, and offenders alike. He is described as hard working, dedicated, and a true professional, whom fellow staff are proud to work with. He exhibits pride, integrity, and professionalism; and strives to promote a positive image at work, at home, and in the community (Washington Department of Corrections, 1999: 2).

Alternative imagery can be created through a three-pronged approach that involves corrections professionals obtaining membership in community service organizations, being involved in the community's public education system (K-12 and college), and organizing fund raising and "sweat equity" services.

Membership in Community Organizations

Participation in community service organizations such as the Lions, Kiwanis, and Rotary will provide influential members of the community the opportunity to gain contextual information about corrections through social interaction with correctional managers during formal meetings and attendance at organization-sponsored events. Corrections professionals should strive to assume a leadership position within their service organization as Dr. Jane Young of the North Carolina Department of Correction did in 1998. The director of educational services for the Department of Correction, Dr. Young was elected to be the first female president of the Raleigh Host Lions Club in seventy-five years (North Carolina Department of Correction, 1998a: 1). Once a corrections professional is in a leadership position in a service organization, it will be much easier for that individual to disseminate contextual information.

Community involvement is not limited to service organization membership. Correctional manager and line staff participation in local activities such as school board elections, citizen advisory councils, petition drives, town meetings, school activities, coaching and refereeing sporting events, and school sports fund-raising events will signal an interest in serving the community. The more active corrections professionals are in supporting community events, the more likely it is that the individuals they are meeting will be inclined to reject negative stereotyping.

Correctional Involvement at the K-12 Level

Participation in the public education system should occur at two levels: the K-12 grade level and the college level. At the K-12 level, there are three useful initiatives: school-based probation, the speaker's bureau, and contributions to the classroom.

School-based Probation. School-based probation programs target at-risk youth by assigning juvenile probation officers to public schools on a full-time basis for monitoring the activities of students who have been placed on probation. The monitoring and intervention activities of these officers are designed to help at-risk youth reduce the number of disciplinary referrals, detentions and suspensions, days missed, and referrals for intensive supervision probation they incur, and increase the number of positive school reports, completed homework assignments, and completed grades (Hazelton and Shaffer, 1999: 1).

School-based probation programs help challenge negative stereotyping by exposing school personnel, students, and parents to probation officers and the contribution they are making to the community. This information then may be generalized to influence their perception of other correctional employees.

The Speakers' Bureau. The speakers' bureau is composed of corrections professionals who are articulate, at ease with public speaking, and interested in presenting contextual information about corrections. The participants in a speakers' bureau should be volunteers because employees uncomfortable with public speaking tend to present poorly when they are forced to speak to the public. The speakers' bureau can be used effectively at either the K-12 level or the college level.

The K-12 Level. The children of today will be the crime control policy makers of tomorrow. Early personal exposure to a positive image of corrections will help mitigate the negative impact of the popular culture of corrections on young minds. The speakers' bureau at the K-12 level should target general students as well as students who are defined as being at-risk. The format of the presentation can take on as many forms as correctional employees are able to devise. Box 8-1 provides a small sample of speakers' bureau activities.

Box 8-1 Speakers' Bureau Activities

In Maryland, at St. John Neumann School, Officer Ronald Smith shared his experiences as a correctional officer with a first-grade class and Sergeant Terry Beal provided a demonstration of his drug detection dog, Bear, by leading the animal through a series of drug detection exercises. Both officers are pursuing the possibility of working with police officers in the Cumberland City Police D.A.R.E. Program. The article covering this event noted: "Many students responded favorably when Officer Smith asked who was interested in becoming a correctional officer or a police officer" (Desaulniers, 1998: 3).

The Federal Bureau of Prisons has long been a leader in promoting corrections through use of a speakers' bureau. For example, on January 28, 1998, Federal Correctional Institution Dublin employees met with 275 middle school students at Cesar Chavez Middle School in Hayward, California. Employees discussed "the Bureau of Prisons, the importance of a good education, and how to achieve personal and professional success" (Federal Bureau of Prisons, 1998a: 2).

In October, 1999, ten inmates from Federal Prison Camp Loretto participated in the Annual Red Ribbon Campaign, a project which involved giving presentations on the negative consequences of substance abuse to approximately 7,000 students at 15 schools in three Pennsylvania counties (Federal Bureau of Prisons, 1999d: 3).

In Colorado, the warden of the U.S. Prison Florence and members of his staff have been speaking on a regular basis with at-risk youth "about the dangers of a criminal lifestyle and the consequences of bad decision making" (Federal Bureau of Prisons, 1999e: 2). These talks have included visits to the administrative section of the U.S. Prison Florence so the children could get a taste of prison.

Inmates in the Speakers' Bureau. Many departments of corrections use offenders, particularly inmates, as part of their speakers' bureau program. This approach of hearing "it like it is" from a convicted felon can pay excellent dividends. A special education teacher in Kansas was so impressed by this approach that after inmates talked to a group of sixth, seventh, and eighth graders he wrote to tell the commissioner of corrections that the inmates had:

. . . delivered excellent messages on how poor choices can affect you, your family, and your friends for a lifetime. They stressed the importance of staying in school, staying off drugs, and learning to communicate your feelings to others in a positive and supportive way.

We feel the Stop Violence Coalition is and has been a very effective tool not only for these students but for the speakers involved as well. Our middle school principal is requesting them to present their program to our Board of Education (Kansas Department of Corrections, 1998: 1).

Contributions to the Classroom. In Maryland, correctional employees donated more than 10,000 books (28 books for each of approximately 500 students) to Johnston Square Elementary School:

Staff who worked with the children were moved by the affection and gratitude of the children and school employees. The project has great moral value and provides positive role models in the form of correctional employees (Stritch, 1998: 3).

In Delaware, ten inmates at the Delaware Correctional Center near Smyrna translated 60,000 pages of textbooks into braille for blind and visually impaired students at public, private, and religious schools. The inmates are members of the "Men with A Message" program, which started over eight years ago. Nine to twelve months of training are required for certification in braille. Only the Library of Congress can grant certification (Mace, 1997).

In Minnesota in 1999, inmates at the Minnesota Correctional Facility received a $3,000 grant from the Education Minnesota Foundation for Excellence in Teaching and Learning to write and illustrate a book of personal stories about why they are in prison and the experiences they have had during incarceration. Inmates at a Florida correctional facility are to print and bind copies of the book. The books will be provided free of charge to at-risk youths in the Minnesota public school system (Minnesota Department of Corrections, 1999a: 2).

Bringing Students into Corrections: "Shadowing." K-12 students can be invited to enter the correctional environment. For example, in Louisiana, on February 2, 1998, Captain Keith Deville was an active participant in "Shadow Day" at the Work Training Facility North. "Shadow Day" provides students the opportunity to observe correctional employees during the performance of their duties. Captain Deville had four eighth-grade students with him for his shift. The students watched Captain Deville and "At the end of the day the students said they had enjoyed the day and were surprised by what they learned a correctional officer's job is like," reported the Warden (Louisiana Department of Public Safety and Corrections, 1998a: 1).

The Federal Bureau of Prisons also provides public school students the opportunity to participate in a "shadowing day." On November 18, 1999, seven ninth-grade students spent the day at Federal Detention Center-Philadelphia learning about the Bureau. They "observed the workplace culture, interacted with staff, and learned about the education and skills that are needed to work for the BOP" (Federal Bureau of Prisons, 1999f: 2).

Correctional Involvement at the College Level

Historically, corrections professionals and college faculty have found it difficult to trust each other. A 1995 survey reached the following conclusions about criminal justice practitioners' perceptions of how they are viewed by academicians:

> Most of the practitioners were positive toward ademicians but there were some common perceptions among some of the practitioners. Some practitioners felt that academicians had a disdain for practitioners. There was a feeling that this disdain was less among the academicians that had been practitioners at some time in their career. There was also a feeling among practitioners that academicians did not communicate with practitioners often enough. However, the most common feeling expressed by practitioners was that academicians were too theoretical and lacked contact with the real world. There were also several practitioners that felt that their graduate education had been useless for them in their criminal justice positions (Caldwell and Dorling, 1995: 110).

Although corrections was not singled out in this study, it is reasonable to conclude that a survey of corrections professionals would yield similar conclusions. On the other hand, faculty often complain of bureaucratic delays created by correctional policy and procedures. A professor writing a book on corrections finds it frustrating to call a human resources officer in a department of correction, ask for something as basic as a correctional officer job description, and be told: "You will have to submit an official request in writing on a university letterhead before we can make a decision whether or not to release that type of information."

However, corrections and academia do not have to be mutually exclusive entities. There are six mutually beneficial activities in which corrections professionals and academics can engage: the corrections internship; professional conferences; collaborative research; teaching partnerships; creation of a National Corrections Explorers Conference; and new prison siting.

The Corrections Internship

Internships are an important component in the process of preparing students for service in the criminal justice system because "They serve as an important bridging experience between students' academic careers and their careers as criminal justice professionals" (Parilla and Smith-Cunnien, 1997: 225). For the vast majority of students, the internship represents their first opportunity to work in corrections. If the internship experience is properly structured, these students will be able to "make a connection between experience-based learning and more traditional 'academic' learning" (Parilla and Smith-Cunnien, 1997: 229).

A high degree of structure is essential if an internship is to effectively introduce a student to the complexity of corrections. A written internship policy should establish guidelines for selection, supervision, evaluation, and early termination. Development of this policy requires the collaboration of the academic supervisor and the agency site supervisor.

The Intern Selection Process. The selection process begins with the academic supervisor interviewing those students who have expressed an interest in doing an internship. The interview should be standardized and designed to establish:

1. The reason the student wants an internship

2. The rationale for selection of the internship site in which the student is most interested

3. The student's goals and expectations for the internship

4. Academic preparation for the internship experience

5. Future goals and the role the internship is expected to play in achieving these goals

Once the academic supervisor is satisfied that the student is an appropriate candidate for an internship, the student should submit an application to the internship site. Agencies differ in their application requirements. A formal written application, transcript, and criminal record background check by the agency are frequently the standard requirements to be completed before the site supervisor will conduct an interview. Once a student has been tentatively accepted by the internship site, there needs to be a personal interview with the site supervisor. The purpose of this interview is to provide the site supervisor with a "feel" for the student's:

1. Rationale for the internship site selection

2. Knowledge of the agency

3. Expectations and goals for the internship

4. Ability to work with agency personnel and clients

5. Ability to take direction

Students and site supervisors typically view the internship as preparation for future work in that, or a similar, agency. For the vast majority of students, the purpose of the internship is to make "themselves as attractive as possible to potential employers" (Parilla and Smith-Cunnien, 1997: 231). And the agency regards the interns as members of a future applicant pool.

The Role of the Site Supervisor. Site supervisors should be volunteers who understand the importance of the internship and their responsibility to make it a successful experience for both student and agency. To be effective, the site supervisor must be an individual who is comfortable responding to questions and will not hesitate to quickly correct any inappropriate student behavior. The focus of supervision is to evaluate how well the student adapts to the culture of the organization. Site supervisors have the responsibility of providing interns a maximum degree of exposure to as many aspects of the work environment as possible. Agency liability concerns may limit some types of exposure, but it has been this author's experience that liability issues rarely, if ever, arise during an internship. Hands-on experience must be emphasized, but this does not mean students should be used as secretaries or filing clerks. An internship that uses students as a source of cheap labor is an internship that is wasting the time of all concerned.

Orientation of the Student. Effective site supervision requires the site supervisor to orient the student to the realities of organizational bureaucracy and working with offenders. This is done most effectively through a formal orientation backed up by written rules of conduct. It is not enough to provide written information to the student or volunteer. There must be a follow-up discussion during which points can be clarified and questions or concerns addressed. The orientation should include a review of a work schedule for the intern, which encourages site supervisor-student interaction on a daily basis.

The Evaluative Role of the Academic Supervisor. The academic supervisor should make at least one visit to the internship site to meet with both the student and the site supervisor to discuss the student's progress and to detect, and confront, any behavior that is inappropriate. Weekly phone contact should be maintained with the student so issues can be addressed as they arise. The overall evaluation of the student is the responsibility of the academic supervisor. This evaluation should be based on a review of the student's daily journal of activities; department of correction's documentation of performance during formal training provided by the agency during the internship; a written overall performance evaluation provided by the site supervisor; and a critical analysis paper. The critical analysis paper is particularly useful in evaluating the intern because it establishes how well the student has integrated academic and work experiences. Writing the paper also can be a useful mechanism for decertifying correctional stereotypes. Box 8-2 presents guidelines for the critical analysis paper.

Box 8-2 Guidelines for the Critical Analysis Internship Paper

I. Introduction:

   A. Brief overview of the agency, including:

   1. Type of agency (local, state, federal, law enforcement, court, corrections, and any other relevant descriptive information)

   2. Location (including address)

   3. Size of the agency (number of personnel, offenders, geographical area served, and any other descriptive information)

   4. History

   5. Special accomplishments or recognition

II. Organizational culture and structure:

   A. Expected employee behavior:

   1. Mission statement

   2. Official goals statement

   3. Official values statement

   4. Code of ethics/conduct

   B. Organizational structure:

   1. Agency organization chart

   2. Organization chart for your unit (include number of employees)

   3. Agency relationship to other elements of the criminal justice system. Students may use a flow chart to illustrate this relationship.

III. Agency placement: observations and findings:

   A. What are the most important staff functions in the unit to which you are assigned?

Continued on the next page

Box 8-2 Guidelines for the Critical Analysis Internship Paper (continued)

    B. Prioritize the functions by calculating the percentage of employee time spent on each function.

    C. Which of these functions are you allowed to perform?

    D. Describe your typical day.

    E. Which functions are most interesting to you? Why?

    F. Which functions are least interesting to you? Why?

IV. Personal development:

    A. What impact has this internship had on your ability to relate to a diverse group of people?

    B. What have you learned about your personal strengths and weaknesses?

    C. What actions will you take to correct personal weaknesses?

V. Summary and discussion on integration of courses and internship:

    A. Based on your course work, discuss the issues and challenges most relevant to the agency (such as budget constraints, legal changes, increasing or decreasing crime rates, effects of jail/prison crowding, changing area demographics, effects of get tough on crime policies, impact of the media on the public perception of the agency, and so forth).

    B. According to the agency, which of these issues and challenges has the greatest impact on the ability of the agency to accomplish its mission? What is the nature of this impact?

    C. How does the agency address these issues and challenges?

    D. What criminal justice themes developed in your courses were verified by your internship? What themes were not?

    E. In view of your agency experience, what works in the criminal justice system? What does not work? Is this what you had expected to find? Why or why not?

    F. What impact has this internship had on your career goals?

    G. How can the internship experience be improved for future students?

    H. What can the criminal justice department do to better prepare students for both the internship and future criminal justice employment?

Many students return from the internship amazed at the degree of professionalism they encountered in the agency. They simply had not expected it. Nor were they prepared for the contrast between Hollywood corrections and modern corrections.

The Internship Open House. One effective way to communicate correctional support for internships is to host an internship open house. For example, the Cook County Department of Corrections, in November, 1997, sponsored their second annual

Internship Program Open House. This six-hour program introduces "academic heads from the social work, criminal justice, law library and library science fields of numerous schools" (Cook County Department of Corrections, 1997: 1) to the availability of internships in the facilities of the Cook County Department of Corrections through the use of a tour and staff presentations.

Participation in Professional Conferences

Correctional employees who are specialists in fields that have a membership outside of corrections (psychologists, educators, physicians, dentists, counselors, chaplains and so on) are often members of professional organizations that hold annual conferences to discuss issues of concern to that profession. These employees should take every opportunity to play a key role in sponsoring sessions at those professional conferences. For example, Dr. Linda Richardson, a Louisiana Department of Public Safety and Corrections clinical psychologist, chaired a symposium entitled "So You Want To Be a Correctional Psychologist" at the annual meeting of the American Psychological Association in San Francisco. More than 100 people attended the symposium and:

> With Dr. Richardson's assistance, the annual APA meeting provided the opportunity for the department to receive some positive attention as well as to be portrayed in a leadership role in the field of correctional psychology (Louisiana Department of Public Safety and Corrections, 1998b: 2).

Corrections professionals also should seek out opportunities for their organization to work with community organizations to jointly sponsor professional conferences of interest to the employees of both groups. In many states, the department of corrections and victim rights groups are jointly sponsoring conferences to address the issues involved in meeting the needs of the victims of crime.

Collaborative Research

There are so many pressing issues in corrections that there is no lack of potential research projects of interest to both academia and corrections. The executive managers of correctional organizations (especially department of corrections) are generally open to the idea of research, but it will be permitted only after an appropriate research proposal has been submitted to the organization's research and planning unit (or other qualified individual(s)) for review. This will be the case even if the research will be jointly conducted. The proposal must contain, at minimum, the area of research, the methodology to be used, and the rationale for conducting the research. If a research proposal is rejected, the researcher should be informed of the reasons for rejection. If the proposal is accepted, every cooperation should be extended to facilitate the research.

Joint Authorship. Whenever possible, there should be an opportunity for joint authorship of any articles resulting from the research. Even if this is not an option, it is important that the academic(s) conducting the research meet with correctional managers and other interested staff to share the results of the research before it is published. This allows the corrections professionals the opportunity to identify and advise of any perceived flaws in methodology, discussion, or conclusions. This opportunity to review should not be considered censorship. It is an expression of professional courtesy. On a more pragmatic level, pre-publication review may be a condition to be agreed to before permission to conduct the research will be granted.

Teaching Partnerships

Faculty and corrections professionals can create teaching partnerships in a number of interesting ways. Corrections professionals can be invited to team teach corrections-related courses with faculty, a process that can open the door to a more exciting level of student discussion than might otherwise occur. Team teaching can take place in both the campus classroom and the prison classroom. Faculty can be invited to lecture at correctional training academies on specialized subjects such as correctional law, courtroom behavior, principles of effective verbal and written communication, stress management, ethics, and conflict resolution techniques.

Those colleges and universities that have a University Day (a day in which classes are suspended and outside speakers are invited in to talk about their professions) can invite corrections professionals to speak to students in criminal justice, social work, sociology, and psychology. In addition, executive managers in corrections can actively encourage subordinate managers and line staff to enter degree programs. And, of course, corrections can invite faculty and students to tour prisons and community corrections facilities and allow them the opportunity to talk candidly with both staff and offenders. After the tour, both faculty and corrections professionals can field questions and integrate the information learned on the tour with the information previously presented in the classroom.

All of these activities will bring corrections and academia together in an interaction format well suited to question and answer sessions that can identify and decertify stereotypes. A particularly useful teaching partnership is one that brings faculty, students, and offenders together in the classroom. Such an approach has been pioneered in Maryland.

Inmates Teaching Ethics to College Students. An extremely valuable teaching partnership exists between the Federal Bureau of Prisons and the University of Maryland at College Park. On May 4, 1998, two business administration professors and eighty graduate business administration students went to the Federal Correctional Institution Cumberland to listen to three white collar offenders discuss the illegal business practices that had resulted in their incarceration. On May 5–6, an additional 120 students and 4 professors toured the Federal Prison Camp-Allenwood and spoke with other white collar criminals about their illegal activities. Prior to that experience, two Federal Prison Camp-Allenwood inmates were escorted to Susquehanna University to speak to seventy business law students about ethics in the workplace (Federal Bureau of Prisons, 1998b: 3).

Other universities have been quick to appreciate this approach of "hearing it from the horse's mouth." As of November 23, 1998, Susquehanna University, Bucknell University, and Pennsylvania State University have requested to participate in this program that teaches college students about the legal and ethical issues they will have to be prepared to face in the business world (Federal Bureau of Prisons, 1998c: 2).

The National Law Enforcement Explorers' Conference

Another example of university involvement in the criminal justice system also involves the University of Maryland at College Park. In 1998, the university hosted the July 20–25 National Law Enforcement Explorers' Conference. This conference brought together 3,500 Law Enforcement Explorers (Boy Scouts of America) and 1,000 police officer advisers for the purpose of a career fair and conference (Higginbotham, 1998). The event provided students with the opportunity to view law enforcement innovations and meet with career professionals to discuss the significant issues of the field. There is no reason corrections cannot participate in this type of activity. It would take a great deal of work with the Boy Scouts of America, but the American Correctional Association is in an excellent position to approach that organization and work with it to develop and sponsor a future National Corrections Explorers' Conference that could be hosted by a major university.

New Prison Siting

An outstanding example of a successful working relationship between corrections and academia is the State Correctional Institution-Pine Grove Task Force composed of representatives of the Pennsylvania Department of Correction and Indiana University of Pennsylvania. In Indiana, Pennsylvania, Indiana University of Pennsylvania faculty and corrections professionals have worked together to plan the siting and operation of the State Correctional Institution-Pine Grove: a new maximum-security institution for young adult offenders located a short distance from the Indiana University of Pennsylvania campus.

The State Correctional Institution-Pine Grove task force created a 135-page concept paper, "Models of Collaboration Between the Pennsylvania Department of Corrections, Indiana University of Pennsylvania, and the Indiana County Community" (Wells, 1998: 1) in which Indiana University of Pennsylvania faculty presented a wide range of theoretical and legal issues to be considered during planning and operation. This document has given the Department of Corrections the ability to more accurately anticipate future problems and act to reduce their impact.

It is anticipated that Indiana University of Pennsylvania faculty will be involved in the daily operation of many of the State Correctional Institution-Pine Grove's programs. This involvement will provide an excellent opportunity for faculty to get a firsthand look at the operation of a state prison. It also will give offenders and correctional personnel the opportunity to see faculty as individuals instead of stereotypical professors. The opportunities for consultation, joint research/publication, and team teaching will be remarkable. All of these processes will allow the Department of Correction to educate the faculty who will influence thousands of students over the life of their careers. After this experience, the faculty involved in this partnership should be less likely to promote negative correctional stereotypes.

Nontraditional Decertification Initiatives

Providing contextual information to decertify correctional stereotyping is not a process limited to academic settings. It can take place in a variety of other settings.

Having a Booth at the County Fair. The North Carolina Department of Correction in 1997 set up a Department of Correction booth at the Mountain State Fair near Asheville; the Dixie Classic in Winston-Salem; the State Fair in Raleigh; and the Columbus County Fair (North Carolina Department of Corrections, 1998b: 9). The employees staffing these booths were able to provide interested citizens with a broad range of written information about corrections as well as answer their questions.

The Inmate Job Fair. It is important to expose the business community to corrections because business professionals are influential members of the community. One method for increasing exposure is the inmate job fair. Many employers who once spurned the idea of recruiting inmates became receptive to viewing inmates as potential employees when a tight job market developed in the 1990s. Regardless of the level of corrections involved, job fairs are remarkably similar in structure. Typically, the inmates selected to participate in inmate job fairs have: attained pre-release status (usually defined as being within one-to-two years of release); completed prerequisite employment skills classes; written a professional resume; and practiced their interview skills with other inmates and correctional vocational counselors. Representatives of area companies are invited to interview the inmates for anticipated job vacancies. Prior to the actual job fair, inmates can hone their interviewing skills in a mock job fair. Employer reaction to inmate job fairs has been positive:

> In Austin (Texas), for example, Faulkner Construction Company has hired about 150 ex-offenders since 1992. At first, executives at other companies scoffed when they learned the company was recruiting at a jail house job fair, said Brian Faulkner, president of the company's concrete-pumping affiliate. "Now, I don't tell them," said Faulkner, adding that ex-offenders have preformed as well at their companies as people hired off the street. "I look at it as an untapped gold mine. . . . I'm thinking I don't want this to get out, or everyone and his dog will be going there, too" (Grimsley, 1998: A01).

The Prison Museum. The Louisiana State Penitentiary at Angola formally opened its prison museum on April 9, 1999. The purpose of the museum is to "preserve the prison's past and to educate all who visit, as to the role the prison has played in our state's history" (Tanner, 1999). The Louisiana State Penitentiary Museum's photographs and exhibits cover 130 years of correctional history. Angola also educates the public by allowing thousands of visitors to enter the prison for annual events such as the Angola Prison Rodeo in October and the Arts and Crafts Festival held on a spring weekend.

The Inmate Publication. A significant contribution to the prison literature has been created by inmates at Angola who publish a unique prison news magazine called *The Angolite*. This publication provides a wealth of information to readers. For example, the January/February 1998 issue noted on its "In This Issue" page a synopsis of the following articles:

DEATH AMONG US—Lane Nelson
At Louisiana State Penitentiary more lifers are dying than are being released. The population is aging, and death by natural causes is common. Hospice care for terminally ill patients has come to Angola. Specially trained inmate volunteers care for the dying, the system's alternative to compassionate release.

HIGH RISK-HIGH REWARD—Kerry Myers
For an ex-convict, odds for success are low. All too often they leave prison no better than when they entered, recidivism statistics waiting to happen. A novel experiment is underway in Angola called the Pre-Release Exit Program. Its purpose—to help releasees beat the odds. Only time can prove its worth.

OUT OF SIGHT—Lane Nelson
Hollywood came to Angola with a big budget movie, an award-winning director and celebrated actors. As a location site, the sprawling 18,000-acre prison proved far too good to pass up. Hundreds of prisoners were used as extras in the film, and the movie crew was amazed by what they learned at Angola.

The seventy-two pages of the January/February issue covered a variety of other events and issues in sections labeled: Mailbox; News Briefs; Death Watch; Inside Angola;

Book Review; Sports Front; Religion in Prison; Club News; Sounding Off; and Expressions. *The Angolite* provides valuable insights into corrections without reinforcing the negative stereotypes that are a cardinal feature of the traditional prison literature. Thus, it serves as a counterbalance to such works as *On the Yard*.

 The Angolite also has the distinction of having had many of its columns reprinted in a book, *Life Sentences: Rage and Survival Behind Bars* (Rideau and Wikberg, 1992). This book presents prison life from the view of the inmates and the chapter titled "The Sexual Jungle" provides a graphic account of prison rape that is frequently referenced in academic discussions of prison deprivation. Rideau is one of the most famous prisoners in the United States because of his ability to contribute to the prison literature. That contribution includes a movie, *The Farm*, about life at Angola that shared the Sundance Film Festival Grand Prize Award and was a 1999 Oscar nominee for the best documentary.

Providing Direct Services to the Community

Corrections can help the community by providing direct services to those community groups that have the greatest need for assistance. By helping others, corrections helps itself because acts of assistance encourage the general public to redefine their perception of corrections in nonstereotypical terms. Direct services are grouped into two broad categories: fund raising activities and sweat equity services.

 Fund Raising Activities. These activities assist special needs groups in the community to meet their basic life needs by providing them with additional financial resources that have been obtained through public and/or correctional employee contributions. Box 8-3 provides a random sampling of correctional fund raising activities. Many fund raising teams compete with each other to see who can raise the highest amount.

Box 8-3 Fund Raising Activities of Departments of Correction

In Maryland

Children with special needs are a favorite with correctional fund raisers. For example, Maryland Division of Correction employees:

> participated in Somerset County's first "Relay for Life" to benefit the American Cancer Society. Employees joined several hundred walkers who raised over $60,000 for this worthwhile cause. The $20,000 collected by seventeen ECI/PHPRU teams was from food sales, raffles, a car wash, individual solicitations and from ECI's Casual Day contributions (Miller, 1998: 5).

In Missouri

Eight Department of Corrections correctional centers took part in the "Cops and Lobsters" promotion during March to raise money for the Special Olympics. "Cops and Lobsters" involves law enforcement personnel serving as waiters/waitresses at area Red Lobster restaurants for a week, with the tips they receive going to benefit Special Olympics. Correctional officers raised a total of $3,184 for this worthy cause this year. Officers also raised additional money by selling T-shirts (Missouri Department of Corrections, 1998: 3).

In Washington

On July 21, 1998, Special Emergency Response Team members climbed Mount Saint Helens for a special fund raiser for the Special Olympics. The 8,365 foot climb raised over $2,500.00 for the Special Olympics (Glebe, 1998: 2).

In addition, the Coyote Ridge Corrections Centers' Combined Fund Drive raised $2,433.45 through such activities as: "a pool tournament, basketball tournament, volleyball tournament, bake sale, luncheon, potluck breakfast, pumpkin carving contest, pie in the face, paint ball tournament, baby picture contest, and a silent auction" (Martin, 1999: 7).

In Ohio

Director Reginald A. Wilkinson declared the week of July 5 "DRC Flood Relief Week" during which employees could "dress down" for a donation of $10 toward flood relief. Donations were collected from all 30 prisons, the eight regional parole offices and the central office divisions. The grand total collected reached almost $20,000 (Dean, 1998: 2).

Sweat Equity Services

Sweat equity is a term that refers to the labor of individuals being invested in a community. These services include responding to community emergencies; assisting low income and other needy groups with housing and home-related services; and reducing the cost of government. Sweat equity services substitute physical labor for money. A variety of physical activities can be undertaken to build equity in the community. The personal interaction that occurs between provider and recipient during these activities can change the recipients' perception of corrections.

Responding to Community Emergencies. Given the magnitude of many community emergencies, corrections professionals by themselves cannot provide the high level of assistance a community struck by disaster requires. Instead, they recruit offender volunteers (primarily inmates) to assist the communities through such activities as removing snow and ice, building flood levees, cleaning up natural disasters, and fighting forest fires. To cite only three examples out of an impressive list in 1998:

In Minnesota, Sentencing to Service offenders spent more than 8,000 hours helping to clean up the damage caused by the devastating tornados that struck Southwestern Minnesota in March. These offenders handled debris cleanup, tree and brush removal from roads and yards, and cleared power line easements so electrical power could be restored to communities (Minnesota Department of Corrections, 1998a: 3).

In North Carolina, inmates provided a full range of emergency assistance services under very difficult circumstances after Hurricane Bonnie battered North Carolina's coast for three days in late August. One hundred and two work crews with more than 1,000 inmates worked 12-hour days in heat indexes that rose as high as 105 degrees. Inmates from 29 prisons and the department of correction's IMPACT program participated in the community cleanups that lasted several weeks (Hardee, 1998: 1,7).

In Kansas, 36 minimum-custody inmates performed 384 hours of work sandbagging and cleaning up from flooding in the El Dorado area in early November, 1998. During four days of flooding along the Walnut and Arkansas Rivers near Winfield, 159 inmates spent 2,220 hours sandbagging and performing other flood-related activities (Kansas Department of Corrections, 1999: 9).

Providing Services to Community Special Needs Groups. Probationers, inmates, and parolees can create community service projects as diverse as: organizing runathons to solicit contributions for victims of disease; making Christmas toys for needy children; giving arts and crafts to sick children in a children's hospital; helping individuals with mental or physical disabilities; assisting the elderly; educating public school students about crime and drugs; translating books into braille for the blind; and building homes for the needy as part of a vocational training curriculum (Freeman, 1998).

Additional projects can include such activities as: donating money to food pantries; working with Habitat For Humanity; creating floral arrangements for the elderly in nursing homes; growing produce in prison gardens to supplement the diets of poor citizens; planting trees along highways; and engaging in a variety of home renovation projects for the poor and elderly.

Inmates can be very creative in providing direct services. For example, in California, inmates are involved in a unique program that provides wigs to children who have lost their hair because of illness. Inmates can donate braids, ponytails, and long hair to "Locks of Love," a company in Florida that makes children's wigs (California Department of Corrections, 1998).

In Minnesota, female inmates at the Minnesota Correctional Facility-Shakopee have volunteered to raise and socialize puppies for the first eighteen months of their lives for an organization called the Canine Companions for Independence (CCI). This organization is a nonprofit provider of service dogs for children and adults with disabilities. Shakopee inmates have raised seven puppies since their involvement with Canine Companions for Independence began in 1994. The program now has "two puppy-raisers, four puppy-sitters, three puppy-walkers, a waiting list of eighteen inmates who want to be involved in the program . . . "(Minnesota Department of Corrections, 1999b: 2).

Reducing the Cost of Government. Many inmate work programs are touted as reducing the cost of government. In Minnesota, for example, offenders working on Sentencing to Service (STS) crews during the 1996–97 biennium completed projects with an estimated market value of $11.6 million. Typical projects included river and park cleanup and improvement, trail development, including walking bridge construction, and litter pickup. The cost to the community for civilian workers would have been $8.4 million (Minnesota Department of Corrections, 1998b: 18).

In North Carolina, the Marion Minimum Security Unit's community work program completed 186 projects and saved taxpayers $452,751 in labor costs on such projects as installing roofs for local fire departments, renovating the county courthouse library and the Old Fort Police Department, building nature trails, installing carpet, and cleaning 100 buses for the county school system (Hardee, 1999: 12).

In Pennsylvania, inmates at the State Correctional Institution in Albion's vehicle restoration unit spent a year transforming an old bus pulled from a junkyard into the Department of Transportation's Mobile Driver and Vehicle Services Unit. Creation of this mobile driver services unit was accomplished for $107,000. The cost of a new bus, before conversion costs, would have been $250,000 (Hahn, 1999: 1B).

Every effort should be made to publicize offender activities with which the reasonable reader could identify or perceive as being beneficial to the community. There is, of course, a danger inherent in placing inmates on community work details: an inmate working in the community who escapes from the work detail, or escapes and commits a crime, or commits a crime while on the detail will not improve the public perception of corrections. Therefore, the decision to take inmates outside of the facility always should be based on the need to achieve legitimate penological goals, such as rehabilitation or community service. Inmates should never be placed outside of the facility solely for community education purposes.

Increasing Community Involvement in Corrections

Increasing community involvement in correctional activities can be accomplished in a number of different ways: community volunteer participation in correctional services delivery; community open houses; friend and family tours; youth tours; and citizen advisory boards.

Community Volunteers. Community volunteers possess a broad range of skills that will complement the activities of treatment staff. In addition, volunteers can benefit corrections by telling other citizens about their positive experiences with corrections professionals. They can provide correctional managers with feedback about the public's point of view on corrections-related issues and raise concerns which corrections professionals, upon reflection, decide they need to revisit. Volunteers are a bridge between corrections and the community.

Minimal effort is needed to develop a good working relationships with local Alcoholics Anonymous (A.A.), Narcotic Anonymous (N.A.) groups, and other self-help groups interested in working with offenders who have special problem areas, such as domestic violence, parenting problems, depression, and sexual disorders. Volunteers can provide chemical dependency support groups, anger and violence management groups, one-to-one mentoring, esteem building, and tutoring programs. A valuable source of volunteers are the local churches whose leaders fill prison chaplaincy positions and recruit volunteers interested in working with inmates who have turned to religion to address their problems.

Volunteers' contributions to corrections should be officially recognized during a ceremony and or dinner hosted by the organization's executive leadership. This recognition can take place during National Volunteer Month or as a special session of an Employee of the Month/Year Awards Ceremony. Appropriate certificates and/or plaques should be accompanied by a writeup about the volunteer in the organization's newsletter and a glowing press release sent to local and statewide news media.

Hosting the Community Open House. The community open house brings general members of the community into the correctional environment. The first element in conducting a successful community open house is to advertise the dates of the open house in the local newspapers. This advertisement can use the same provocative format as the Oregon Department of Corrections uses in advertising its legislative and media tours (*see* Chapter 6). The advertisement should note that visitors must submit their names far enough in advance that a national and local police check can be run to screen out individuals with criminal records. The name and phone number for the security person responsible for conducting these checks should be included in the advertisement. Visitors will be informed by letter that they have permission to enter the facility.

The second element is a security procedure that requires all visitors to sign in and be processed into the facility through a metal detector at the front gate. Drug dogs can be in the area, but great sensitivity must be exercised in the manner that these dogs are used. Too forceful a use of the dogs will reinforce smug hack imagery. Every visitor should be issued a readily identifiable visitor's pass which they must wear at all times. The number of badges issued will be recorded and this figure checked (and double checked) when the last visitor turns in his or her pass at the end of the tour. The right hand of each visitor should be stamped with an ink that is only visible under blue light. Inmates should not be permitted near the entrance to the prison when visitors are entering and leaving.

The third element is constant supervision by correctional officers during the tour. Officers should be at the front and rear of each tour group with no more than fifteen visitors in each group. After every stop, the rear officer should conduct a standing head count to make sure that no visitors have drifted away from the group. Any visitor who needs to use a restroom should be escorted to and from that restroom by a same-sex officer who ensures that the visitor returns to the group. Another officer should immediately search the restroom to ensure that no contraband has been dropped off. Close supervision of the visitors, without being threatening, is the key to maintaining tight security on a tour. All security procedures should be performed with courtesy so there will be no suggestion of smug hack corrections.

The Staff Family and Friends Tour. This is a variation on the community open house. Security concerns are considerably less because the visitors are the family members and personal friends of the correctional employees. This type of tour allows these individuals to see where the correctional employee works. The security precautions taken during the tour should, however, be the same because of liability issues.

The Youth Tour. Many jails, prisons, and juvenile correctional facilities allow public school students to tour their facilities, especially if those students have been defined by the school as at-risk youths. The idea is to show youth what is awaiting them if they violate, or continue to violate, the law. However, a Scared Straight approach is not recommended because experience has found this strategy to be relatively ineffective in changing juvenile behavior. All of the procedures noted for general community and family and friend tours also apply to the youth tour, but a special emphasis must be placed on supervision. Otherwise, a negative event can occur. Such an event occurred at the State Training Center in Monroe, New Jersey in the spring of 1999. Six high school students were separated from the sixteen-student group and "The mother of one student who participated in the tour told the Bergen Record that four inmates stripped her son and tried to sexually assault him, causing him to run naked from a housing unit" (*The Corrections Professional*, 1999: 2).

The media, legal, and public perception consequences of such an event are obvious. The strict supervision of all visitors is a critical requirement for any successful open house or tour.

The Citizen Advisory Board

The citizen advisory board can exist at two levels: central office and the field. The composition of the citizen's advisory board should reflect "a diverse membership with statewide representation. . . . that encompasses the legislature, the teaching profession, educational administration, criminal and juvenile justice, and a wide variety of community programs" (Minnesota Department of Corrections, 1999a: 1). The function of the advisory board is to provide the community a formal forum for expression of their perspective on correctional activities and advice on improving community-corrections relations. Therefore, different perspectives should be represented on the board.

The Impetus for Advisory Board Creation. Braunstein and Tyre (1994) report that citizen advisory boards are traditionally borne out of a sensational incident (a trigger incident) that grabs the community's attention in a sensationally negative way. This is a reactive approach that puts the correctional agency on the defensive. A more effective course of action for corrections is the proactive creation of a citizen advisory board long before a trigger incident occurs.

Representation on the Advisory Board. Corrections' representation always should include executive managers. Community groups that have expressed an interest in corrections should be invited to have representatives on the advisory board. However, the different perspectives of community representatives may create internal conflict. Elected officials may try to use the advisory board to promote a specific crime control agenda. American Civil Liberties Union representatives will want an emphasis placed on organizational behavior being consistent with due process requirements. Religious leaders will want corrections to strive to infuse spiritual values into the rehabilitation process. Liberals will want a maximum amount of resources channeled into rehabilitation. Conservatives will want those same resources dedicated to ensuring that security is the primary concern. Inmate family advocacy groups will want corrections to maximize the opportunity for inmate visits and other forms of family contact. As a result, meetings can be time-consuming and correctional managers may become frustrated by what appear to be an endless series of unproductive meetings in which the same arguments are repeated ad nauseam. This is frequently a negative result of encouraging a diversity of membership, but strong leadership by corrections can create a positive working environment.

Conducting the Advisory Board's Business. The advisory board's meeting schedule should be flexible, but there should be a minimum number of times the board meets: six times a year is common, although more meetings may become necessary if there is a trigger incident or serious community concerns expressed about policy changes that might affect the community. Meetings can be held in the community, within the correctional organization, or they can alternate between the community and corrections. A system of meeting alternation is best because it indicates that community and correctional needs are being given equal weight.

Advisory Board Activities. Quinn (1999) reports that advisory boards can engage in a variety of helpful activities. In Texas, advisory boards (Community Participatory Councils) involved in the parole process engaged in the following projects:

> . . . toured a treatment facility, conducted a training seminar for police, distributed crime avoidance pledge cards to local schools, submitted statements on victims' concerns to state's Attorney General, participated in vigil for victims, provided juice packets for victims, created a spiritual reintegration directory, created a resource directory for officers, created a resource pamphlet for releasees, created a job board for releasees, surveyed area employers for employment opportunities, hosted a community forum, held a job fair, cleaned/painted waiting and classroom areas in district field office, sponsored releasee art show, offered dress for success program, initiated scholarship fund for releasees' children, held agency information fair, produced video to recruit volunteers, used volunteers to create women's, family and spiritual support groups, and created and ran a speakers' bureau (Quinn, 1999: 83).

Advisory board involvement in the ACA accreditation process and in facility emergency plan development, testing, and evaluation also should be encouraged.

Although the advisory board is made up of volunteers and only has an advisory role, any correctional rejection of community suggestions should be explained carefully. For example, if there are substantial reasons for rejection of a citizens' request that a local prison install a whistle to be blown in the event of an escape, the reasons for that rejection should be carefully articulated. It is not enough to simply say "We don't think that's a good idea."

As Quinn (1999: 80) has noted: "The most fundamental goal (of the advisory board) is to provide a channel of communication between the field offices of a centralized state agency and the communities they serve." Curt responses and a failure to listen to legitimate community concerns will result in the disbanding of the board, the creation of hard feelings, and a confirmation that the popular culture of corrections has been right all along.

Points to Consider

1. In addition to the activities noted in this chapter, what activities would you suggest for increasing the general public's contextual information about corrections?

2. What challenges would be presented to a correctional employee participating in a speakers' bureau at the K-12 level? At the college level? How would you meet these challenges?

3. What challenges do internships present to faculty, practitioners, and students? How can these challenges be met?

4. What areas of research would be most beneficial to corrections? Why?

5. What other nontraditional educational initiatives can corrections develop?

6. What other sweat equity projects do you think would benefit the community?

7. What are the pros and cons of using prison inmates to assist communities during an emergency? How should these inmates be selected?

8. What will be the most important challenges during any type of community open house? How can these challenges be met?

9. What are the pros and cons of instituting a citizen advisory board?

References

American Prison Association. 1939. Presidential Address. *Proceedings of the Sixty-ninth Annual Congress of the American Prison Association.* New York, New York: American Prison Association.

Braunstein, S. and M. Tyre. 1994. Selling Your Community on a Citizen's Review Board. *Public Management.* 76(1): 12–15.

Caldwell, D. and E. W. Dorling. 1995. Networking Between Practitioners and Academics in Law Enforcement. *Public Administration Review.* 55(1): 107.

California Department of Corrections. 1998. California Inmates Donating Their Hair To Sick Children Who Need Wigs. News Release. February 18.

Cook County Department of Corrections. 1997. Program Services Sponsors 2nd Internship Open House. *The Key.* October.

The Corrections Professional. 1999. Juvenile Facility Tours Halted After Assault. 4 (17): 2.

Dean, A. 1998. DRC Flood Relief. *The Communicator.* Summer.

Desaulniers, K. A. 1998. WCI Sends K-9 Dogs To School. *Division News.* 5(10). Maryland Division of Correction.

Federal Bureau of Prisons.1998a. Dublin Staff Attend Career Day at Local School. *Monday Morning Highlights*. February 9.

———. 1998b. Allenwood, Cumberland Participate in Ethics Program. *Monday Morning Highlights*. May 18.

———. 1998c. FPC Allenwood Expands "White Collar" Ethics Program. *Monday Morning Highlights*. Nov. 23.

———. 1999d. FPC Loretto Inmates Participate in Red Ribbon Campaign. *Monday Morning Highlights*. November 8.

———. 1999e. USP Florence Staff Speak with At-Risk Youths. *Monday Morning Highlights*. January 11.

———. 1999f. FDC Philadelphia Participates in Shadowing Day. *Monday Morning Highlights*. November 23.

Ferrell, J. 1998. Criminalizing Popular Culture. In F. Bailey and D. Hale, eds. *Popular Culture, Crime and Justice*. Belmont, California: West/Wadsworth Publishing. pp. 71–83.

Freeman, R. M. 1998. Public Perception and Corrections: Correctional Officers as Smug Hacks. In F. Bailey and D. Hale, eds. *Popular Culture, Crime, and Justice*. Boston: West/Wadsworth.

Glebe, P. 1998. SERT Raises Money For Special Olympics. *The Communique*. 17(9). September.

Graber, D. 1989. *Mass Media and American Politics*, 3rd edition. Washington, D.C.: Congressional Quarterly Press.

Grimsley, K. D. 1998. A Job Fair's Captive Audience: Employers Resort to Wooing Inmates. *Washington Post*. September 7:A01.

Hahn, T. 1999. Albion Inmates Turn Junk Into Bus. Erie, Pennsylvania. *Morning News*. February 15.

Hardee, C. 1998. Bonnie Batters the Coast: Staff and Inmates Help Communities Clean Up the Damage. *Correction News*. October. North Carolina Department of Corrections.

Hardee, C. 1999. Poteat, Franklin Take Marion Work Program to Next Level. *Correction News*. January. North Carolina Department of Corrections.

Hazelton, J. S. and B. D. Shaffer. 1999. Unpublished paper.

Higginbotham, C. E. 1998. Personal correspondence. March 18.

Kansas Department of Corrections. 1998. *Monthly Newsletter*. 3(52). December.

———. 1999. Community Assistance During 1998 Flooding. *Monthly Newsletter*. 3(55). April.

Lopez, S. 1998. It's No Party in the County Jail: A Tough Sheriff's Inmates Live in Tents, Eat Ostrich Meat and Wear Pink Undies. *Time*. March 2, 151(8): 4.

Louisiana Department of Public Safety and Corrections. 1998a. Anyone at Your Place Get Shadowed on Ground Hog's Day? *Fax Facts*. February 16.

———. 1998b. *Fax Facts*. September 8.

———. 1998c. *Angolite*. January/February.

Mace, B. 1997. Bringing Braille to Delaware's Visually Impaired Students. *Smyrna Clayton Sun Times*. December 24.

Martin, J. 1999. CRCC Combined Fund Drive. *The Communique*. 18(2). February. Washington State Department of Corrections.

Miller, M. 1998. ECI/PHPRU Employees Raise $20,000 For Cancer. *Division News*. 5(10). Maryland Division of Correction.

Minnesota Department of Corrections. 1998a. Tornado Cleanup. *Perspective*. Volume 24. May-June.

———. 1998b. *1996–1997 Biennial Report*. St. Paul, Minnesota: Minnesota Department of Corrections.

———. 1999a. *Hotline*. 27: 4.

———. 1999b. *Hotline*. 27: 8.

Missouri Department of Corrections. 1998. Correctional Centers Raise Thousands for Special Olympics. *The Horizon*.12(2).

North Carolina Department of Correction. 1998a. Young Becomes First Female President of Lions Club. *Correction News*. September.

———. 1998b. It's Fair Time. *Correction News*. September.

Parilla, P. F. and S. L. Smith-Cunnien. 1997. Criminal Justice Internships: Integrating the Academic with the Experiential. *Journal of Criminal Justice Education*. 8(2): 225–241.

Quinn, J. 1999. Community Participation in the Parole Process: Texas' Community Participatory Councils. *Corrections Management Quarterly*. 3(2): 77–83.

Rideau, W. and R. Wikberg. 1992. *Life Sentences: Rage and Survival Behind Bars*. New York: Time Books.

Stritch, A. 1998. Division Continues to Reach Out to Johnston Square Elementary School—Receives Recognition in Baltimore Sun. *Division News*. 5(10). Maryland Division of Correction.

Tanner, N. 1999. Personal correspondence.

Washington Department of Corrections. 1999. *The Communique*. 18(5): 2.

Wells, R. 1998. Local Partnership with Prison Sought. Task Force: Indiana University of Pennsylvania Could Provide Many Services. Indiana, Pennsylvania. *Indiana Gazette*. February 17: 1–3.

Ethical
Employee Behavior:

The Foundation for the Decertification of Negative Stereotyping

During their examination of the relationship between the news media and the public perception of the police, Ericson, Baranek, and Chan (1989: 97) noted that "be cause [police] are in the media spotlight constantly, [they] are especially vulnerable to having their procedural strays focused upon. . . ." Although correctional employees are not in the "media spotlight" to the extent that police are, they are equally as vulnerable to public humiliation when their "procedural strays" are documented by the news media. This is particularly true when those "procedural strays" fall into the category of criminal behavior.

Crimes committed by correctional employees can be classified as being relatively rare and Websdale and Alvarez (1998:124) have noted that "Rarer forms of crime are newsworthy in part because of their rarity, but also because they lend themselves to graphic and sensationalistic reporting, which sells newspapers." Reporters are extremely interested in correctional employee misconduct, particularly if it involves violence or sex, especially forced sex, because of the inherent irony of a keeper of criminals being in the awkward position of having to prove that he or she does not belong on the other side of the bars with those criminals.

Creating a Double Echoing Loop. Manning (1998) defines a phenomenon called a *double echoing loop* in his discussion of the role of the news media in creating popular culture. This phenomenon has two elements. First, an actual event is reported by the news media in a manner that makes the viewers feel as though they are bearing personal witness to the event (Manning uses the example of the April 11, 1995, Oklahoma City bombing). Second, that event is framed by the news media in the context of a much larger category of similar events (Waco and Ruby Ridge provide the context in the Oklahoma City bombing example). The result of this framing is a "coherent sequence illustrating a type of event that is both fateful and consequential" (Manning, 1998: 34). The creation of a double echoing loop results in a restructuring of social reality. This concept is useful in examining the impact of job-related employee misconduct on the public acceptance of negative correctional stereotypes.

Employee Misconduct on the Job. Corrections professionals frequently express indignation when reporters use the descriptive title "guard." They complain that this is a word with negative connotations that is an inadequate descriptor in an era that has allocated resources to a professionalization of the correctional security work force that requires correctional officers to engage in human service activities and a level of employee-inmate interaction far more complex than the term "guard" suggests. In their efforts to remove this offensive word from the public's vocabulary, many correctional managers require their organization's publications to use the title "corrections officer" or "correctional officer." These same managers frequently will conduct a personal lobbying campaign to persuade news media reporters, editors, and directors to avoid the use of the stigmatizing title "guard" in their articles and newscasts.

In many U.S. newsrooms, these efforts have paid off and "guard" has been removed from the reporter's lexicon and replaced with the more positive title sought by corrections professionals. The anticipated payoff for corrections is seeing security staff referenced by a title that connotes a level of professionalism far above the level required of mere "guards." So, what happens next? On Wednesday, June 9, 1999, Bill Miller of the *Washington Post* reported:

> A former D.C. jail inmate told a jury yesterday that she once got an $825 tip from a corrections officer after performing a striptease. Now she is seeking millions of dollars in civil damages, saying she was forced to strip and subjected to other abuses during her incarceration four years ago. Jacqueline Newby said she felt "humiliated, embarrassed and stupid" after shedding her clothes in a dance for corrections officers in July 1995. She said she performed on three nights that month, including one evening in which she and other inmates covered themselves with baby oil. "It was getting real crazy," said Newby, adding that officers were rooting for the strippers as they danced atop a table. "It was pretty much out of control" (Miller, 1999: B06).

Yes, the reporter has been receptive to the efforts to educate him to employ the term corrections officer instead of guard, but where is the victory for corrections? In this case, the term corrections officer is being used in the context of an ugly, degrading story that supports so many negative stereotypes about corrections that it easily could have been the product of a Hollywood writer. A title intended to create a public perception of professionalism and respectability now becomes just another synonym for smug hack corrections. This particular association of title and negative imagery will be an enduring one because of the sensational nature of the factual knowledge in the newspaper article. Sex sells: the erotic image of lusting guards forcing sexy captive women to expose bodies glistening with baby oil as they dance on a table within the stark confines of a jail will remain in the public mind long after the names of all of the participants and location of the incident have been forgotten.

The Double Echoing Loop. The Miller article is balanced. It points out that the jail managers admit to having problems with "rogue officers" and have taken appropriate disciplinary action against twelve corrections officers accused of this misconduct. Ms. Newby's criminal history, use of illegal drugs since the age of thirteen, and history of being an exotic dancer who engaged in sexual activity with members of her audience for money is presented in the article. There is no attempt in the article to cast Ms. Newby as an innocent victim forced into deviant behavior she would otherwise shun by a corrupt system.

The problem for corrections is that other reporters may broaden the perspective of the Miller article by framing its content within the context of a larger social issue, such as sexual abuse in domestic violence situations, or the sexual abuse of women in the military, or national examples of sexual abuse of female inmates such as the Georgia sex scandal noted in Chapter 4. Radical feminist groups may decide to use the article to bolster their argument that men regard women as sexual objects and nothing more. There are any number of ways that the Miller article can be placed in the context of a larger social issue with similar themes. The result is a magnification of a single instance of employee misconduct that will tarnish the reputations of correctional employees in general.

In addition, the alleged activities of the jail correctional officers will remain in the public view long after the Miller article has been read. At the time the article appeared, a second inmate had already received a $5.3 million verdict in a civil suit filed in response to sexual abuse by the jail employees and two other lawsuits had been filed: one by an inmate who said she also was forced to perform stripteases, another by an inmate who said she was beaten because she refused to perform. Each time there is a public hearing on these lawsuits, it is likely that the sexual abuse imagery once again will be presented to the public, especially if the plaintiffs win, and the potential for creation of a double echoing loop will increase with each presentation.

Image Damage Even if the Double Echoing Loop Is Avoided. Although the article does not raise this subject, there are a number of dispositions possible in these lawsuits. Ms. Newby and the other two plaintiffs may not be victorious. The $5.3 million verdict won by the second inmate may be overturned. It almost certainly will be reduced by an appellate court if the verdict is upheld.

But none of this will matter to the general public even if the news media reports these outcomes if and when they occur. The reason it will not matter is because the public's initial perception of the D.C. jail correctional officer's alleged behavior has been negative, and this behavior will have contributed one more ugly example of "guard" misconduct to the vast depths of the popular culture of corrections long before the appellate courts are able to render a decision. Even if the news media does not frame the misconduct of the jail correctional officers in the context of a larger social issue, and a double echoing loop is not created, the imagery contained in the Miller article will resonate with the imagery of B-Class prison movies already firmly embedded in the minds of the readers of the article.

Stereotypical Employee Behavior in the Community. Correctional employees also can undergo public scrutiny when they are off the clock and engaging in normal community activities. The old chestnut about an organization's employees being its ambassadors when they are in the community is worth remembering:

> When it comes to promoting the image of corrections, they are always on duty. Courtesy and professionalism must always be the watchwords. Whether line staff are greeting visitors to the facility, chasing escapees, attending PTA meetings, coaching Little League, basketball, and soccer games, on duty in community hospitals, testifying in court, or simply commuting to and from the job, they must be professional in their community interaction (Freeman, 1999: 32).

Unfortunately, when correctional employees in a community setting engage in inappropriate and offensive behavior and that behavior is witnessed by members of the general public, a social phenomenon similar to a double echoing loop can occur. The only difference in this situation is that the news media does not initiate the loop process by reporting some distant event, although it, undoubtedly, will play a role in reinforcing the imagery of the event. Therefore, the dissemination of negative imagery that is created by the witnessed event will be to a much smaller audience. However, the basic principle is the same.

For example, this author was in a bookstore one day after work in 1998 when at least fifteen patrons waiting in line at the cash register at the front of the store observed four state prison correctional officers, in uniform, standing at the rear of the store in front of a rack of hardcore men's magazines. One correctional officer, a big-bellied sergeant with garish female tattoos on both forearms, was holding open an issue of *Hustler*, and commenting graphically on the women displayed inside. The other correctional officers were laughing loudly, making obscene comments, and, generally, behaving like adolescents. A grandmotherly woman who was tightly holding the hand of a young girl while waiting to make her purchase turned to the other customers standing in line at the checkout register and loudly proclaimed: "Isn't it just grand to know that we have perverts guarding the perverts?"

This event was the personal witnessing element of the creation of what could be termed a double echoing loop for the store patrons. The larger context for this inappropriate behavior will eventually be supplied by the news media and/or the entertainment media. The next evening news segment highlighting allegations of female inmates being abused in a state prison and/or the next prison movie that shows prison or jail "guards" forcing female inmates to participate in unsavory sexual activities is likely to be uncritically accepted by those witnesses as an accurate portrayal of correctional officers, especially if they have also read the Bill Miller article.

After all, their experiential knowledge now validates the factual knowledge in the news media report. And if these witnesses hear discussions about female sexual abuse in domestic violence situations or any other issues involving the sexual abuse of women, this event may inform their acceptance or rejection of the arguments being presented by the discussants. For the patrons of that store, a "coherent sequence" was created by those four correctional officers and their adolescent enjoyment of *Hustler*. Another element was added to their social construction of corrections.

Creating a Perceptual Ripple Effect. In addition, when any member of the general public personally witnesses disturbing correctional employee behavior, the result is acquisition of an interesting anecdote for discussion with friends and family. This will create a perceptual ripple effect. A single incident of personally witnessing inappropriate behavior or misconduct by a correctional employee can influence the perception of dozens of people who did not actually witness the behavior. As a result, all the employee-of-the-month award press releases, glowing articles about fund raising and sweat equity events, and human interest stories about personal service to the community will not undo the reinforcement of negative stereotyping accomplished by the correctional officers in the bookstore and the Washington D.C. jail.

Employee Language as a Reinforcer of Stereotypical Imagery. It is not just behavior that reinforces negative stereotyping. The language correctional employees use in discussing their work also can contribute to the constructed image of corrections. Many correctional officers, especially males, relish the imagery of a tough officer doing a demanding job in a dangerous environment that a weaker individual could never handle. They enjoy telling frightening war stories that demonstrate their physical toughness and ability to control very dangerous inmates. In telling these war stories, officers often exaggerate the personal dangers to which they are exposed. For example, note the exaggeration in the words of a male correctional officer who is protesting the hiring of female officers:

A lot of things can happen to you in here—guards get killed every day. When I go into a dangerous situation, I want to know that my partner is going to be there to help me. You just can't count on a woman. And even if you can, what is she going to do? Is she going to be able to pull an inmate off my throat before he has the chance to kill me? No way in hell! (Zimmer, 1986: 55).

Obviously, there is no prison in America (nor has there ever been) where "guards get killed every day." For whatever reason, this correctional officer needed to present the image of masculine toughness so characteristic of the prison movie guard. And the anti-woman sentiment being expressed certainly runs counter to the executive managers' emphasis on women being equal partners in corrections. It is also interesting that this particular individual seems to prefer the use of the word guard. Some correctional officers may consider guard to be a more masculine descriptor than correctional officer.

A New Set of Images: The Ethical Employee

In his comprehensive review of the numerous prison movies made between 1929 and 1995, Derral Cheatwood (1998) notes that one of the fundamental structural elements of the prison film has been a powerful theme of injustice, either justice denied or "a surrealistic, malevolent, or abstracted justice that has little concern with individual lives, or is a dictatorial force that confronts the individual" (Cheatwood, 1998: 214). The heart and soul of smug hack corrections is immoral employee behavior in the consistent service of "malevolent" injustice. The recurring and primitive structural themes of physical brutality; exploitation of inmate labor; racial prejudice; sexual abuse of female inmates; staff incompetence, corruption, and cruelty; and the condoning of homosexual rape involve destructive activities that debase and degrade individuals by denying them the most basic human dignity, destroying their potential to grow and change, and promoting injustice. These activities are the epitome of the immoral behavior that is the hallmark of systemic injustice. They are the antithesis of behavior based on religious principles and community values. Because of the power of Hollywood, and the seductiveness of the theme of "malevolent" injustice, community education strategists must present to the general public an alternative set of equally powerful images: correctional employees as ethical individuals.

The creation of these alternative images will occur only if corrections' executive managers are successful in developing and maintaining an organizational culture that nurtures and rewards ethical behavior. An ethical organizational culture is a culture in which both employee behavior and system behavior are guided by the goal of doing justice, a goal that requires adherence to the fundamental moral principle that personal conduct must be fair and not unlawfully harm others. The centerpiece of an ethical organizational culture is the code of ethics: a written policy that articulates the promotion of justice as an element of the mission of corrections.

The Code of Ethics/Code of Conduct

Because correctional organizations are located in every county in the United States, it is appropriate that there be national guidelines to help structure the code of ethics for individual organizations. National guidelines have been provided by the American Correctional Association's Code of Ethics (*see* Box 9-1). The ACA code acknowledges the rule of law, is periodically revised to reflect changing conditions in the work and external environment, and provides guidelines for doing justice.

BOX 9-1 American Correctional Association Code of Ethics

PREAMBLE
The American Correctional Association expects of its members unfailing honesty, respect for the dignity and individuality of human beings and a commitment to professional and compassionate service. To this end, we subscribe to the following principles.

Members shall respect and protect the civil and legal rights of all individuals.

Members shall treat every professional situation with concern for the welfare of the individuals involved and with no intent to personal gain.

Members shall maintain relationships with colleagues to promote mutual respect within the profession and improve the quality of service.

Members shall make public criticism of their colleagues or their agencies only when warranted, verifiable, and constructive.

Members shall respect the importance of all disciplines within the criminal justice system and work to improve cooperation with each segment.

Members shall honor the public's right to information and share information with the public to the extent permitted by law subject to individuals' right to privacy.

Members shall respect and protect the right of the public to be safeguarded from criminal activity.

Members shall refrain from using their positions to secure personal privileges or advantages.

Members shall refrain from allowing personal interest to impair objectivity in the performance of duty while acting in an official capacity.

Members shall refrain from entering into any formal or informal activity or agreement which presents a conflict of interest or is inconsistent with the conscientious performance of duties.

Members shall refrain from accepting any gifts, service, or favor that is or appears to be improper or implies an obligation inconsistent with the free and objective exercise of professional duties.

Members shall clearly differentiate between personal views/statements and views/statements/positions made on behalf of the agency or Association.

Members shall report to appropriate authorities any corrupt or unethical behaviors in which there is sufficient evidence to justify review.

Members shall refrain from discriminating against any individual because of race, gender, creed, national origin, religious affiliation, age, disability, or any other type of prohibited discrimination.

Members shall preserve the integrity of private information; they shall refrain from seeking information on individuals beyond that which is necessary to implement responsibilities and perform their duties; members shall refrain from revealing nonpublic information unless expressly authorized to do so.

Members shall make all appointments, promotions, and dismissals in accordance with established civil service rules, applicable contract agreements, and individual merit, rather than furtherance of personal interests.

BOX 9-1 American Correctional Association Code of Ethics (continued)

Members shall respect, promote, and contribute to a work place that is safe, healthy, and free of harassment in any form.

Adopted August 1975 at the 105th Congress of Correction

Revised August 1990 at the 120th Congress of Correction

Revised August 1994 at the 124th Congress of Correction

(Source: American Correctional Association, 1997.)

Every code of ethics is unique because it is the product of an organization's unique priorities, challenges, and history. However, all codes specifically reject the themes and behavior of "malevolent" injustice that form the core of the popular culture of corrections. They all mandate that employees are to conduct business in a way that does not reinforce negative stereotyping. A good example of a department of corrections code of ethics is that of the Kansas Department of Corrections. Box 9-2 shows this code, which was adopted in December, 1998. Note that the code is applied to contract personnel and volunteers as well as correctional employees.

Once the code of ethics has been formally published, all employees, current and new, should be required to sign a statement that they intend to govern their professional behavior in accordance with the provisions of the code of ethics.

The Code of Conduct. The code of ethics is only the first step. Many of the phrases used in that policy statement can be subject to differential interpretation. Therefore, the code of ethics must be reinforced by creation and dissemination of a second document that operationalizes its spirit and intent by providing specific examples of acceptable and prohibited behavior. This document is the code of conduct.

Translating the Code of Ethics into Personal Behavior

Because many applicants will have preconceived ideas about correctional work based on the popular culture of corrections, preemployment interviewers should be on the alert for any suggestion that an applicant is interested in corrections because of a desire, or proclivity, to engage in stereotypical behavior. This requires the development of comprehensive recruiting, interviewing, and hiring procedures that rely on psychological testing, making extensive background checks, and using ethics-based interview questions. Hiring individuals with a high potential for ethical behavior reduces the probability of the occurrence of individual misconduct or participation in a corrections horror story.

Executive managers also can promote ethical employee behavior by making personal adherence to ethical principles one of the official criteria for promotion. Promoting individuals whose personal integrity is outstanding, and letting it be known that ethical behavior is one of the criterion for promotion, will pay dividends in encouraging staff to engage in ethical behavior.

Introducing the Code of Ethics. Corrections' executive managers always should take the lead in introducing new employees to the ethical principles defining the organizational culture. This leadership is critical because stated expectations for ethical behavior will be given the greatest credibility if they initially come from the manager at the top of the organization. An example of this type of leadership is shown in Box 9-3.

BOX 9-2 Kansas Department of Corrections' Code of Ethics

As an employee, contract personnel or volunteer of the Kansas Department of Corrections, I will value and maintain the highest ideals of professionalism and public service in carrying out my duties and responsibilities.

I will respect the dignity of individuals, the rights of all members of society and the potential for human growth, development and behavioral change. I accept that it is my fundamental duty to serve the public; to safeguard lives and property; and to maintain an environment free of deception, oppression or intimidation, violence or disorder. I will exercise power and authority prudently and within the limits of the law.

I will recognize the fact that I have power over the lives of offenders, and will not abuse that power in any way, including by attempting to establish any form of personal relationship with an offender, or take any action toward or concerning an offender which advances a personal interest or cause of my own.

I will be constantly mindful of the welfare of others. To the best of my ability, I will remain calm in the face of danger and maintain self-restraint in the face of ridicule.

I will treat all persons with respect and dignity, and will not mistreat any person based on that person's race, gender, nationality or religious beliefs. I will not engage in any conduct that results in hostility or offense on the basis of sex, nor in any way improperly introduce any sexual material or activity into the workplace.

I will be honest and truthful. I will be exemplary in obeying the law and following the rules and regulations of the Department. I will promote honesty and ethical behavior over loyalty to individuals. I will immediately report dishonest or unethical conduct or any violation or apparent violation of the department's rules and regulations.

I will use public funds in a fiscally responsible manner. I acknowledge that I have been selected for a position of public trust. I will constantly strive to be worthy of that trust and to be true to the mission and values of the Department of Corrections (Kansas Department of Corrections, 1999: 2. Reprinted with permission of the Kansas Department of Corrections).

The next step in creating an ethical organizational culture involves reinforcing the fundamental principles of those codes. This is accomplished through a schedule of employee training that begins with the new recruits and is periodically repeated in the form of inservice training held at least every two years.

Employee Ethics Training

Correctional employees at every level require training in the principles governing ethical behavior. Ethics training should begin during the initial training phase when the new employee is introduced to the correctional environment. The most effective ethics training starts with a five-to-six hour series of courses that are part of the basic training core curriculum. These courses cover the basic principles of ethical behavior, the organization's code of ethics/conduct, and the opportunities for unethical behavior that are most likely to be encountered in the daily routine. The trainers should use a lecture-group discussion-scenarios format. After the lecture and discussion portion of the class, new employees can

BOX 9-3 Letter From the Superintendent of
State Correctional Institution-Albion to New Employees

Dear New SCI Albion Employee:

What is a prison? What is SCI-Albion about?

Prisons are complex human organizations which attempt to simulate normal society within an abnormal environment. SCI-Albion is a "normal" prison with a difference. It has an environment in which the staff tolerate the defects of the human condition, yet strive toward being firm but fair while maintaining the highest level of security. It is a community within a community, a microcosm of the general society reflecting its defects and its accomplishments. SCI-Albion's mission is not only to protect society but also reflects a value system which recognizes the ability of the individual to change. It is not intended to be a "nice" place to live yet always holds the carrot of freedom beyond the razor ribboned fence. It is, however, a place of hope—a place where an individual's responsibility for their actions will be a primary precept and self-change can be accomplished. SCI-Albion is a reflection of the community at large and will be held to the highest standard of integrity and human dignity. Staff are valued, their input given the highest credibility. Inmates are accountable and their future lives returned to their hands. Hopefully, the staff and inmates will see that there is a common ground in which they both have an equal stake for survival. Their lives interact on a daily basis, creating a mini society in which individual behavior is reflected in mutual respect.

So what is a prison? A prison is a reflection of us, the society which created it. It is as good as we are and as bad. Since it does reflect the best and the worst of us, we must always strive to ensure that the good prevails. I assure you, SCI-Albion will always strive towards being the "Best."

These are my goals for SCI-Albion, a correctional facility which will fulfill the objectives which our society has set for it, and which will at the same time, present new opportunity and challenges for its residents. They will leave sober, with improved educational abilities, and ready to work.

As Martin Luther King once said, "the time is always right to do what is right." Correctional employees must always be guided by our Code of Ethics, our Standards and Beliefs on the Treatment of Inmates, and good old common sense. The job we have is a noble one, it serves and protects our society. Always be proud of your role as Corrections' Professionals.

Sincerely,
Edward T. Brennan
Superintendent

(Source: Pennsylvania Department of Corrections, 1999. Reprinted with permission of the Pennsylvania Department of Corrections).

be provided a series of scenarios based on real life situations and given the opportunity to debate the most ethical course of action in each situation. The Minnesota Department of Corrections uses scenarios that create the opportunity for new employees to choose ethical behavior that advances the mission or unethical behavior that advances the popular culture of corrections.

Ethics Refresher Training. At least every two years every correctional employee should attend a two-to-four hour ethics refresher course. The lecture-group discussion-scenarios format can be used, but the scenarios should be updated to reflect the employee's higher level of experience. In addition, every employee promoted to a supervisory position should be required to take a special supervisor's ethics course that focuses on the potential for personal abuse of their new authority, identification of subordinate ethical violations, and techniques for correcting unethical employee behavior. Executive managers are not exempt from ethics training. There should be special courses for ensuring that top managers are also up-to-date on the best techniques for defining and promoting ethical behavior.

Ethics training reinforces the principles, rules, and regulations contained in the code of ethics/conduct, but these also must be reinforced outside of the training environment. There needs to be a structural mechanism available to help keep the issue of ethics alive in the minds of employees after they have completed their latest round of training.

The Ethics Committee. Dr. Sam Souryal, a criminal justice professor at Sam Houston State University in Huntsville, Texas, has suggested that one way of making ethics a permanent part of the employee's work orientation is for correctional managers to create an ethics committee, the membership of which is elected by the employees, not appointed by the managers. This committee can function as an advisory board that is charged with the responsibility to "identify problems, potential problems and ethical trends. It can also produce advisory opinions on discipline, punishments and policy changes" (quoted in *The Corrections Professional,*1998: 7). The members of the ethics committee also can plan and host ethics workshops and seminars, put information about ethical issues on employee bulletin boards, and include stories about ethical and unethical behavior, both inside and outside of corrections, in employee newsletters. All of these activities will act as a continuous reinforcement of the lessons learned in formal training.

The Executive Manager as Ethical Role Model

Every correctional manager has a professional obligation to act as a positive role model that offenders and line staff will want to emulate as they go about their daily routine. When it comes to promoting ethical employee behavior, managers must talk the talk and walk the walk.

Talking the Talk and Walking the Walk. It is the fundamental responsibility of every correctional manager to be a positive role model for both line staff and offenders. Talking the talk, but not walking the walk is always a mistake. Managerial lapses in ethical behavior are destructive because of the authority, power, and high degree of visibility possessed by these individuals. For example, in 1998 a major at an Eastern maximum-security prison received a fifteen-day suspension for his behavior during a cultural sensitivity class. The major:

> walked into the class wearing a white paper lunch bag with eye holes over his head and sat down. . . . sat in the seat for about five minutes, did not say a word, then stood up and left the room. Black employees in the class told their bosses that they viewed the incident as racially insensitive because the white bag resembled the hoods worn by members of the Ku Klux Klan (Bucsko, 1998).

This behavior is especially repulsive because of the theme of racial prejudice that has always been woven through the tapestry of smug hack corrections. The result of this type of ethical lapse may well be the promotion of racial bigotry among line staff. When managers are unethical, the constructed image of corrections gains vitality.

Policy Responses to Identified Ethical Violations

Executive managers must identify and develop a plan of action for managing specific categories of unethical behavior whenever examples of that behavior appear. This requires the use of the full range of resources available to the organization. Take, for example, the sexual abuse of female inmates by correctional employees. The Michigan Department of Corrections has developed an effective model for confronting this serious problem. Box 9-4 provides the Michigan Department of Corrections' description of that model.

This policy identifies the violation of ethical principles and defines a course of systemic activity to reduce the potential for a type of abusive behavior that is presented in prison movies and prison literature as commonplace. Unfortunately, the Michigan Department of Corrections continued to receive allegations of sexual misconduct by its employees after formulation of this policy. And this raises a critical point.

Policy created for the purpose of preventing employee misconduct must be developed and presented in ethics training before the new recruit begins service or prior to the opening of a new facility. The reason why proactive policy development is critical can be easily illustrated by one example. In December, 1999, thirteen employees at the Virginia Department of Corrections' Fluvanna Correctional Center for Women reportedly resigned or were fired for "allegedly sexually assaulting, harassing or fraternizing with inmates" (*USA Today*, 1999). The facility had been open for only five months. As this example demonstrates, deviant employee behavior symptomatic of ethical rot can develop very quickly. And the most serious ethical rot will be manifested in the corrections horror story.

Policy to Prevent the Corrections Horror Story

Corrections horror stories always involve gross violations of the code of ethics. It is incumbent upon correctional managers to identify those correctional initiatives that have the highest potential for becoming a corrections horror story and initiate proactive action through the creation and dissemination of policy designed to mitigate the development of group ethical violations. The first potential corrections horror story to be examined involves the supermax prison.

The Supermax as the Next Big Corrections Horror Story. Supermax prison inmates are kept in their cells twenty-three hours a day and allowed no physical contact with other inmates and only minimal contact with correctional employees. Because of these conditions, the supermax prison is generally acknowledged as effective in reducing institutional violence. For example, in the 1970s, before California built its first supermax prison, one out of every 1,200 inmates was murdered by another inmate. As of 1996, that statistic had changed to one out of every 12,000 inmates (Gavora, 1996: 7).

However, the nature of the inmates confined in the supermax prison and the punitive control orientation that emphasizes security above every other consideration has had the unintended consequence of creating a fertile breeding ground for employee misconduct. State Correctional Institution-Greene, mentioned previously, has already seen what can happen when group ethical violations occur in a supermax prison. However, it is unlikely that Pennsylvania will be the only supermax horror story. In fact, the ACLU's National Prison Project, the National Campaign to Stop Control Unit Prisons, and the Clinton Justice Department already have signaled their concern about the proliferation of supermax prisons across the county and the manner in which they are being operated (Gavora, 1996: 7). For

**Box 9-4 The Michigan Department of Corrections'
Sexual Misconduct Management Model**

Michigan's efforts in dealing with sexual misconduct include:

- Defining improper relationships with prisoners for employees in the employee handbook.

- A clear policy on dealing with allegations of such conduct.

- Giving inmates procedures for filing complaints in the prisoners' guidebook and giving inmates access to outside counseling, the Corrections Ombudsman and court monitors.

- Sanctions for sexual harassment and misconduct, including dismissal.

- Lobbying for passage of a state law which makes such behavior a fourth-degree Criminal Sexual Conduct crime for employees. But the department helps employees avoid such behavior in the first place through a variety of training courses.

- Anatomy of a Set-Up is a six-hour mandatory class for new prison employees telling them what to watch for to avoid being used and manipulated by prisoners. This includes watching out for sexual innuendos and overfamiliarity which can lead to compromising security as well as sexual misconduct.

- New employees are also required to take a four-hour class explaining the department's policies on sexual harassment. The class tells employees what constitutes sexual harassment and gives them information on how to report it and how to prevent it. Existing employees are given a two-hour refresher course every two years.

- All employees are required to take a three-hour course in the employee handbook, which reviews all department work rules, including improper relations with prisoners including sexual conduct. Employees are told and given the handbook which says that sexual contact with a prisoner is a criminal offense.

- All employees who work in women's prisons must complete a 40-hour course on the Special Needs of the Female Offender. This class teaches professionalism in dealing with women offenders. It provides information on how women offenders act in a prison setting, their psychological and mental health problems and why they act the way they do.

- There is a four-hour mandatory inservice class for non-custody staff in avoiding over familiarity with prisoners, and an 11-hour mandatory inservice class for custody staff on how to manage prisoners safely. This class focuses mostly on crisis intervention techniques but can deal with over-familiarity issues

(Quoted from the Michigan Department of Corrections, 1998: 20. Reprinted with the permission of the Michigan Department of Corrections).

example, in 1996, the Assistant Attorney General for Civil Rights in the U.S. Department of Justice, Patrick Deval, charged in a thirteen-page letter to Governor Parris Glendening that Maryland's supermax prison (the Maryland Correctional Adjustment Center) was:

> . . . violating inmates' constitutional rights through a range of offenses from inadequate exercise equipment to lukewarm meals. He gave the state 49 days to comply with a three-page list of "necessary remedial measures," or else face a federal lawsuit (Gavora, 1996: 6).

Maryland Division of Correction officials expressed outrage at the accusations. But expressions of outrage do not prevent a correctional program from becoming fodder for a news media expose. Correctional managers can minimize the potential for supermax horror stories by developing specific written policy. An example of the content of this type of policy is found in Box 9-5.

The aggressive managerial approach to the operation of a supermax facility demonstrated in Box 9-5 will not guarantee that employee misconduct will never occur, but it certainly will reduce the potential for that misconduct and the news media documentation of the corrections horror story (soon to be optioned by Hollywood) that will follow.

A Rapidly Expanding Corrections Horror Story: The Juvenile Boot Camp. Since Louisiana opened the first juvenile boot camp in 1985, more than 60 of these facilities have come on line. In January, 2000, Maryland's governor ordered the closing of the Savage Leadership Challenge Camp after a state task force found "29 possible cases of excessive force, child abuse and simple assault" (*The Corrections Professional*, 2000: 4). The report:

> . . . documented juvenile's bloodied heads, head lacerations and frostbite caused by guards' discipline. Guards also reportedly used racial slurs and one was fired for beating a youth on the torso with a steel arrow. The report concluded that most of the abuse went unpunished (*The Corrections Professional*, 2000: 4).

The article noted that the FBI was also investigating allegations of physical abuse at other youth boot camps in Maryland. At roughly the same point in time, the director of California's youth corrections agency was forced to resign "following an investigation that revealed a pattern of brutality at one of the state's facilities" (APBNews.com, 1999). Creation and dissemination of policy along the lines suggested in Box 9-5 would be useful in preventing juvenile boot camp horror stories.

Given human nature, there always will be a small subset of correctional employees who will ignore policy and training and the actions of role models and choose to engage in unethical behavior. This is the rationale for department of corrections' and large county jail systems creating internal affairs units. Often, these units are designated as the Office of Professional Responsibility or Special Services Unit, and one of their primary responsibilities is to administratively remove unethical employees from the correctional system. However, if all of the elements of an ethical organizational culture presented in this chapter are fully embraced, the workloads of these special units will be reduced significantly.

Ethical Behavior and Community Education

A written code of ethics/conduct provides correctional managers with an opportunity to increase the level of contextual information possessed by the publics that are of concern to community education strategists. The codes provide written evidence of the organization's desire to discharge all of its responsibilities in an ethical manner.

Box 9-5 Creating Policy to Prevent the Supermax Horror Story

The authors of this policy should remember the worst prison movies they have ever seen and then ask the question: What can we do to reduce the potential for that kind of employee behavior in our new supermax prison? To counter the potential for smug hack corrections behavior, the policy should, at minimum, include:

1. A written mission statement for the supermax prison

2. Definition of the categories of inmates to be confined

3. A well-designed classification and referral system, which ensures that only the most dangerous (as objectively defined) inmates are sent to supermax. The effectiveness of this system should be reviewed on an annual basis.

4. A well-designed behavioral evaluation system to ensure that inmates are kept in supermax status only until it has been determined that they can be transferred to a less secure facility. The effectiveness of this system should be reviewed on an annual basis.

5. Definition of the qualifications of the correctional employees who will staff the prison

6. Written policy and procedures governing every aspect of the facility operation with an emphasis on use-of-force policy

7. A code of ethics/conduct to govern employee behavior with an emphasis on use-of- force policies

8. Specialized training for all supermax employees with periodic inservice training to reemphasize the code of ethics/conduct and organizational policy

9. An aggressive central office investigation of all inmate complaints, no matter how farfetched

10. A policy of rotation of employees to prevent the development of a negative organizational culture

11. Frequent, unannounced central office inspections to ensure employee compliance with the code of ethics/conduct and all organizational policy

12. Full managerial accountability for the unethical behavior of subordinates

13. Access of the news media and inmate advocate groups to the facility

14. Annual evaluations of every facet of the operation by central office managers with the immediate correction of deficiencies

In addition, ethical employee behavior based on those codes supports a community education strategy in three ways. First, ethical behavior will deny the news and entertainment media the vivid examples of current employee misconduct that support the constructed image of corrections. Second, ethical behavior will create a steady and readily available supply of factual material for the press releases, human interest articles, annual reports, and employee-of-the-year award ceremonies that are now a standard feature of community education. Third, those employees who embrace the need for ethical behavior will actively work to create a humane correctional environment. Visitors coming into this environment will witness all of the positive elements to be found in an ethically managed correctional organization. Experiential knowledge will reinforce factual knowledge.

Correctional employees whose personal and professional behavior is incongruent with the stereotypical behavior of the popular culture of corrections will provide the general public with a reservoir of contextual information that decertifies the negative correctional stereotypes presented so skillfully in prison movies and the prison literature.

Points to Consider

1. Can one negative personal encounter with correctional officers, such as the one described by the author at the beginning of this chapter, really persuade members of the general public that the constructed image of corrections is an accurate reflection of corrections? On what do you base your answer?

2. How widespread is the type of inappropriate employee behavior described at the beginning of this chapter? On what do you base your answer?

3. If you were a corrections superintendent, what actions, in addition to those discussed by this author, would you take to promote an ethical organizational culture?

4. Is ethics a more difficult issue in institutional corrections than it is in community corrections? Defend your answer.

5. Is ethics a more difficult issue in a women's prison than it is in a men's prison? Defend your answer.

6. What specific behaviors can a correctional manager engage in to set a personal example of ethical conduct?

7. If you are a correctional manager and you discover that your best friend on the job has been engaging in unethical behavior, what will you do? What factors will play a role in your decision? At this stage in your career, can you answer this question with any degree of certainty? Why or why not?

8. Does the correctional environment offer greater obstacles to promoting an ethical organizational culture than other work environments? Defend your answer.

9. What potential corrections horror stories other than the supermax prison and juvenile boot camp can you identify?

10. What actions can managers take to prevent these corrections horror stories from occurring?

11. What actions should a correctional manager take to reduce the potential of the juvenile boot camp horror story from occurring?

References

American Correctional Association. 1997. *Directory of Juvenile and Adult Correctional Departments, Institutions, Agencies and Paroling Authorities.* Lanham, Maryland: American Correctional Association.

APBNews.com. 1999. Youth Jails Chief Quits: Probe Finds Brutality at California Facilities. December 24.

Bucsko, M. 1998. Prison Officer is Disciplined in Race Incident. *Pittsburgh Post-Gazette.* June 9: 1.

Cheatwood, D. 1998. Prison Movies: Films About Adult, Male, Civilian Prisons: 1929-1995. In F. Bailey and D. Hale, eds. *Popular Culture, Crime and Justice*. Belmont, California: West/Wadsworth Publishing. pp. 209-231.

The Corrections Professional. 1998. Ethical and Moral Dilemmas: A Constant Challenge in Corrections. December. 47: 7.

————. 2000. Abuse Reports Close Maryland Youth Boot Camps. January. 7: 4.

Ericson, R.V., P. M. Baranek, and J. B. L. Chan. 1989. *Negotiating Control: A Study of News Sources*. Toronto: University of Toronto Press.

Freeman, R. M. 1999. *Correctional Organization and Management: Public Policy Challenges, Behavior, and Structure*. Woburn, Massachusetts: Butterworth-Heinemann.

Gavora, J. 1996. The Prisoners' Accomplice: Clinton Justice Department Alleges Violations of Prisoners' Rights in Supermax, Maryland's Prison for the Most Dangerous Prisoners. *Policy Review*. September/October. No. 79: 6-7.

Kansas Department of Corrections. 1999. A Message From The Secretary: Ethics. *Monthly Newsletter*. March, 355.

Manning, P. K. 1998. Media Loops. In F. Bailey and D. Hale, eds. *Popular Culture, Crime and Justice*. Belmont, California: West/Wadsworth Publishing. pp. 25-39.

Michigan Department of Corrections. 1998. Working with Female Inmates Presents Special Challenges. *Signal*. January. 51: 19-20.

Miller, B. 1999. Ex-inmate Tells Court of Forced Striptease, "Out of Control" Jail Scene. *Washington Post*. June 9: B06.

Pennsylvania Department of Corrections. 1999. Letter From the Superintendent of SCI-Albion To All New Employees.

Pollock, J. M. 1994. *Ethics in Crime and Justice: Dilemmas and Decisions*, 2nd Edition. Belmont, California: Wadsworth.

USA Today. 1999. Virginia, December 23.

Websdale, N. and A. Alvarez.1998. Forensic Journalism as Patriarchal Ideology: The Newspaper Construction of Homicide-Suicide. In F. Bailey and D. Hale, eds. *Popular Culture, Crime and Justice*. Belmont, California: West/Wadsworth Publishing. pp.123-141.

Zimmer, Lynn E. 1986. *Women Guarding Men*. Chicago: University of Chicago Press.

Zinn, Lorraine M. 1993. Do the Right Thing: Ethical Decision-Making in Professional and Business Practice. *Adult Learning*. 52: 7-8.

Expanding the Community Education Resource Base

Gauging the Potential for a Positive Public Response

Criminal justice system visionaries have concluded that sweeping changes in the criminal justice system in the twenty-first century will "demand more accountability and offer new challenges" (Muraskin and Roberts, 1999: 3). Large-scale social change and technological innovations in every component of the criminal justice system are anticipated. Morgan-Sharp and Sigler (1999) in a discussion of sentencing structures suggest that one of the most profound changes in the twenty-first century will be a shift from the current preference for punishment of the criminal offender to a preference for a more treatment-oriented approach to changing criminal behavior. They argue that this shift will occur because the current punishment paradigm "will fall out of favor with the public and will be replaced by the treatment or rehabilitation paradigm" (Morgan-Sharp and Sigler, 1999: 351). If this paradigm shift does occur, there will have to be an increasedx allocation of resources to community corrections and concurrent changes in sentencing structures and restrictions on parole eligibility.

There is a growing body of literature on public attitudes toward crime control that supports the Morgan-Sharp and Sigler perception of a shift in public preference in the direction of community corrections. Cullen and Gendreau (1988), in a review of the literature, concluded that the public's attitude toward the treatment of convicted offenders is not as punitive as the news media or elected officials believe it to be.

For example, *The Figgie Report* (1985) found that only 8 percent of the public believed that parole should be abolished, 24 percent of the public believed that the parole system should be retained in its present form, 61 percent of the survey respondents, while they supported the basic concept of parole, did express a concern that the current parole system needs to be reorganized. However, *The Figgie Report* provides no evidence that the general public is clamoring for parole to be eliminated. Mande and English (1989) conducted a study for the Colorado Department of Public Safety and reported a public acceptance for the community treatment of offenders. Public support for the use of sanctions other than incarceration has been documented by at least one national poll: "A national poll taken by the Wirthlin Group in 1995 found that three out of four Americans favored a balanced approach of prevention, punishment and treatment rather than imprisonment alone to reduce crime" (American Correctional Association, 1995: 58-59). And Applegate, Cullen, and Fisher (1997) reported that Ohio citizens expressed strong support for correctional treatment programs and a philosophy that offender rehabilitation should be the goal of incarceration.

As to the debate over crime control through incarceration versus crime prevention through the remediation of social problems, research shows that the public is not uniformly in favor of a purely criminal justice system solution to crime. For example, Doble (1987) reported finding public support for crime prevention through the remediation of criminogenic social problems. Doble's findings are in stark contrast to the widely held political perception that the general public will reject prevention initiatives as being soft on crime. In his analysis of a growing public reaction against "get tough on crime" public policy, Currie notes:

> By the end of the decade, majorities of the American public according to opinion polls, supported greater investment in educational, employment, and health care strategies to help the disadvantaged into more productive roles in American life (Currie, 1997: 64).

Such a shift in public attitudes could significantly impact corrections and create dramatic changes in its mission and system functions, especially if this shift is communicated effectively to elected officials who respond by modifying the draconian crime control policies created in the last three decades of the twentieth century. However, while the public's attitude toward crime control may be shifting, and this shift may improve the political environment in which corrections must function, there remains a serious challenge that has not been discussed by criminal justice visionaries. At the end of the twentieth century, the evidence that the popular culture of corrections would continue to reinforce a negative public perception of corrections was incontestable.

The Continuing Influence of Hollywood. In the Sunday, May 16, 1999, edition of the *Pittsburgh Post-Gazette*, Stephen Schurr reported that *The Shawshank Redemption* has been ranked by web surfers as one of America's favorite films. According to Schurr, this 1994 movie is so popular that there are at least twelve web sites devoted solely to what film fans refer to as "Shawshankmania." The Internet Movie Database (www.imdb.com), which encourages web users to cast their votes for the top 250 movies in America, reports that *Shawshank* has been among the top ten movies since its release and has been ranked number one for nearly two years. One web site that is dedicated to spiritual issues (Hollywood-jesus.com) raves that *Shawshank* should be viewed as "a Christian allegory about hope, faith and perseverance" (Schurr, 1999: E5).

The comments made by web site voters when they are ranking the movies do not reflect admiration for the correctional staff portrayed in *Shawshank*. Voter admiration is reserved for inmate Andy Dufresne, "a banker convicted of murder who triumphs over the adversity and hopelessness of a harsh prison through perseverance. . . ." (Schurr, 1999: E4). Significantly:

> One site reviewer, commenting on the Christ-like qualities of the Tim Robbins character, wrote that when in a terrible situation, one should ask, "What would Andy Dufresne do?" (Schurr, 1999: E5).

A movie that does not even have the distinction of being based on a true story still has the power to create the imagery of a courageous prison inmate beating a system full of prison guards and a warden who fully deserve the public's contempt and ridicule. Given the proclivity of television program executives to rebroadcast popular movies long after their theater release date, *Shawshank* undoubtedly will continue to influence the public perception of corrections well into the twenty-first century.

The Continuing Influence of the News Media. Munro-Bjorklund (1991) emphasizes that the public perception of corrections has been shaped by news media events such as the 1971 Attica riot and media looping such as the politicalization of Willie Horton. This trend undoubtedly will continue. For example, a 1997 news article guaranteed to reinforce smug hack corrections imagery is aptly titled "Brutality Reigns in Georgia Prisons":

> If you've ever seen a prison movie, you've probably seen a prison riot. In the Hollywood version, hardened thugs—some with legitimate complaints, some without—go on a rampage, setting fire to bunk beds, knifing their inmate enemies, clubbing prison guards.
>
> Here, in Georgia, the truth is stranger than fiction. Exactly a year ago, on July 10, 1996, according to several reliable witnesses, the guards at Hays State Correctional Institute near Trion went on a rampage— kicking, beating and clubbing restrained prisoners, bashing some so badly that blood spurted up the prison walls. It was such a revolting spectacle that even longtime prison employees— no wimps, these—were sickened. It was impossible for many of the beaten inmates to offer resistance since they were bound—shackled, or as one witness put it, "hog-tied" (Tucker, 1997: A6).

Tucker has chosen to directly relate the reported behavior of Georgia Department of Corrections correctional officers to the prison movie theme of out-of-control inmates in a prison riot. This is clever. It makes the point very effectively that correctional officers also can riot and be just as savage, if not more so, than the inmates. Thus, the repulsive images of smug hack corrections are reinforced by this article.

This reinforcement of negative correctional stereotyping in the twenty-first century will not rely exclusively on corrections horror stories. Reinforcement will be subtly created through the hundreds of five- or six-line fillers about instances of "minor" correctional employee misconduct that newspaper editors routinely use to secure their word count for the daily issue. For example, on January 2, 2000, the *Tribune-Democrat* in Johnstown, Pennsylvania, reported that two "guards" employed at the Fort Dodge Correctional Facility in Iowa were fired for using handcuffs to secure an inmate in a stairwell so he could be spanked by other inmates as part of the inmate's birthday celebration (*Tribune-Democrat*, 2000). These types of "minor" incidents will accumulate in the public mind like sediment at the bottom of the ocean and eventually form a solid layer of reinforcing imagery that will encourage public acceptance of the negative stereotypes supported by the larger and more graphic displays of unethical behavior documented in sensational articles like "Brutality Reigns in Georgia Prisons."

Creating Additional Community Education Resources. Adoni and Mane (1984) have stated that the influence of popular culture on public perception increases as alternate sources of influence decrease. The seemingly unlimited ability of Hollywood and the news media (and some correctional employees) to continue to contribute to the popular culture of corrections sends a clear message to corrections' executive managers that they must do more than continue their efforts to decertify negative correctional stereotyping. They must intensify those efforts by seeking and securing the assistance of community groups that have the ability to provide additional resources for the broad dissemination of contextual information. The four community groups whose resources may be most readily available to corrections include: the technology industry, private corrections and corrections-related businesses, legal watchdog/inmate advocacy groups, and the victims of crime.

The Technology Industry

The community education resources to be found in the technology industry consist of the sophisticated products that booming industry is marketing to corrections. In view of the current overwhelming interest in maximizing the use of technology in every sphere of American society, it is safe to predict that corrections will continue to be courted by technology specialists intent on placing their technological innovations in such areas as: internal and external institutional security, employee protection and self-defense, record keeping, offender location tracking, data storage and processing, research and development, and correctional industries, at a minimum. The message the technology industry is continuously promoting is that corrections should maximize its use of innovative technology in pursuit of the goal of achieving a high-tech corrections:

> Picture a criminal justice community working together, sharing offender information electronically. Picture a corrections department that trains its staff through virtual reality technology, using laser technology for firearm training and non-lethal weapons for safety. Picture a department that incarcerates only the uncontrollable, violent offenders, placing its emphasis on intermediate punishment programs (McQuillan, 1998: 1).

Even if this vision is never fully realized, technology can make a significant contribution to community education, and that contribution can be made today.

Technology's Contribution to Community Education. Technology can contribute to community education in four ways. First, the use of innovative technologies can make correctional employees at every level of their organization function more effectively by increasing their ability to deliver high-quality services with efficiency and accuracy. For example, William Archambeault (1999) suggests that computer-based technologies will allow corrections to "manage its huge offender data systems" more efficiently and "lead to more secure correctional facilities and more effective treatment programs" (Archambeault, 1999: 286). The end result of technological innovation may be a reduction in the potential for the routine bureaucratic foul-ups that the news media is so quick to report. As employee foul-ups decrease, the potential for adding current examples of employee incompetence to the popular culture of corrections concurrently decreases.

Second, the general public is impressed with technology and the people who know how to use it. The electronic surveillance and motion/sound detection systems, smart cards, electronically controlled gates and doors; stun shields, belts, and guns; telemedicine; satellite tracking of sex offenders and other high-risk probationers and parolees; and all the other shiny technological innovations being pitched to correctional managers suggest to the public that the users of this technology must be intelligent and sophisticated. Whereas smug hack corrections has an unappealing grit and dirt feel associated with its imagery, the inherent sophistication of an increasingly high-tech corrections can create a sparkling image of gleaming professionalism for the members of the various publics as they tour correctional facilities during their open house visits. This image will confer upon correctional employees the desirable mantle of competence and intelligence that the average citizen associates with individuals who use technology in their work. This new set of images will produce an automatic questioning of the popular culture of corrections' stereotype of uneducated, illiterate guards characterized by strong backs and weak minds.

Third, technological innovations in communication such as the Internet can enhance the ability of community education strategists to do a more effective job of disseminating contextual information. For example, those members of the general public who want to learn about corrections easily could access a variety of Internet sources of information by the beginning of the twenty-first century (*see* Box 10-1). Many of these web sites were created and maintained by corrections professionals or organizations that possess an intimate knowledge of corrections.

Fourth, as corrections becomes more technological, the workforce will need to be better educated. Managers and line staff alike will have to possess the educational background necessary to understand, and fully use the technology that is flooding the corrections market. A criminal justice visionary has noted that "Modern information systems and scientific classification procedures" have helped create "a need for better-educated modern correctional 'managers' who can anticipate and prevent problems" (Welsh, 1999: 302). The creation of this need for educated correctional managers is a positive development because the better educated the correctional manager, the more likely that he or she will strive to promote the ethical organizational culture that is the ultimate antidote to negative correctional stereotyping. This statement will be especially true if future college criminal justice curriculums are revised to include a high level of instruction in ethics and its role in the modern correctional system.

The Potential Dark Side of Technology

Technological innovations that have the potential to greatly increase organizational effectiveness while improving the image of corrections will be welcome in a business that believes the news media is always gunning for it. However, some categories of technology have a high potential for the type of misuse that will reinforce the public's perception that smug hack corrections is alive and well in America. To cite just one example, there is a growing controversy over the use of such inmate control technology as the stun belt.

The Stun Belt. The stun belt is a physical control device designed to deliver 50,000 volts, and three to four milliamps, of electricity for a period of eight seconds to disruptive individuals. The shock produced by the device is sufficient to render any individual, no matter how strong, incapable of launching a physical attack. According to the manufacturers, this incapacitating shock is not fatal because of the low milliamperage that is involved; however, it is quite painful and the recipient of the shock falls to the ground, twitches spasmodically, loses muscle control, and even may lose control of bladder and bowels. The stun belt has some equally persuasive cousins: the taser, the stun gun, and the stun shield.

While it can be argued that the use of these devices is a more humane control alternative than the use of batons or lethal force, the potential to use them in an unethical manner cannot be ignored. All of these devices have a high potential for gross misuse. If the decision is made to add any of them to the control arsenal, then there is an ethical responsibility to try and limit their potential for abuse through the promulgation of policy and

Box 10-1 Internet Sources of Information about Corrections as of January 17, 2000

American Bar Association, Criminal Justice Section, Committee on Corrections and Sentencing
      http://www.abanet.org/crimjust/corrsent.html

The American Correctional Association
      http://www.corrections.com/aca

The American Institute of Architects, Architects for Justice
      http://e-architect.com/pia/caj/home@asp

The American Jail Association
      http://www.corrections.com/aja

American Probation and Parole Association
      http://www.appa-net.org/

California Probation, Parole, and Correctional Association
      http://www.cppa.org

Correctional Education Association
      http://www.jhkeeley@aol.com

Correctional Industries Association
      http://corrections.com/industries

Family and Corrections Network
      http://www.fcnetwork.org

International Brotherhood of Correctional Officers
      http://www.ibco.org

International Prison Ministry
      http://www.ipm.org

National Association of Blacks in Criminal Justice
      http://nabcj.org

National Commission on Correctional Health Care
      http://www.ncchc.org

The Prison Issues Desk
      http://www.prisonactivist.org

    Two additional web sites can be helpful. The first web site, Prisons.com (http://www.prisons.com), provides a broad range of information on current events in corrections, links to other criminal justice system web sites, and a directory of correctional organizations. The second web site, Corrections Connection Network (http://www.corrections.com/state.html#state) provides a direct linkage to every department of corrections website currently in existence. Department of corrections' web sites provide a wealth of contextual information about the sponsoring agency and its role in crime control and prevention.

training that clearly defines when, where, how, and by whom these devices can be used. The failure of management to be proactive inevitably will result as in the type of corrections horror story that always has been so effective in promoting smug hack imagery.

The Internet. The ability of community education strategists to use the Internet as a fresh forum for presenting contextual information to the general public is most certainly a positive. This powerful form of communication has enormous potential for good; yet, this technology can be easily abused by employees who choose to surf the net and engage in activities (such as spending time in sexually oriented chat rooms) that can embarrass the organization if they are discovered by the news media. An example of the embarrassment an organization can suffer from employee abuse of the Internet occurred at the Naval Support Station in Camp Hill, Pennsylvania on December 3, 1999. Five hundred and twenty four federal employees were disciplined for transmitting e-mail messages that contained sexually explicit graphic cartoons, photographs, and suggestive jokes and stories. The federal employees were charged with "misconduct involving misuse of a government computer system by distributing sexually explicit and inappropriate material to individuals in the work environment" (Graybeal, 1999: A1). The discipline administered to the employees ranged from fourteen-day suspensions to letters of admonishment.

Subsequent articles following this headline story provided similar examples of employee misconduct at a wide range of private and public work sites. If corrections is to prevent employee access to Internet technology from being converted into a negative news event, its executive managers must anticipate the types of abuse that are most likely to occur and formulate policy to prevent those abuses. No employee Internet access should be permitted prior to written policy dissemination and training.

Regardless of the type of technology that is under discussion, the potential for misuse and abuse always will be present. Correctional managers must be alert to this double-edged dimension of technology and formulate policy to clearly define the purpose of the equipment and the manner in which it is to be used. It does take time to develop appropriate policy and train employees, but it takes even more time to try to undo the public image damage created by just one ugly incident.

Private Corrections and Corrections-related Businesses

Effective community education requires the use of nontraditional resources in the quest to gain political support and shape public perception. A potentially large, and relatively untapped, resource is to be found in the private sector corporations that provide contractual services and goods to public corrections. Many of these corporations have annual revenues in excess of a billion dollars. Public corrections managers can seek the cooperation of these corporations in their promotion of community education.

What the Private Sector Offers. Correctional managers should seek to achieve more than the delivery of professional service and quality products from the private sector. They should actively encourage their vendors to consider volunteering to make a firm commitment to assist in community education efforts. The American business community has become quite sophisticated in using the news and entertainment media to market its products. This time-tested expertise should be defined as a resource to be used for the benefit of community education. Vendors should be requested to consider the ability of their organization to:

- participate in American Correctional Association accreditation activities
- assist in correctional publicity efforts to promote a more positive view of inmates, staff, and organizational contributions to the public welfare

- promote prisons as a source of jobs, income and a positive economic force in the community
- agree to allow reporters to cover the activities of the private contractor
- provide information to researchers, including those in the academic community
- provide speakers for the speaker's bureau and other public presentation events
- present public information seminars in their area of expertise
- provide information to elected officials at the request of correctional managers (Freeman, 1999b: 34)

All of these voluntary private sector activities will demonstrate the positive aspects of public corrections. They also will associate public corrections with private sector corporations that enjoy a good reputation in the community. In addition, the private sector is a fertile recruiting ground for corrections' public information officers and directors of communication since a solid marketing background prepares public information officers and directors for the task of "selling" corrections.

The Downside of Association with the Private Sector. There is, however, a potential drawback to promoting an association with the private sector. In the late 1990s, disturbing reports about private prison abuses began to surface in the news media. For example, in 1999, a professor at Columbia University School of Law wrote an article on private prisons whose lead paragraph started with: "Privatization has undeniably led to problems of gross mismanagement, brutality and across-the-board skimping" (Berger, 1999: A26). The author at another point in the article flatly stated:

> Although the jury is still out, it's fair to say that privatization has not fulfilled its advocates' more extravagant promises. Worse, scandals, abuses and sheer incompetence have dogged the business since its modern inception in the mid-1980s. Based on this, a go-slow policy is plainly warranted (Berger, 1999: A26).

By the end of the twentieth century, the literature was beginning to fill with articles that called into question the ability of private prisons to provide a high level of control and service in a humane, safe, and orderly manner:

> But privatization has undeniably led to problems of gross mismanagement and brutal treatment too grave to ignore. Texas, which houses one-fourth of its prisoners in private facilities, presents an especially appalling picture. For instance, a videotape revealed guards in one detention center kicking inmates when they were down, siccing dogs on them and shooting them with stun guns (Berger, 1999: A27).

Yes, the paragraph clearly states that the incident happened at a private prison. But does the public clearly differentiate between public and private prisons? It is highly unlikely that the general public will make a mental note that this repugnant event took place at a private prison and not at a public prison. What is more likely is that after viewing the news media coverage of this particular event (and remember that television newscast producers love videotapes) the public will retain the following words and phrases: "detention center;" "guards" (at least they were not referred to as corrections officers); "kicking inmates when they were down;" "siccing dogs on them;" and "shooting them with stun guns." In addition, the public now has been exposed to factual information that encourages it to associate the "humane" technology of stun guns with the good old-fashioned kicking of inmates when they are down and siccing dogs on them that is highlighted in the most violent prison movies.

Public corrections does not need the onus of being tarnished with the same brush that may be liberally applied to private prisons in the twenty-first century. Because the public is unlikely to differentiate between public and private prisons when it reads or hears about an incident of private prison brutality or corruption, any disturbing news story about private corrections will cast a negative reflection on public corrections. Community education strategists must watch the evening news, read the professional journals and news magazines, and lobby against their organization establishing an association with any private contractor that has been the center of scandal.

In the event that a negative news media event does occur after a contract has been approved, the public corrections manager should have the authority to activate the equivalent of a moral turpitude clause. That is, every contract with a private corrections contractor should have a morality clause that releases the contracting agency from the contract if the vendor engages in behavior that has the potential to damage the reputation of the contracting agency. Obviously, there are a variety of potential problems, legal as well as pragmatic, associated with this type of action, but corrections receives enough bad press on its own without taking on the additional burden of being associated with the unethical conduct of private contractors.

Recognizing the Good Private Contractors. It is always important to officially recognize the efforts of business people who have actively assisted corrections. For example, in 1998, the Kansas Department of Corrections selected James V. Laubach, president of Century Manufacturing, to receive the 1998 Menninger Award. The basis for the award selection was Mr. Laubach's commitment in 1993 to establish a prison-based lucite products industry at Ellsworth Correctional Facility. In 1997, he opened a second industry at El Dorado Correctional Facility. Inmates as well as taxpayers have benefitted from the income generated by these industries (Kansas Department of Corrections, 1998: 4). And the Kansas Department of Corrections has benefitted from the good press accompanying this association.

Legal Watchdog/Inmate Advocacy Groups

Groups such as the American Civil Liberties Union and various inmate advocacy groups such as the Pennsylvania Prison Society traditionally have been viewed with suspicion by correctional employees because they are seen in absolute terms as pro-inmate and anti-corrections. And that suspicion is frequently returned by members of those groups who believe that the popular culture of corrections is telling it like it is when it comes to corrections and its treatment of convicted offenders.

This does not have to be the case. The American Civil Liberties Union and inmate advocacy groups share many of the concerns that are uppermost in the minds of corrections professionals: the creation and efficient delivery of offender services, fairness in decision making and the use of discretion, effective allocation of scarce resources, creation of humane prison environments, and the elimination of punitive sentencing structures and legislation aimed at getting tough on inmates. For example, on March 26, 1998, the American Civil Liberties Union urged the Crime Subcommittee of the House Judiciary Committee in Washington D.C. to reject H.R. 2070, which would require HIV testing and disclosure of HIV status for any federal inmate whose bodily fluids have come into contact with a nonincarcerated individual. Citing confidentiality concerns, fear of discrimination, and the possibility of violence or abuse directed at correctional officers, the American Civil Liberties Union opposed the legislation, a position consistent with that articulated by many corrections professionals (American Civil Liberties Union, 1998).

In addition, negative reports generated by the American Civil Liberties Union and inmate advocacy groups can be referenced by correctional budget planners to justify the creation and funding of new programs. For example, an American Civil Liberties Union report critical of a department of corrections' management of mentally ill inmates can provide the foundation for a department of corrections' request for creation and funding of mental health units in selected prisons within the system. American Civil Liberties Union concerns about supermax prison policies may lead to a review and modification of specific policies before a trigger incident that causes painful publicity occurs.

Honoring the American Civil Liberties Union. The value of groups such as the American Civil Liberties Union to corrections has been recognized by at least one department of corrections. In the Spring of 1999, the Utah Department of Corrections honored the American Civil Liberties Union and the Disability Law Center, "two of its most persistent watchdogs," (*The Corrections Professional*, 1999c: 4) during a department of corrections banquet. What were the reasons for honoring these watchdog organizations?

> Both the American Civil Liberties Union and DLC, through lawsuits, have forced Utah lawmakers to pump millions of dollars into prison medical care and sex-offender treatment and have forced policy change governing inmate restraints, the care of HIV-infected prisoners and the forced medication of mentally ill inmates. . . . Corrections officials have used the court battles as a means to shift policies (*The Corrections Professional*, 1999c: 4).

Working with watchdog groups also provides an invaluable opportunity to educate individuals who can be the fiercest organized opponents of corrections if they are operating on the basis of negative correctional stereotypes. Allowing watchdog groups into the facilities, letting them talk to inmates and employees, inviting them to corrections-sponsored seminars and professional conferences, and having correctional representatives attend watchdog group seminars and conferences can help bridge a gap that often has seemed insurmountable, but which can be crossed.

The Victims of Crime

It is quite likely that many crime victims have a negative view of corrections because of their negative experiences with criminals and the criminal justice system, in general. A negative experience with one element of the criminal justice system, such as the courts, can create negative emotions that carry over onto other elements of that system. A crime victim who feels further victimized by plea bargaining, for example, can feel hostility for corrections when the issue of parole must be considered by an institutional treatment staff and the parole board. In addition, even crime victims who have had a positive experience with the police and courts can demonstrate a dislike for corrections if they have uncritically accepted the country club corrections' stereotype of corrections as an agency that coddles inmates and then returns them to the community where they are free to create more victims. This dislike, even when it becomes open hostility, should not be ignored because victims constitute a valuable potential resource for community education if they can be taught to understand, and appreciate, the mission of corrections. This element of community education relies extensively on exposure to programs of department of corrections' victim services.

Victim Services and Restorative Justice. Victim services programs rapidly are becoming an integral function of state departments of corrections. These programs are rooted in the increasingly popular philosophy of restorative justice: the concept that offenders, victims, and community representatives can work together to develop a mutually satisfactory response to the offender's crime and the victim's pain.

A national teleconference sponsored by the National Institute of Justice in December, 1996, created seven principles of restorative justice that provide the foundation for programs of victim services:

1. Crime is an offense against human relationships.

2. Victims and the community are central to justice processes.

3. The first priority of justice processes is to assist victims.

4. The second priority is to restore the community, to the degree possible.

5. Offenders have personal responsibility to their victims and communities.

6. Offenders will develop improved competency and understanding as a result of the restorative justice experience.

7. Stakeholders share responsibility for restorative justice through partnerships for action (Gregorie, 1998: 1).

Victim services programs founded on these principles represent an excellent opportunity to educate the general public and provide them with a better understanding of the role of corrections in crime control.

The Missouri Victim Services Program. The efforts of the Missouri Department of Corrections to educate crime victims is particularly impressive. The Department of Corrections provides crime victims with *A Handbook for Crime Victims* that has information organized in the following categories: mission statement; vision statement; introduction; probation and incarceration; truth-in-sentencing laws; victim rights and parole hearings; parole, including assessment, supervision, termination, and conditions of probation/parole; and victim services. In Missouri, victim service specialists are expected to do the following things:

- coordinate the victim notification process

- attend parole hearings with victims, if requested

- support family members of victims at executions

- serve as an advocate for victims within the department

- ensure departmental policies and procedures are sensitive to the needs of victims

- arrange personal meetings for victims with members of the division of probation and parole

- provide information regarding inmates' incarceration

- provide referrals to other victim-service agencies

- respond to questions from victims and prosecuting attorneys

- engage in public speaking
- provide staff training to increase sensitivity to the needs of victims (Missouri Department of Corrections, 1999)

The Crime Victim as Community Education Resource. Every contact between a victim and victim services specialist can be a positive experience because each contact is designed to assist the victim in managing an emotionally difficult situation. The more positive the contact between victim services personnel and victims, the higher the probability that these individuals will form a positive image of corrections. Positive interactions with crime victims provide the victim services specialist a valuable opportunity to disseminate contextual information about corrections that can reduce the crime victim's potential for antagonism and confrontation. In addition, victims who believe corrections is on their side can begin to think of themselves as being on corrections' side. This can be a helpful attitude in two ways.

First, when crime control policy and corrections-related issues are being publicly debated, a positive personal exposure to corrections, especially if it had not been anticipated prior to the initial interaction with the victim services specialist assigned to their case, may encourage crime victims to challenge the stereotypical statements about corrections that elected officials present in their campaign rhetoric. If elected officials are challenged frequently enough, they may be more receptive to learning about corrections from sources other than the mass media. They may decide to increase their experiential knowledge. This, in turn, may help them shape a more rational crime control policy that is of benefit to both corrections and society.

Second, even if crime victims choose to remain aloof from political debates, routine interaction with their peer groups and families will provide numerous opportunities to talk about their positive experience(s) with corrections. These discussions will provide an additional source of contextual information to correctional outsiders that contradicts negative stereotyping. Just as the negative behavior of the four correctional officers in the book store presented in Chapter 9 can initiate a social phenomenon similar to a double echoing loop, the positive behavior of victim services specialists can initiate an equally powerful positive perception of corrections that can help reduce the influence of subsequent news media reports of correctional employee misconduct on both the crime victim and the individuals with whom the crime victim has shared his or her positive experiences with corrections.

Is Community Education a Viable Approach? The influence of Hollywood and the news media on public perception is so powerful and pervasive that it can appear to be inviolate. The wisdom of committing scarce resources to community education in the twenty-first century is an issue that requires an examination of the research literature on the ability of community education to change the public perception of corrections. The literature on this subject is more positive than might be anticipated.

The Public Potential for Receptivity to Community Education

The proposition that the creation of a contextual information base concerning corrections effectively can influence the public's understanding of the role of corrections in crime control has been demonstrated in several studies. Doble and Klein (1989) studied the attitudes of Alabama citizens and found that educating the public about the high costs associated with incarceration and the nonstereotypical nature of offenders resulted in the public acceptance of a much lower rate of incarceration than had been reported previously. This level of acceptance included public approval of a variety of work and community service programs. An Ohio study revealed public support for early parole as long as that privilege was conditioned on inmates meeting the criteria of good behavior and participation in prison education and work programs (Skovron et al., 1989). In other words, early release from prison is acceptable if the inmate has worked to earn that release instead of it being given as a "right."

The value of creating a contextual information base through community education was most dramatically demonstrated by Bennett (1991) in his report on an American Justice Institute study that surveyed 1,000 residents in the six metropolitan areas of California that provide approximately 65 percent of the annual commitments to the California Department of Corrections. The initial results showed that if given a choice between prison and probation for twenty-five crime vignettes ranging from petty theft to rape, 63 percent of the respondents felt prison was the best option. This appears to represent strong public support for the "get tough on crime" policies developed since the early 1970s. But, appearances can be deceiving.

Bennett reports (1991: 92) that changing the structure of the survey significantly changed the responses. In the revised format, the respondents were first asked to read brief descriptions of a number of community-based programs such as Intensive Supervision Probation, boot camp, drug treatment programs, and restitution centers. The descriptions included estimates of the relative effectiveness and costs of each program. Then, the respondents reviewed the twenty-five vignettes with the assumption that the community programs that had been described to them were available at the time of sentencing, were appropriately financed and managed, and had adequate levels of professional staff.

Once the vital information about program structure, cost, and effectiveness that had been left out of the initial survey was provided, only 27 percent of the survey respondents agreed that incarceration was the most appropriate disposition. This reduction of support for incarceration as the only solution fell from 65 percent to 27 percent. This suggests that correctional community education strategists reasonably can conclude that many members of the general public are indeed receptive to contextual information. Otherwise, Bennett's survey respondents would not have changed their opinions after their receipt of relevant information about correctional programming.

Elected Officials: Contradictory Indications. The receptivity of elected officials to contextual information is much less certain. Legislative activity at the end of the twentieth century provided mixed signals. For example, in Missouri, the state Senate passed a law giving state judges more discretion in sentencing by abolishing mandatory minimum sentences of three years for crimes committed with guns by first-time offenders. In addition, the state Board of Probation and Parole will have new authority to reduce sentences for drug crimes. These political actions were taken despite the objections of critics who "said the proposal disregards widespread concern about crime and gives criminals a bad message" (*The Corrections Professional*, 1999b: 2). Missouri's legislative changes are in the best interests of corrections and they possibly may have been influenced by contextual information received through community education.

However, in Kansas, the Sentencing Commission recommended a marked increase in parole eligibility from forty to fifty years for offenders convicted under the "Hard 40;" an increase in parole eligibility from fifteen to twenty years for offenders convicted of felony murder; and a 20 percent increase in the length of sentences for Severity Level III crimes. Yet, this same Commission proposed reducing by 20 percent the length of sentences for Severity Level I and II crimes as well as reducing the sentence for offenders convicted of indecent liberties who have had voluntary sex with a fourteen- or fifteen-year-old but who are not more than three years older than the victim (Kansas Department of Corrections, 1999: 7). This type of contradictory crime control policy suggests that while there may be some receptivity to community education, the "get tough on crime" perspective is still powerful in political circles.

The fact that there are elected officials who are beginning to advocate crime control policy that does not rely exclusively on the overuse of incarceration provides corrections' executive managers and their allies an incentive to interact with those officials, advise them, and seek their support in the education of the general public about crime control policy. But it must be noted that some elected officials may remain difficult to convince. For example, in 1999, New York Governor George Pataki urged the state legislature to adopt determinate sentencing, to institute parole supervision for felons released from state prisons after completing their determinate sentences, and to abolish the parole board (*The Corrections Professional*, 1999a: 2).

The Public Perception of Corrections at the End of the Twentieth Century

As the twentieth century drew to a close, two rigorous attitude surveys that covered a broader geographical area than the surveys previously referenced in this book documented the public perception of corrections. These surveys are the 1996 National Opinion Survey on Crime and Justice and the 1996 Gallup Poll.

The National Opinion Survey on Crime and Justice. In 1996, the Survey Research Program of the Criminal Justice Center at Sam Houston State University designed the National Opinion Survey on Crime and Justice to test attitudes about the criminal justice system. The sample consisted of 1,085 randomly selected American adults. The sampling and data collections were conducted by the Public Policy Research Institute at Texas A&M University. The National Opinion Survey on Crime and Justice found an overall general decline in the public belief that the criminal justice system adequately can protect citizens from criminal predators. The findings were remarkably similar to the findings reported in Chapter 1. Sixty percent of the respondents said they had either a "great deal" or "quite a lot" of confidence in the police. Thirty-four percent of the survey respondents expressed confidence in the courts. However, only 26 percent had confidence in "your community probation system" and "your state prison system." The only rating lower than that given for corrections was the 24 percent vote of confidence in the criminal justice system as a whole (Flanagan, 1996).

The Gallup Poll. The 1996 survey of public attitudes toward American institutions conducted by the Gallup Organization asked randomly selected Americans the degree of confidence they have in fourteen American institutions: the military, the police, the church or organized religion, the presidency, the U.S. Supreme Court, banks, the medical system, public schools, television news, newspapers, organized labor, Congress, big business, and the criminal justice system (Gallup, 1997). In the Gallup Poll, the police rated a 60 percent vote of confidence, but the criminal justice system as a whole received only a 19 percent confidence rating:

> The 19 percent rating for the criminal justice system was the lowest of any institution in the Gallup poll; Congress registered 20 percent, big business had 24 percent, and organized labor had a 25 percent confidence rating (Flanagan, 1996: 5).

Televisions news received a 36 percent vote of confidence, and newspapers received 32 percent approval. Although corrections was not listed as an institution to be ranked, it is safe to assume that it significantly contributed to the dismal overall approval rating of the criminal justice system. To argue otherwise would fly in the face of both the principles of rational analysis and the results of the other surveys that have been referenced.

Clearly, there is a long way to go when the goal is changing the public perception of corrections. If the current efforts to provide community education are intensified, then it is possible that the public perception of corrections in the twenty-first century will be more positive than they have been in the twentieth century. However, changing the public perception of corrections is not an easy task. It is a major challenge. In fact, it may be easier to manage inmates than it is to successfully challenge the grip the popular culture of corrections has on the public perception of corrections. But it is a challenge that must be met because it is in the best interests of corrections and society to do so. It is incumbent upon corrections professionals to educate the general public of the twenty-first century so they can understand the mission, functions, and challenges of corrections accurately.

The General Public of the Twenty-first Century Already Exists. The general public of the next century are the readers of this book, students in K-12 and college, young adults just beginning their careers, older adults thinking about retirement, retirees, and the young children who are only now getting their first exposure to corrections through television news broadcasts and prison movies. Some of these individuals already have a negative image of corrections so firmly in place that no amount of community education will change their minds. But there are other citizens who remain open to being influenced by contextual information about corrections. If the challenge to provide this information is not met through the commitment of an increased allocation of organizational resources to community education, then the powerful influence of the popular culture of corrections on the public perception of corrections is likely to remain unabated.

If the nature and character of corrections remains tarnished in the public eye during the twenty-first century because of correctional inaction, then corrections has nobody to blame except itself. The responsibility for community education cannot be delegated to any other group in American society, nor should it be.

Points to Consider

1. What additional challenges to improving the public perception of corrections can you foresee in the twenty-first century?

2. In the future, will the news and entertainment media continue to be as powerful as they are today? Or will they be replaced by some other form of communication technology? If so, what form do you think that technology will take? What will be its impact on the public perception of corrections?

3. If you were a commissioner of corrections, what would you include in a policy governing the use of such devices as the stun belt and its cousins?

4. If you were a commissioner of corrections, what would you include in a policy governing employee use of the Internet?

5. What are the pros and cons of asking the private corrections industry to share resources with public corrections for facilitating community education?

6. What are the pros and cons of seeking the support of watchdog and inmate advocacy groups?

7. How can victim services specialists contribute to community education?

8. What is the single most challenging aspect of community education? Why?

9. Can community education actually succeed or is it just an exercise in futility? Defend your answer.

References

Adoni, H. and S. Mane. 1984. Media and the Social Construction of Reality: Toward an Integration of Theory and Research. *Communication Research*.113. (July): 323-340.

American Civil Liberties Union. 1998. ACLU Urges House Panel to Preserve Safety, Privacy of Corrections Officers. March 26. http://www.aclu.org/congress/t032698.html.

American Correctional Association. 1995. Wirthlin Poll, Part of the National Quorum program conducted by the Wirthlin Group. Laurel, Maryland.

Applegate, Brandon K., Francis T. Cullen, and Bonnie S. Fisher.1997. Public Support for Correctional Treatment. *The Prison Journal*. 773: 237-258.

Archambeault, W. G. 1999. The Impact of Computer-based Technologies on Criminal Justice: Transition to the Twenty-first Century. In R. Muraskin and A. R. Roberts, eds. *Visions for Change: Crime and Justice in the Twenty-First Century*. Upper Saddle River, New Jersey: Prentice Hall. pp 275-292.

Bennett, Lawrence A. 1991. The Public Wants Accountability. *Corrections Today*. (53)5: 92-95.

Berger, Vivian. 1999. Private Prisons: Bad Idea? *The National Law Journal*. March 22. A26-27.

The Corrections Professional. 1999a.. NY Governor Asks State to End Felony Parole. January 22. 49: 2.

———. 1999b. Missouri Senate Passes Sentence-Cutting Bill. April 23. 415: 2.

———. 1999c.Utah DOC Honors Watchdogs. June 4. 418: 4.

Cullen, Frank and Paul Gendreau. 1988. The Effectiveness of Correctional Rehabilitation: Reconsidering the "Nothing Works" Debate. In Lynn Goodstein and Doris Layton MacKenzie, eds. *The American Prison: Issues in Research and Policy*. New York: Plenum Press.

Currie, Elliott. 1997. Crime, Justice, and the Social Environment. In Barry W. Hancock and Paul M. Sharp, eds. *Public Policy, Crime, and Criminal Justice*. Upper Saddle River, New Jersey: Prentice Hall. pp. 51-67.

Doble, John. 1987. *Crime and Punishment: The Public's View*. New York: Public Agenda Foundation.

Doble, John and Josh Klein. 1989. *Prison Overcrowding and Alternative Sentences: The Views of the People of Alabama*. New York: The Public Agenda Foundation.

Figgie Report. 1985. *Part V: Parole: A Search For Justice and Safety*. New York: Research and Forecasts, Inc.

Flanagan, T. J. 1996. Community Corrections in the Public Mind. *Federal Probation.* (60)3: 3-9.

Freeman, R. M. 1999. Challenging the Negative Public Perception of Corrections: Guidelines for Implementing a Community Outreach-Based PR Strategy. *Corrections Management Quarterly.* 33: 28-36.

Gallup, G., Jr. 1997. Confidence in Institutions. In *The Gallup Poll: Public Opinion, 1996.* Wilmington, Delaware: Scholarly Resources. pp.77-81.

Graybeal, L. 1999. E-mail Spells Woe at Navy Base. Harrisburg, Pennsylvania. *The Patriot-News.* December 3. A1.

Gregorie, T. 1998. A Road Map to Restorative Justice in Corrections. *Networks.* 133. National Victim Center.

Kansas Department of Corrections. 1998. Menninger Award. *Monthly Newsletter.* 350. October.

———. 1999. Proposed Amendment to the Sentencing Guidelines Act. *Kansas Department of Corrections Monthly Newsletter.* 354: 7.

Mande, Mary J. and Kim English. 1989. *The Effect of Public Opinion on Correctional Policy: A Comparison of Opinions and Practice.* Colorado Springs, Colorado: Colorado Department of Public Safety, Division of Criminal Justice.

McQuillan, P. 1998. Corrections 2025. *Correction News.* February. North Carolina Department of Corrections.

Missouri Department of Corrections. 1999. *A Handbook For Crime Victims.* Office of Victim Services. *Correction News.* March.

Morgan-Sharp, E. and R. T. Sigler. 1999. Sentencing into the Twenty-First Century: Sentence Enhancement and Life Without Parole. In R. Muraskin and A. R. Roberts, eds. *Visions for Change: Crime and Justice in the Twenty-First Century.* Upper Saddle River, New Jersey: Prentice Hall. pp. 351-366.

Munro-Bjorklund, V. 1991. Popular Culture Images of Criminals and Prisoners Since Attica. *Social Justice.* 183: 48-70.

Muraslin, R. and A. R. Roberts. 1999. *Visions for Change: Crime and Justice in the Twenty-First Century.* Upper Saddle River, New Jersey: Prentice Hall.

Schurr, S. 1999. Shawshank's Redemption: How a Movie That Got Mixed Reviews and Did So-So Business Found An Amazing Afterlife. *Pittsburgh Post-Gazette.* May 15: E4-E5.

Skovron, Sandra Evans, Joseph E. Scott, and Francis T. Cullen. 1989. Prison Crowding: Public Attitudes Toward Strategies of Population Control. *Journal of Research in Crime and Delinquency.* 25: 150-169.

Tribune-Democrat. 2000. Prison Guards Fired After Inmate Birthday Spank. Johnstown, Pennsylvania. January 2.

Tucker, C. 1997. Brutality Reigns in Georgia Prisons. Harrisburg, Pennsylvania. *Patriot-News.* July 14: A6.

Welsh, W. N. 1999. Court-Ordered Reform of Jails: Past, Present, and Future. In R. Muraskin and A. R. Roberts, eds. *Visions for Change: Crime and Justice in the Twenty-First Century.* Upper Saddle River, New Jersey: Prentice Hall. pp. 295-312.

Index

by Lawrence H. Feldman

About the Author

Robert M. Freeman is an Associate Professor and Chair of the Department of Criminal Justice at Shippensburg University in Shippensburg, Pennsylvania. Dr. Freeman is a recognized authority on correctional management and the complex relationship between crime control policy and correctional system behavior, especially the unintended consequences of that policy. He has extensive personal experience with every facet of correctional management, including the last major prison riot of the 1980s. Dr. Freeman was employed by the Pennsylvania Department of Corrections from 1970 to 1990. He was a psychologist for five years, a deputy superintendent for five years, and a superintendent for ten years. He also has worked in private corrections managing jail and prison health care contracts for a national corporation.

Dr. Freeman is the author of *Strategic Planning for Correctional Emergencies* (published by the American Correctional Association) and *Correctional Organization and Management: Public Policy Challenges, Behavior, and Structure*. This book, *Popular Culture and Corrections*, is the final book in a management trilogy designed to provide students, academicians, and even the most seasoned corrections professionals with a comprehensive understanding of the multifaceted elements of correctional management in an increasingly volatile political and financial environment.